The Edge of War

The Edge of War

by James David Atkinson

FOREWORD BY
Admiral Arleigh A. Burke

 HENRY REGNERY COMPANY

CHICAGO • 1960

Library of Congress Card Catalog Number: 60-14054

Copyright © 1960 by Henry Regnery Company, Chicago 4, Illinois.
Manufactured in the United States of America.

TO MY BROTHER
EDWARD W. ATKINSON

CONTENTS

Foreword

It is most opportune that a book such as this makes its appearance to remind free men everywhere that conquest need not necessarily take the form of armed aggression. In the pages of this timely book, Dr. Atkinson describes the fusion of war and peace in the Communist conspiracy to rule the world. Unless there is a full understanding of the treacherous techniques of Communism, and of the insidious perversion of every decent concept of civilized behavior which it represents, mankind faces bondage under the most barbarous tyranny the world has ever known.

Inherent in this struggle is a ceaseless pressure applied in every line of human endeavor, psychological, political, ideological, economic, diplomatic. It appears in the arts, in the sciences, in sports, in cultural activities, in education, in commerce and industry. It is a struggle of ideas, of ideals, and of philosophies. It can be countered only by an equally dedicated conviction in the moral principles and ethical values which underly the concept of human liberty.

The enemy has conducted his aggressive campaign in such a manner as to take every possible advantage of our own idealism and high principles. We are forced to deal with a sworn enemy to whom the simplicity of truth, the standards of morality, and the ethics of moral responsibility are meaningless. The arena in which the Communists have chosen to wage their eternal struggle is one in which there are no ground rules but the law of the jungle, the primitive law of survival without regard to integrity or to decent standards of human conduct.

The author brings home to the reader the fact that in these circumstances we cannot be aloof from the hard reality of a determined and ruthless foe. The concept of freedom has been challenged, hence the right of free men to personal liberty, indeed to their very lives, is seriously threatened.

The Communists owe a large part of their success to a willingness to roll up their sleeves and take their credo to the common man in the rice paddies, factories, cottage shops, and farms. It is here that free men must meet the challenge, among ordinary people throughout the world. To many, Communism offers a change from unacceptable conditions. It offers the security of slavery.

The common man must understand that freedom offers opportunity, the chance to grow, to create, and to develop by his own efforts the fuller life which he seeks. It offers him responsibility. Western civilization is a living monument to this simple truth, and unless the free world develops this understanding, it will be seriously handicapped in its struggle with the hardened and trained revolutionaries who are dedicated to destroying the civilized society which has taken mankind nearly two thousand years to build, a crusade which is not yet complete.

It is a privilege to have the opportunity to state my agreement with Dr. Atkinson's general thesis and especially his observation that "warfare of the latter part of the 20th Century is, above all, a battle of the spirit, of ideas, and of the human will." This battle will be fought in the hearts, in the minds, and in the souls of men everywhere. It is hoped that this book will serve to awaken many to this fact.

Dr. Atkinson is exceptionally well qualified to write on this very important subject. His service in the Military Intelligence Branch of the Army during World War II provided him with a basic understanding of the tactics used by Communists. This experience also enabled him to arrive at a realistic appraisal of the devious and insidious methods used by the proponents of Communism in their all-out efforts to spread their false ideology.

Dr. Atkinson has been director of a special course in Psychological Warfare conducted by the Georgetown University Graduate School for the Armed Services.

He has also served as a consultant to the Psychological Strategy Board, the Operations Research Office, the Department of the Army, Department of the Navy and other department agencies.

Dr. Atkinson has also written numerous articles concerning foreign policy and military affairs and was a member of the faculty of the National Strategy Seminar at the National War College. He has established himself as one of the foremost authorities in this vital area.

ARLEIGH A. BURKE
Admiral, U. S. Navy

Preface

An English poet of the First World War wrote that the "top of sovereignty" was "to bear all naked truths." Nothing, it would seem, is harder for many Americans today. In our search for easy and comfortable solutions in a world of conflict we have often avoided the naked truth that there *is* an irrepressible *conflict* between the Communists and ourselves. This conflict is not less real because it is often masked by fair words about peaceful coexistence. Nor is it less real because today's warfare is not limited to battles between armed groups. Much more, warfare is now a contest between peoples —and their civilizations—whose whole physical and moral forces are mobilized with all of their economic, industrial, military and moral resources. The naked truth of the conflict in which we are now engaged cannot be swept under the rug by "Marches for Peace," endless remarks that nuclear war would be terrible (who doubts it?), or repetition about improved relations and mutual confidence.

This book is an attempt—however fragmentary—to spell out some aspects of the new warfare in which we are engaged. It is also an affirmation of faith (however pretentious such may appear on my part) that the American system will ultimately triumph over a faceless despotism. John Stuart Mill once wrote that "a State which dwarfs its men in order that they may be more docile instruments . . . will find that with small men no great thing can really be accomplished." Surely the true glory and continuing strength of Americans has been that we saw the State small and man big.

To Admiral Arleigh A. Burke, Chief of Naval Operations, United States Navy, I owe a great deal. He graciously wrote the Foreword for this book. Additionally, from conversation with him I have derived much that was highly valuable with reference to military and naval affairs.

To Georgetown University and to its administration and faculty, I am greatly indebted. The generosity of the Georgetown University Alumni Annual Giving Fund helped make publication a reality. The Rev. Brian A. McGrath, S.J., Academic Vice President, gave me every encouragement and support, and the Rev. James B. Horigan, S.J., Dean of the Graduate School, the Rev. Joseph A. Sellinger, S.J., Dean of the College of Arts and Sciences, and Professor Howard A. Penniman, Chairman of the Department of Government, aided me at every turn. Professors John H. McDonough and Stefan T. Possony gave much of my manuscript the benefit of a careful reading, and their emendations have been of the highest order. The Rev. Joseph T. Durkin, S.J., Professor of American History, made many valuable suggestions and graciously made available to me some unpublished letters of General William T. Sherman. I am also indebted to Professors Eugene H. Bacon, Thomas P. McTighe, Rev. F. William O'Brien, S.J., Rev. Daniel E. Power, S.J., Bernard M. Wagner, Walter W. Wilkinson, Rev. Gerard F. Yates, S.J., and Rev. James V. Scholl, S.J., and Rev. Richard C. Spillane, S.J., for many excellent comments and for sound advice. All writers are forever indebted to librarians. I am doubly so to Mr. Salvatore Costabile, Miss Carol Evans, Mr. Joseph E. Jeffs, Mr. Peter J. Laux and Mr. M. Richard Wilt of the Georgetown University Library.

It would be difficult adequately to express my indebtedness to all of the many people in the armed forces who, at various times, gave freely of their advice and assistance in a multitude of ways. Among Army people I wish to thank especially Lt. General James M. Gavin, USA (Ret.), Major General Charles H. Bonesteel, III, USA, Colonels Otis E. Hays, Jr., USA, William R. Kintner, USA, Virgil Ney, USAR (Ret.), Tobias Philbin, USA, Donovan P. Yeuell, Jr., USA, Lt. Colonels Harold R. Aaron, USA, William M. Calnan, USA, Albert Hunter, USA, Francis Kelly, USA, William D. Neale, USA, William B. Rose, USAR, Miner L. Weems, USA, Majors George Daoust, USA, Henry G. Morgan, Jr., USA, Samuel J. Tobin, USAR, Captain Robert T. Crowley, USAR, and 1st Lieut. Francis S. Gospodarek, USAR. From the Navy and Marine Corps: Vice Admiral John T. Hayward, USN, Rear Admiral Thomas H. Moorer, USN, Captains Nils Johnson, USN, Raymond E. Peet, USN, Gilven M. Slonim, USN, Comdr. Frances E. Biadasz, USN, Lt. Commander William Barnes, USNR, Lieutenants Roy Fell, USN, Duane Thorin, USN, Major T. Paul Riegert, USMC, and Capt. James Munson, USMC. I am especially grateful to the Navy Department and to the officers and men of USS INDEPENDENCE for the insight into carrier operations furnished during an eight day cruise aboard INDEPENDENCE during September, 1959. From the Air Force: Colonels John Baer, USAF, Charles Hale, USAF, William Heimlich, USAFR, Charles W. Hostler,

USAF, William J. Jones, USAF, James G. L. Kellis, USAF, and Major Eugene M. Emme, USAFR, and Colonel Leslie Norton, USAF, and others of the Air War College faculty and staff.

The wise counsel of friends has been of great help. Among them are: Dr. David M. Abshire, Brig. General Donald Armstrong, USA (Ret.), Mr. Karl Baarslag, Colonel Nicholas Beckett, USAR (Ret.), Colonel Leo A. Codd, USA (Ret.), Captain Victor Gondos, editor of *Military Affairs*, Mr. Dayton M. Harrington, Rear Admiral John D. Hayes, USN (Ret.), Mr. Peter Healey, Mr. L. Eugene Hedberg, Mr. Irving Herschbein, Professor Tibor Kerekes, Dr. Robert Killmarx, Captain John O. Marsh, Jr., Virginia National Guard, Mr. John W. McConnell, Mr. Robert L. Miller, Mr. Charles Relihan, Professor William H. Russell, Mr. George Stansfield, and Professor Charles C. Tansill.

The patience and generosity of the publisher, Mr. Henry Regnery, have made him a friend indeed. My thanks to Mrs. Paul A. Conlin for typing the bulk of the manuscript.

I am happy to record the assistance of an old friend, classmate, and fellow West Virginian, the Rev. Edward A. Griffin, nor can I overlook the inspiration of Mrs. Edward W. Atkinson, Mr. and Mrs. Walter M. Matthews, Mr. and Mrs. Thomas E. Nutter, and David, Margaret, Mary, and Elizabeth Atkinson. My brother, Edward W. Atkinson, has been of the very greatest assistance in reading the manuscript and in offering invaluable suggestions for revision. My wife has assisted in the research involved in preparing the manuscript and has helped in revising my work. Here, as always, I am perpetually in her debt.

The help that I have received in the preparation of this work has been generous indeed. Without the kindness and gracious advice and assistance of those whom I have named (and, undoubtedly, of some whose names have inadvertently been omitted), this work would be even less worth while than it is. While, therefore, much is owed to many, all expressions of opinion and all sins of both commission and omission throughout the manuscript are mine alone.

JAMES DAVID ATKINSON

The Edge of War

CHAPTER 1

The American Approach to War

"The successful development of the Bolshevist doctrine throughout the world can only be effected by means of periods of rest during which we may recuperate and gather new strength for further exertions. I have never hesitated to come to terms with bourgeois governments, when by so doing I thought I could weaken the bourgeoisie. *It is sound strategy in war to postpone operations until the moral disintegration of the enemy renders the delivery of a mortal blow possible.*"* So wrote Lenin. We Americans have often acted as though warfare were a matter of bullets, bombs, and bloodshed. It may be all of these. But long before nuclear weapons or guided missiles, warfare was also ideas. Nuclear weapons and guided missiles have not changed the power of ideas. They have, instead, raised them to a higher threshold of man's consciousness. Today, as Lenin recognized, the ideas which soften up a nation for the knockout blow may be more important than the blow itself.

For in either the long or short run, it is ideas, not material things, which are portentous for right or wrong. It has not

*Emphasis supplied.

been until our own times that men generally have come to see how intimately their own daily lives may be affected by the theories—often seemingly esoteric—propounded by ideologues remote from the seats of power and responsibility. It is, perhaps, grimly paradoxical that in an age when scientific endeavor has reached undreamed of heights of achievement, ideas have become even more portentous for human destiny. This is so because political and military theorists more and more direct, guide, and condition the awesome forces of the atom and the mechanical creations of man in the latter part of the twentieth century. Twenty years ago who among us would have attached much significance to the theories of war and politics propounded by an almost unknown Chinese named Mao Tse-Tung? And even today Americans tend to be much more concerned about the fact that Sputniks have been put into orbit rather than about the *implications* which such devices may have as regards the creation of a fear psychosis, the creation of a feeling of insecurity and lack of confidence in our American government and way of life, and in the possibilities thereby raised for Communist nuclear blackmail.

Americans have, in general, been more inclined to disregard theoretical concepts in this way than have Europeans or Asians. The story is told of the famous Madison Avenue tycoon who, in the midst of a business conference, rushed to a dictating machine and bellowed, "Have somebody give me a memo on what this philosophy of Thomas Aquinas is all about." Whether apocryphal or not, the story is revealingly typical of our approach toward speculative thinking generally. It can even be more strongly underscored with refcrence to the American attitude towards speculative thinking about warfare. Sir Charles Oman, the British military historian, declared that not only the historians of medieval days but also the nineteenth- and twentieth-century historiographers had no precise understanding of the true nature of war. They often did not look beyond the aspect of losses or brutalities. Medievalists and moderns alike tended to cover up their lack of knowledge or often their disdain of military affairs by downgrading the historical significance of such events.

Sir Charles' observations are even more valid with reference to the United States, since our historians, and our writers generally, have, with some exceptions, given scant attention to military history and even less to philosophical speculation about war. As the brilliant historian of naval affairs Professor Samuel Eliot Morison has said, there has been, especially in the historical writing in the United States in the 1920's and 1930's, a trend that has "ignored wars, belittled wars, taught that no war was necessary and no war did any good, even to the victor." Happily, an opposite tendency has been developing in intellectual circles within the past decade; yet even today military history often remains a minute chronicle of commanders, battles, and places; and many of us still shy away from speculative thinking about war. This tendency may be, in part, because the study of the history of ideas has only recently attained a firm place among thinkers and critics. Now that many scholars are at work exploring the ideas behind literature and the fine arts as well as all forms of scientific endeavor, it would seem that the time is ripe for broad investigations into the ideas behind

3

military strategy and tactics and the development of weapons and communications.[1]

THE ROLE OF FORCE IN AMERICAN THOUGHT

The American intellectual heritage has been to regard warfare (that is, organized force) either as absolutely immoral and hence to be abolished—root and branch—or as so unreasonable and repugnant to those of intellectual attainments that it will, in some mysterious way, be exorcised by the spirit of reason. Those of our philosophers who have taken up the study of war have usually been content either to dwell on its immoral nature and to look to some legal means for suppressing it or to view war as so unreasonable that it will eventually disappear or can, in some way, be driven from the minds of men. "The fatalistic view of the war-function is to me nonsense," declared the American philosopher William James, "for I know that war-making is due to definite motives and subject to prudential checks and reasonable criticisms, just like any other form of enterprise. And when whole nations are the armies, and the science of destruction vies in intellectual refinement with the sciences of production, I see that war becomes absurd and impossible from its own monstrosity. Extravagant ambitions will have to be replaced by reasonable claims and nations must make common cause against them."[2] Remarkably, we see in the world of the latter part of the twentieth century echoes of this view that war has become absurd and impossible from its own monstrosity.

Today such views take as their basis the idea that the terrible destruction which would be wrought by the use of

4

large-scale nuclear weapons has brought warfare to a dead-end street. Thus, much credence is given to expressions in the press, over the air waves—and especially in intellectual circles—that war is unthinkable, that war is too horrible to contemplate in the nuclear era, and, wonder of wonders, that war has finally abolished itself! The unfortunate fact is that while war may have reached a stage in which it is unthinkable to many in the civilized world, war, or at least new forms of warfare, may still remain thinkable to Russian, Chinese, and other Communist leaders. This tendency to consider war as unthinkable is, however, not really new in the American experience. Despite Jefferson's suggestion that military affairs should constitute a definite part of American education, we have often looked askance at the role of military power—of organized force—in human affairs and, as a result, have usually failed to understand the *raison d'être* for the employment of force. When the preponderance of the intellectual climate of opinion regards warfare as intrinsically evil, there is apt to grow up, equally, a climate of opinion which does not understand how force can best be employed and which therefore may oscillate between the extremes of abdication of the use of force in any eventuality and the unlimited use of force.

Although not an American, Lord Bertrand Russell, the well-known philosopher, might be said to exemplify one extreme attitude toward the employment of force in the present nuclear age. He has been reported as having stated in an interview that it would be preferable to live in a Communist-dominated world rather than risk a nuclear war. While it is difficult to quarrel with Lord Russell's efforts to obtain peace,

5

it would appear that such efforts are out of touch with reality. In fact, one might employ the idiom of that well-known television and screen personality, Mr. Elvis Presley, to ask the noble lord whether existence under Soviet control would really be living? The student of military affairs must refuse to accept such a simple answer to a problem so complex as modern warfare. In the first place, the values at stake—human dignity itself and a host of others precious to our heritage—are so great that the risk even of an all-out war is far preferable to an abject surrender. More probable, also, is the fact that the warfare of the future *will not* involve a nuclear holocaust since the parties involved will retain their freedom of action to prosecute the war by measures short of total destruction.

That the problem is by no means a simple question of either total submission or total destruction has been presented in a challenging fashion by Pope Pius XII, who speaking on the subject of war stated: "the battlefield and the weapons ready for use are of unimaginable power. Thus the problem of national defense assumes an ever increasing importance, its problems are as complex as they are difficult to solve. This is why no nation which wishes to provide for the security of its frontiers, as is its right and absolute duty, can be without an army proportionate to its needs, supplied with all indispensable material; ready and alert for the defense of the homeland should it be unjustly threatened or attacked." The prevention of the dilemma of having to choose between surrender in the face of nuclear blackmail threats on the one hand and total nuclear war on the other may, therefore, be precluded by the maintenance of powerful defense forces which possess a wide range of capabilities—land, sea,

6

air, and unorthodox warfare combat potentials. Equally essential for survival—and almost infinitely more basic—is the possession of a philosophical approach which recognizes, above all, the necessity for the defense of the values of our Judaeo-Christian civilization and which, secondly, prepares an intellectual atmosphere conducive to the selection of the proper amount of force for the needs of the particular situation which arises. We will not be well served, however, by the dogmatic acceptance of the idea that *any* use of force is to be avoided under *any* circumstances.

AMERICAN MILITARY THINKERS

American scholars—whether philosophers, historians, or political scientists—have in the past tended to avoid coming to grips with the theoretical side of warfare. This has perhaps been the result of the seeming security, throughout our history, offered by the vastness and the geographical location of America. In his classic history of the United States during the administrations of Jefferson and Madison, Henry Adams held that in the American mentality repugnance to war held first place among political characteristics. As a result of their relative security most Americans looked at war in a peculiar light.[3] In addition to this antipathy of the American character towards war—which observers from De Tocqueville onwards have noted—there has been a somewhat opposing tendency noted by some writers. This might be called the myth that a million men will spring to arms and that one true-blue American is, at least in military matters, a match for ten other men. Nothing has been so persistent in our mythology; yet nothing has been so lacking in actual fact. As that peculiarly American genius Homer Lea wrote in the early twentieth century, "the modern American's conception of military efficiency is but a succession of heroics culminating in victory. This heroism of dreams, this valor of the rostrum, is based, not upon the real history of past military achievements, but upon the illusions of them . . . [and] as the social and industrial, ethical and political organism of this nation becomes more and more complex . . . the self-deception of the people as regards their inherent military capacity becomes more dominant and unreasonable."[4] And he went on to issue the warning, more prophetic for the 1960's than for the early 1900's, that "the self-deception of a nation concerning its true militant strength increases at the same ratio as its actual militant capacity decreases."[5]

Thirty-eight years and two world wars after Homer Lea's prophetic words, Americans in Korea were confronted with a display of force by a ruthless and determined enemy. Once again we had failed to remember that blind confidence in our industrial superiority or the wonders of our twentieth-century civilization was not a substitute for armed might.[6] In spite of the terrible lessons of two world wars, we neglected to do our homework in the vital area of military thinking. Americans still possessed, as they had from Bunker Hill to the Battle of the Bulge, courage to fight against odds, but their country still retained the tradition of unpreparedness for war.[7]

Thus two essentially opposing currents of thought in the American heritage—the concept of warfare as essentially evil and hence to be avoided by pretending that it is not there, and the concept of a million men springing to arms (sometimes to nonexistent arms) and winning glorious victories—would seem to have hindered the development of speculative thinking among our scholars and publicists about the nature

8

of warfare. One might add, too, a third factor: geographic location, which has long been embodied in the concept that America's remoteness from the rest of the world and her boundaries with relatively weak and friendly powers offered us long-range security. This has permitted American scholars and thinkers to speculate along almost any lines except those of a military nature and has led them to regard the necessity for military studies as something in the nature of a temporary aberration which could be quickly disposed of to permit a return to more pleasant pursuits of the mind.

Since the armed forces of a nation are an outgrowth of the national character and of the total cultural heritage of the nation, it might be expected that our professional soldiers, sailors, marines, and airmen would, as a reflection of that national character, likewise tend to avoid coming to grips with the theoretical side of warfare. Such has been the case. Americans have distinguished themselves in the fields of military tactics, ordnance, engineering—indeed, in the military arts in almost every area—but we have contributed much less to the speculative side of warfare. Our outstanding contributions to war have been in the areas of logistics, tactics, and technics. When forced into a war, however, we have been more than a match in intellect, resourcefulness, and resolution than those with whom war is an avocation. But Admiral Mahan remains our sole military philosopher of a stature comparable to Clausewitz or Jomini.[8]

ADMIRAL MAHAN

With the possible exception of General William "Billy" Mitchell, the only American who stands out as a great military theorist in the ranks of those philosophers or theorists

9

of warfare on a global basis is Admiral Alfred Thayer Mahan. General Mitchell was the first military theorist to conceive of the employment of air power in worldwide terms and, in many respects, must be considered as having contributed more to the theory of air warfare than the other great speculative thinker about air power, the Italian General Giulio Douhet. General Mitchell must be recognized as an original thinker about the military art. He is, however, so close to our own times that it remains rather difficult to obtain a completely fair judgment on his contributions to military theory and his exact place in the galaxy of philosophers of the military art. A detailed scholarly study of General Mitchell's contributions to the theory of war is very much needed.

About Admiral Mahan there is little room for doubt. Historians have rightly assigned to Mahan a place among the greatest of the military theorists of all time. In a series of books and articles which began with his classic *The Influence of Sea Power Upon History* (1890) Mahan not merely developed a historical chronicle of war at sea but evolved theoretical doctrines for the employment of sea power to such an extent that he may well be said to have been the creator of the first unified body of theory and doctrine on this subject. One modern analyst considers that Mahan soon came to hold a place akin to that carved out in the theory of land warfare by Clausewitz and others.[9] Professor Margaret Tuttle Sprout goes even further when she states that "no other single person has so directly and profoundly influenced the theory of sea power and naval strategy as Alfred Thayer Mahan."[10] This is certainly not an extravagant claim, since Admiral Mahan's contributions to military theory went well

beyond his concepts of sea power. The great German authority on geopolitics, General Karl Haushofer, has written that it
was Admiral Mahan who educated America's political leaders
so that they began to think in terms of global power and ex-
panded space, and writers on geopolitics generally have recognized Mahan's contributions to this field. More recently,
one of Britain's most distinguished writers in the field of
strategy, Air Vice-Marshal Kingston-McCloughry, has indicated that he believes Mahan to have been even greater than
Clausewitz, since Mahan's "method resembled a two-way
traffic system: sea-power/history, and history/sea strategy:
Clausewitz's method was almost wholly a one-way system."[11]

Now that the nuclear age seems to offer the United States
even greater possibilities for the exploitation of sea power,
it is perhaps peculiarly appropriate that an American should
have been its great exponent and theorist. For the new technology of the nuclear age has already begun to present problems with respect to the proper posture of national defense
which call for a long, searching look at Mahan's works. Even
now it is clear that these new problems demand not the ignor-
ing of the philosophical approach to sea power but rather a
re-evaluation and extension of Mahan's theories in the light
of present-day scientific and technical achievements. For example, the application of nuclear power to the submersible
vessel so that the underwater craft has now become a true
"submarine" is fraught with great significance for America's
future thinking about national defense. The effect of supplying submarines with nuclear power plants in effect permits
the exploitation of the seas of the world in three dimensions.[12] Conversely, the building of atomic destroyers and

other anti-submarine vessels would give the Navy vastly extended freedom of action to meet the challenge posed by the huge Soviet submarine fleet now in existence.

Equally important in the employment of sea power in the future would seem to be the comparative freedom from land bases offered by nuclear propulsion applied to surface naval vessels. It is possible that the nuclear powered surface craft may be equally as significant as the nuclear submarine. For one thing possession of fleets of such ships would give the United States greater freedom of action and would permit curtailment of dependence upon other nations for base facilities for our naval forces. Outside the rather close limits of territorial waters, the sea, both in international law and in fact, is a vast, almost limitless area in which sovereignty does not run. Hence aircraft carrier and missile striking forces can operate, in effect, as floating airfields and launching platforms without the necessity for political or diplomatic agreements to provide land and air space for their operation from particular countries. In the great age of sail—which Admiral Mahan used to begin his theoretical studies of the influence of sea power—fleets had considerable immunity from the land since they did not have to replenish their fuel. The winds which filled the sails of those far-ranging, storm-tossed ships were a constant, readily available source of energy. In the nuclear age we have again arrived at a point at which surface vessels once more will be able to be largely independent of the land for their supplies of fuel.

Today scientific advances have made it possible for entire fleets to be independent of land bases in ways in which the sailing vessels of the eighteenth century could never have been. Developments in the irradiation of food, making possible its preservation for indefinite periods in less space than required by conventional means, accompanied by new techniques for the packaging and handling of stores of all kinds, have gone far to solve what were once considered well-nigh insuperable problems for provisioning ships at sea.

Equally important have been the advances, both as regards new equipment and new techniques, in repair and overhaul facilities at sea. Nowadays although the fleet train which provides the necessary support for the fleet cannot actually build a new ship while at sea, it can perform virtually every other task necessary to maintain the sea-keeping qualities of the ships of the fleet. The spectacular possibilities which are now being thrown open to surface vessels through the combination of nuclear power plants and new techniques of provisioning, storage, and repair facilities must, however, be considered as operating in concert with what has happened to the submarine now that nuclear power plants are a reality for the underwater craft.

The combination of all of these factors would seem to add up to an immeasurably greater freedom of action in the conjoint fields of military policy and foreign policy for that nation which (1) first thoroughly explores and perfects these new techniques and processes and then (2) develops the theoretical concepts and the body of doctrine which will permit these instruments to occupy their proper place in the national defense structure. On the other hand, to permit these new instruments and techniques to become ends in themselves or, worse yet, to develop them and then fail to understand how best to use them can but lead to mediocrity at best or tragedy at worst. In the area of sea power as well as in other areas of strategy we must avoid the tendency to allow military *thought* to atrophy, for in this direction lies not merely complacency, but madness. It is from theoretical and doctrinal foundations that the correct application of new weapons and techniques of warfare can best be harnessed to the maintenance of the national security. New weapons and new combat methods should not be left to develop independently and, in such a fashion, possibly conflict with the nation's over-all strategy. New advances in techniques and new weapons should be in the service of the grand strategy of the United States and not in conflict with that grand strategy, although proponents of single-weapon strategies sometimes forget this rather elementary fact. And without the development of a body of theory and doctrine such new techniques of war and new weapons are apt to be sterile indeed as servants of national policy.

During the period between the two great wars, for example, the United States Marine Corps pioneered in the development of a body of doctrine and a set of theories for the conduct of amphibious warfare, though there were naval and military people who were skeptical about the *need* for such a doctrine and such theories. Whether in the speculative thinking about sea power so greatly developed by Admiral Mahan, or in the deliberating about land power or air power, military thinking—which means in the long run military practice—must avoid the dead hand of formalism and of an overweening attention to the day-to-day routine of the work of the moment which tends to engulf the military man no less than the scholar.[13]

14

The American Approach to War

THE MILITARY MIND*

In American mythology—and who shall say that this is not one of the most enduring parts of the American heritage—intangible as it may seem—the military officer, whatever his branch of service, has usually been portrayed as an unthinking (or incapable of thinking) martinet. While some novelists, screen writers, and playwrights have contributed a minority view which portrays the military, naval, or air leader in a sympathetic light, the general view and the one which has been most deeply imbedded in our national mythology is that of the brass hat, the my-guts-and-your-blood swashbuckling officer who lacks either sense or sensibility and who, if not watched carefully, will Prussianize a free-born citizenry. That such a mental image bears little resemblance to reality has not at all prevented it from having gained wide currency. Generations of speakers have quoted Dr. Johnson's "patriotism is the last refuge of scoundrels" without inquiring as to the setting within which that great Englishman placed it.

This mental image of the military mind is the result of a queer melange of much fancy and some fact. The traditional fear of military rule—and quite a proper fear—is an Anglo-Saxon one which had, after all, certain grounds. Englishmen, Irishmen, and Scotsmen who had suffered under the Cromwellian rule of the major generals carried something of this distrust with them as a part of their mental baggage to the

*For an interpretative and detailed study in this field see Lieutenant Colonel William D. Neale, U.S. Army, "The U.S. Military Mind," unpublished M.A. thesis, Georgetown University Graduate School, Washington, D.C.: Georgetown University Library, 1958. It is hoped that this analysis of the literature—both fictional and biographical—of the Second World War in its relation to the idea of a "military mind" will be published.

15

New World. Such ideas were powerfully bolstered by the employment of British troops in the coercive enforcement of the restrictive Acts of Parliament on the restive colonists in America. We are pointedly reminded of this fear of possible military rule by the provision written into the Bill of Rights of the Constitution (the Third Amendment): "No soldier shall, in time of peace, be quartered in any house without the consent of the owner, nor in time of war, but in a manner to be prescribed by law." Probably more far-reaching as it concerns the national mythology were, however, some of the irresponsible acts of British officers and soldiers in the days immediately before Lexington and Concord. These wrongs, while not really representative of the British Army nor, indeed, of any military mind, are the very stuff of which myths are made. Thus the great English historian Sir George O. Trevelyan has told us of an incident which occurred on the day ordained by Congress as a day of prayer and fasting in Massachusetts in the spring of 1775. This day was being solemnized in the Boston churches, and to make a mockery of it members of a British unit pitched two tents "within ten yards of the chapel at the West End of the city, and played their drums and fifes as long as the service lasted, while their Colonel looked approvingly on." In the same crude fashion a group of officers shattered the windows in John Hancock's house and cut the fence in front of it with their swords.[14]

This heritage from the rule of the major generals in England and from pre-Revolutionary days in this country must be said to account for a part of the attitude of Americans towards the mythical military mind. To this was added the frontier mythology that viewed any differences in rank, and especially the outward trappings of insignia and badge of office, as representative of the hereditary system of class and caste of the Old World. To the rough-hewn creators of forty-rod Monongahela rye whiskey and similar frontier staples anything smacking of gold braid and epaulettes was indicative of Old World aristocracy and to be viewed with disdain as well as with the suspicion that such trappings might endanger the foundations of the Republic. If, on more extensive reflection, it was realized that the soldierly virtues of discipline, honor, and duty as exemplified in Washington and his Continentals had actually *made* the Republic a living entity, this did little to affect the myth, for the less the amount of solid fact, the stronger the myth. Furthermore, generations of Americans from Bunker Hill to Inchon have been nourished in the belief that the amateur in war has some mysterious, almost magical source of strength and power which enables him to overreach the professional. For a distressingly long time this has been the American mystique as regards national defense, and it has begun to give ground only since the end of the Second World War. As a people, one of our defects has been that, especially in military affairs, we have refused to let the issues be clouded by facts.

The years from the Revolutionary War down through the Civil War marked a curious ambivalence in regard to the American attitude towards the military. That there was no really deep-seated fear of the military is shown by the number of generals, either regular or volunteer, who became President—Washington, Jackson, William Henry Harrison, Franklin Pierce, Taylor, and Grant. Still others—for exam-

17

ple, Winfield Scott and McClellan—received the nomination to that high office. Yet somehow there was the lingering shadow, deeply embedded in American mythology, that there existed a military mind which was alien to this great Republic and which had to be watched carefully lest it undermine our national institutions. The myth that somehow an officer caste might arise and create a dictatorship never, of course, had any foundation in fact, yet it somehow managed to persist. Even in the trying days after the first Battle of Bull Run when McClellan seemed to embody the military virtues which would preserve the Union, neither he nor his staff *did* anything which deviated from their loyal service to the civil authority as represented by President Lincoln and the Congress, although much has been made of a chance phrase in one of McClellan's letters to his wife. It required the cataclysm of war, nevertheless, to make it possible seriously to suspect a general of possessing the *ability* to become a dictator by appealing to the volunteers who had been called to the colors. Yet in the midst of even this great struggle the phantom of a huge regular army still obsessed the nation.[15]

The aftermath of a great civil war found the American people, with the danger past, reverting to the traditional distrust of the military. Only eleven years after the end of the bloodiest conflict ever witnessed in North America, we find the same popular fear of the standing army and its presumed concomitant, the military mind, reflected in a letter by General William T. Sherman, the Army's Commanding General, to his son. Sherman wrote that "had it not been for Custer's affair we could not have warded off the intended reduction of the number and pay of the Army. Now, though

opposed to a small increase of privates to fill up companies,
I believe Congress would vote any number of volunteers, but
we don't want them or need them."[16]

This rather traditional distrust of large permanent armed
forces and especially of the military mind, which was supposedly in back of such forces, could be indulged in time of
peace and when America was far distant from any strong
military power. The neurosis was not apt to be fatal when
our armed forces faced no foes more formidable than the
Arapahoes or the Blackfeet. But with the passing of the nineteenth century and the gradual involvement of the United
States in the ever-widening scope of world politics, such distrust—unless shown to have some real foundation—was liable
to be more harmful than it was to be productive of good.
A certain natural skepticism about the military—as with any
other group—is probably a good thing in a healthy society.
It is, of course, the extremist tendencies in the continuing
creation of the myth of militarism that we need to recognize
and to fear.

To this American heritage of a certain amount of suspicion
regarding the relation of the military and the state—which
was in some ways healthy—was, however, added in the early
years of the twentieth century a body of theory which held
that war itself had never been productive of anything but
evil. This thesis inevitably cast a double shadow on the military mind. For with this rationale not only was the professional officer branded as part of an aristocratic caste, but, even
worse, he was attached to an instrument—war—which was
intrinsically evil and which should be rooted up and cast into
the Pit. This state of mind might be said to have grown out

of the liberalism of the nineteenth century which saw man as moving inexorably toward a final state of perfection in this world. This liberalism seemed to find in the institutions of this world the only things which held man back from a state of ultimate perfection.

For some it was the Demon Rum, as exemplified in the saloon, that barred man's progress to higher things. To others it was monogamy, or the tax system, or some other institution. And to still others it was war as an institution, which meant militarism, the military mind or some other derivative of war. Like many—if not most—battlers for justice and righteousness, those who campaigned in the name of pacifism were motivated by the highest principles. Those who have actually known war could not but agree with the pacifists of the early twentieth century that the abolition of war would remove a great scourge from mankind. But, perhaps because the profession of arms had by its nature made men cautious (and they are usually charged with being over-conservative), the soldiers and sailors of the day were often thought of as being obstructionists because they felt the need for more realistic means to restrain man's very nature rather than merely placing the emphasis on certain of man's institutions. In all fairness it must be remembered, too, that philosophers such as William James recognized that the martial virtues of discipline, devotion to the public good over the private interest, and a keen sense of honor were worthy of admiration and were necessary to the stability of the good society. Indeed, James wrote his famous *The Moral Equivalent of War* with the idea that it might be possible to find during peace some substitute for the martial virtues which he recognized as being called forth by war.

The First World War came, then, as a distinct shock to Americans, and not least to the members of the intelligentsia who, however much maligned (or praised), had pinned their hopes on the apparent steady progress of the world towards perpetual peace through arbitration and other devices of international law as well as the rising standards of communication and education. Nevertheless, the immediate reaction to the First World War was one of exaltation. Americans rejoiced with Englishman Rupert Brooke's lines:

Now, God be thanked Who has matched us with His hour,
And caught our youth, and wakened us from sleeping. . . .

And the concluding words:

If I should die think only this of me
    That there's some corner of a foreign field
That is forever England. . . .

The feeling of exaltation of the war years was followed by a wave of disillusionment in the 1920's which carried over through the 1930's and into the period of the Second World War. Not only did novelists portray the mistakes of the brass hats and revel in the futility of the war to end wars, but the opposition to the armed forces on moral grounds enjoyed a strong revival in the 1920's. One writer somewhat hopefully, if naively, forecast in 1926 that the church could sweep the "Prussian system" out of every college in the United States within a decade if it would fight militarism as it fought the saloon. If such a feeling of moral revulsion against the presence of the Reserve Officers Training Corps units in American universities was indicative of an important section of intellectual opinion, one might well believe that the regular military services enjoyed no immense prestige in America in this era. Certainly the military mind was even more suspect.

The 1920's witnessed also the rise of a body of literature by writers of the Left which has ever since had some influence (although it is difficult to assess fully) on the American climate of opinion vis-à-vis the military. This type of writing sometimes made use of the opposition to so-called militarism on the basis of moral scruples, but more often it scorned any appeal to Christian pleading and used the slogans of democracy, universal peace, and similar themes in portraying those who advocated powerful national defense forces as militarists, men on horseback, enemies of democracy, and other hackneyed names which, although tired, stale, and quite flat, if repeated often enough do eventually carry conviction.

The early thirties supplied much better ammunition for the protagonists of the Left. For the rise of Fascism and, more especially, the gaining of power by Hitler and his followers gave a real basis to some of their claims. The indiscriminate charges against the military mind remained baseless in fact; but a genuine cause for moral indignation, which had previously been somewhat lacking, was then indeed present. From that time on such labels as Fascist, Fascistoid, authoritarian personality, or Nazi could be hurled at those whose concern was a powerful America and who did not discriminate between the evils of Red Fascism of the Soviet Communists or the Brown Fascism of the Nazis. Veterans' organizations such as the American Legion found themselves in that era increasingly portrayed as Blackshirts, American Fascists, and the like. The long-range campaign of Leftist writers and propagandists might well be called Operation Confusion since, at least until that day of June 22, 1941, when the Soviet Union was itself invaded, the aim of these people (whether dupes, fellow-travellers, or outright Party members) seems to have been to confuse and mislead the American people. With regrettable effectiveness they clouded the issues and generated a dense gray fog of confusion and uncertainty about the reasons for the maintenance of national power through armed force, as well as the reasons for the proper use of that force and the distinctions between the use and abuse of military power.

In summing up the climate of opinion that prevailed in the United States on the eve of the Second World War, one is constrained to conclude that the chief forces which conditioned Americans in their attitude towards the military mind were: (1) The long heritage of what might be called frontier democracy's suspicion of the possibility of a military caste. (2) The pacifist/moralist idea—greatly strengthened in the 1920's and early 1930's—that war and the preparations for war were essentially sinful and hence to be extirpated. (3) The Leftist line of thought, especially strong from 1919 onwards, which saw nothing wrong in the possession of force by the Soviet Union, but which felt it a duty or, at least an impulse, to reduce the armed strength of a bourgeois power including that of its own country, the United States. The Leftist, in such a context, really feels no requirement of duty to the land in which he happens to be living, but rather to the world movement of Communism.

To these currents of thought there should probably be

added a fourth, a factor of no little significance in the total current of thought. This was the hard-boiled school of writers and thinkers of the post World War I period. Their style, whether in fiction or in factual writing, was fresh, and after much of the stuffiness of the preceding period, refreshing. Their writing, however, was critically savage. They debunked everything from George Washington to the Christian Church, and in this they resembled the angry young men of the post World War II era except possibly that they had greater craftsmanship in turning a phrase. Perhaps because the great events of the First World War offered such a vast scope for the employment of their talents, or because there had been so many singularly inept commanders on all sides in that war, or because the disillusionment after the Great War so far exceeded that of previous conflicts—for any or all of these reasons, the hard-boiled school turned its pens towards the military mind. Brass hat became a term not so much of opprobrium as of stupidity and, if heroes there were, they were to be found in the ranks. From the collectivity of these writings there emerged the picture of the military man not so much the stern martinet as the unfeeling, unthinking automaton whose bible was the rule book and whose intellectual capacities might, at their highest, permit the writing of some rather stuffy memoirs. It would not seem unfair to say that H. L. Mencken was representative of the hard-boiled school of writing of the period. Writing in the *American Mercury* in September of 1929, the iconoclastic Mencken probably outlined the credo of the thinkers and writers of the time when he said, "the military career tends to slow down the mind, but it may be that the thing works the other way—that it naturally attracts men who are not excessively intellectual." Mr. Mencken went on to opine that "of all the arts practised by man, the art of the soldier seems to call for the least intelligence." The military mind was, in this view, an extremely narrow one. It is consequently small wonder that writers on military affairs in the 1920's and 1930's alike were, at most, barely tolerated and were oftentimes considered as mere spokesmen for a vested interest.

The intellectual ferment of these years may actually be more meaningful than all of the tortuously reasoned and ponderous studies about American isolationism. Many a self-appointed seer has labored mightily to produce still another weighty tome explaining, diagnosing, or interpreting America's alleged withdrawal from international affairs during these two decades. But much of what poured from the presses from 1919 onwards has wordily but unmistakably missed the point, for the history of ideas often tells us more about an era than the history of things. Certainly, with exceptions here and there, the history of the ideas of the years between the two great world wars would reveal an amalgam of distrust and lack of understanding of the military mind. To use Mencken's trend of thought, there was disbelief that any such thing as a mind of the military existed inasmuch as the military could hardly aspire to such high estate.

A realization that this mental attitude existed and a recognition of the events and personalities that produced it are essential for anyone who attempts to perceive the significance of what has taken place in American military thought from the time of Pearl Harbor through the Korean War and into the later 1950's. Robert Sherwood has written, with reference to the period just prior to and also during the Second World War, that in the United States "morale was never particularly good nor alarmingly bad. There was a minimum of flag waving and parades. It was the first war in American history in which the general disillusionment preceded the firing of the first shot."[17] This succinct appraisal portrays rather accurately a distressingly high degree of pseudo-sophistication among the American people; it likewise reveals an unfortunate complacency or disinterest which may well contain the seeds of our national destruction.

Possibly because of the cynicism and debunking of the inter-war years, there was far less disillusionment after the Second World War than there had been after the First World War. And yet there were many who argued that our sacrifices had been in vain once more. Admitting that it was a mistake —we do not yet know whether fatal to our civilization—to crush one form of totalitarianism and not try at the very least to weaken or dissipate the power of the other totalitarianism, can we not still say that the world was the better for the elimination of Hitler and his Brown Fascism? Red Fascism remains in a strengthened and territorially enlarged form, but the elimination of its twin brother can be counted not only as not futile but as having raised up some measure of hope for the future.

The factual writing which followed the Second World War and which has continued down through the Korean War to the present time has, with some exceptions, been much less on the debunking side than that after World War I. Actually we have begun in the past decade to witness the growth of a body of writing about military affairs both by civilians and by military people which has come to appreciate the fact that not only do the military virtues of discipline, duty, and honor have meaning for a modern America, but also that the military mind is apt to be, in intellectual attainments, equally as informed and capable as the civilian mind and sometimes even more flexible. If the free expression and, indeed, the conflict of ideas help provide sustenance for a constitutional and representative form of government such as our own, then the controversies that have arisen among the armed services during the past decade will show that iron dogmatism is not now nor has it ever been a part of American military thought. Still more, they demonstrate clearly that the belief of a military mind which presents a common front against the civilian policy-makers in government has never been more than a myth.

If one turns to the production of the novelist, the screen- and radio-writer, and the television script-writer in the period following the Second World War, a somewhat different picture emerges. The trend in this area of fiction seems to have been not so much disillusionment as futility. One cannot say, of course, that this is an exclusively American affair. It seems to be largely true of the literature of warfare in many other countries. What is interesting on the American scene, however, is the way in which there is something of a repetition of the post World War I themes of the cowardly officer, the stupid general, and the pointlessness of war. Now, however, this is followed—and surrounded—by a feeling of absolute futility rather than the earlier sense of disillusionment. Whether this is the result of the omnipotent state as exemplified in the ever-encompassing Soviet Union (and certainly

George Orwell's *1984* has played some role in this climate of thought), or whether it has been brought on by the advent of the terrifying power of nuclear weapons, or combinations of these and other things of unease in the years after 1945, it is difficult to establish with accuracy. A spate of motion pictures —several of them, incidentally, extremely well-written, forcefully acted, and effectively presented—curiously have one common message: war is futile; war is useless. While no sane person *wants* or *desires* war, it is demonstrably true that war is not necessarily the greatest of all evils. This was true when Hitler was devouring Europe in piecemeal fashion; it is true today. But there the similarity ends.

In Hitler's day writers and movie makers recognized his evil philosophy for what it was. Today a philosophy that is even more evil is coupled to a dynamo—Russian imperialism —that is far more terrifying than Hitler's Nazi war machine. Yet some of those who mold opinion in the United States appear ostrich-like to be completely unaware of these obvious truths, for they do not try to combat the evil that is sworn to destroy them and all their works. The result would appear to be the same as that sought by the Nazi film *Baptism of Fire,* which had as its object the inculcation of fear and defeatism.

Whatever the case may be, there is now less emphasis on the evils of the military mind and more on the futility of war in whatever circumstance. It is interesting to note that in the latter part of the 1950's this rather negative climate of thought of futility, or perhaps of fatalism, has had a tendency to find expression among some philosophers, theologians, scientists, and others in the intellectual community in the United States. Thus a noted clergyman, the Rev. Ernest Gordon, Dean of the Chapel of Princeton University, has written in *The Living Faith for Today* that "war is contrary to the will of God." A scientist, Dr. Robert S. McCleary, in considering "A Christian Answer to Atomic War," has argued that since war in the nuclear age is so terrible to contemplate and a preventive war is, of course, ruled out, the United States should proceed to the complete renunciation of war with unilateral total disarmament.[18] These statements are not isolated ones. They and others like them were uttered by well-educated and respectable persons. Many highly intelligent and well-meaning thinkers and writers in the United States have spoken and written along the same lines, and it is widely known that the great physicist Dr. J. Robert Oppenheimer did not believe it desirable to go ahead with the work which eventually produced the hydrogen bomb. Thus we seem to be edging away from an intellectual climate hostile to the military mind as such and moving more in the direction of accepting as fact the absolute futility of war or the idea that war is evil *in se*. Some speculative thinking has even ventured so far from reality as to be willing to forego any action which would even take any *risk* of war through the employment of limited force or the carrying on of political warfare and diplomatic maneuvering. This brings us, then, to a summation of warfare and the American character.

WARFARE AND THE AMERICAN CHARACTER

The reasons why the United States has developed so few military thinkers (Admiral Mahan, General Mitchell of the Air Corps, General Emory Upton of the Army, and Professor

29

Denis Hart Mahan, of the U.S. Military Academy are exceptions) as contrasted with a host of brilliant tacticians, military
engineers, military scientists, and administrators/organizers
would seem to be the result not merely of the acceptance of
the military mind myth in America, but much more of the
interplay of warfare as experienced by Americans and the
national character. The American national character as related to warfare, though somewhat ambiguous, is composed,
I believe, of at least six elements:

(1) The almost hyper-idealistic attitude that war is immoral. Hence rather than attempt to study warfare and try
to understand it, all efforts should be directed towards its
immediate abolition. This is a noble impulse but, regrettably,
not very productive. It remains, nevertheless, a strong and
continuing drive, as witnessed currently by the numerous suggestions and plans for controlling the world through *law*—as
if all other leaders and peoples understood "law" in the
same sense that we Americans do. The other side of the coin
of this hyper-idealism is also worthy of note. The high sense
of moral values—often criticized by writers of the realist
school and believed by many Europeans and Asians to be
Anglo-Saxon hypocrisy—in behalf of which Americans have
made great military exertions, may well be our greatest single
asset against that modern form of tyranny, the total police
state.

(2) The pragmatic nature of the American mind. One of
the defects of our qualities is a tendency to be excessively practical. In foreign policy this appears as an excessive leaning
toward day-to-day solutions rather than long-range planning,
while in military affairs we incline in the direction of think-

ing that national defense is geared to a profit-and-loss statement. Hence in America the military theorist—or any theorist—is assigned not to an ivory tower, but rather to the
Pentagon's sub-basement. Now the relegation of theorists to
sub-basements even further from Washington than the Pentagon is not necessarily and in all cases a bad idea, but the
tendency as regards the handling of speculative thinking in
such a manner is dangerous. This is not to say that the
American penchant for pragmatism is completely evil. It
is not.

In warfare and in the preparation of a defense policy which
tries to avert war the pragmatic approach with its emphasis
on that which is workable, its stress on the possible, avoids
the trap of the panacea, the one-big-solution or the single-
weapon fallacy in military thought. That wise and witty
Scotsman, Professor D. W. Brogan, has written that "to the
Americans war is a business, not an art." This observation
sums up in a few words a great deal of the story of the American approach to war. This predilection is, of course, intimately related to our essentially pragmatic character and it
has been why, with the tremendous organizational, mechanical, and supply demands of war in the twentieth century,
we have been so often successful. It is not for nothing that
many British and German observers called the Lend-Lease
program of the Second World War one of the decisive—if not
the decisive—elements of that great conflict. For the Lend-
Lease program embodied all of the components of the busi-
nesslike approach to war. Yet again, this pragmatic and func-
tional part of the American character may be carried to such
an extreme that it seeks to secure victory by sheer weight of

materiel alone and hence becomes bogged down in things to the exclusion of ideas. For, as President Wilson said in addressing a group of naval officers early in the First World War, "Somebody has got to think this war out."[19] In the war in which we are now engaged—a war quite as serious and altogether as real as though a formal declaration of war had been issued—the possession of massive *material* engines of destruction *alone* will not be enough. We have got to think things through, and the *best* thinking in America must be brought to bear on the grave and continuing threat which confronts us.

(3) The underlying tenacity and toughness of the American character in war. Under a superficial softness, the American displays in warfare a toughness of character which has surprised many observers from Valley Forge to Pusan. The American's apparent dependence on creature comforts (ice-water was an American phenomenon, for example, in the early nineteenth century) and his tendency to grumble and complain have often led others to think us soft. (For the Nazis and the Communists the word is "decadent.") This, by the way, is not new. A Confederate soldier tells us in his journal that, before the second Battle of Bull Run, "how often was I tempted to lay down my musket and acknowledge myself conquered by the numberless hardships and terrible fatigue of the Campaign."[20] But, like countless other Americans he somehow kept going. And a Union leader who was later the Army's commanding general wrote about the troops who fought in the Indian wars of the 1870's and 1880's that not only should they be supplied with good food, but with every comfort that can be provided. The writer, General Philip Sheridan, could hardly be called soft. This is the American

way, but it can easily be misunderstood. When the United States Navy put soda fountains on shipboard after the First World War, it must have seemed the epitome of ease and comfort, but the Japanese at Midway and Leyte were to find that underneath this exterior appearance of leisure there was a hard core of tenacious endurance. An interesting commentary on the contrast between the American's superficial softness and his interior hardness is to be found in an article in *The Times Literary Supplement* (December 10, 1954) in which the writer reviews and comments on General William F. Dean's autobiographical account of his three years as a prisoner of war in Korea. The reviewer notes some of the qualities which have characterized American military men when he says that General Dean "has something of the dedicated sense of high endeavour and ascetic self-discipline which marked the Roman centurion in the great days of the empire"; but it is in the reviewer's understanding of the military essentials as they would appear to an American that he gives a magnificent analysis of the American character as regards war: "General Dean reminds us, in short, that in spite of its daily ration of ice-cream, its emphatic disinclination to walk and other indulgences the American Army is tough—very, very tough. . . ."

(4) The personalization of the conflict. Americans have a definite tendency to make warfare personal. This is more, perhaps, an Anglo-Saxon characteristic as such, but it has always been strongly evident in the American character. Whether it was Thomas Paine satirizing "His *Mad-jesty*," King George III (a cutting allusion to the King's temporary bouts of insanity), Union soldiers singing "we'll hang Jeff

Davis to a sour apple tree," or the action of later generations embodying the enemy in Kaiser Bill and Hitler,* Americans have tended to personalize their wars. While this may be a safety valve which prevents a rampant and indiscriminate hatred, it may well be more of a weakness than a source of strength because of the high emotional content which is involved. In our own times especially, the impersonal nature of the Soviet and Chinese Communist dictatorships do not seem to produce in the American consciousness the same feeling of revulsion and condemnation as did the similarly committed crimes of the Nazis. This difference seems to stem in part from our tendency towards personalization. Although in Hitler there was an almost perfect target for our wrath, the Communists have furnished us with equally evil but less colorful targets. Stalin seemed in the latter years of his life to be approaching a position in which he would personify the crimes and brutality of Communism, but his death in 1953 put a stop to this tendency. The fact that the inhumanity of the Communists is more cleverly concealed and hence not brought home so much to us is, it would seem, one of the reasons why Americans have been less able to personalize its evil nature.

(5) To the American war is a deadly serious affair. It is not a game. Americans could hardly appreciate, for example, the attitude of Admiral Sir Arthur Wilson of the British Navy, who in the early days of the submarine remarked that the undersea craft were "underhand, unfair and damned un-English." The British, who have shown on a thousand battle-

*It is significant that Hitler was seldom given any appellation which was as mild, comparatively, as "Kaiser Bill."

fields that they are courageous almost beyond belief, nevertheless have a definite tendency to regard war as a game. The Americans, on the contrary, could not be further removed from such a view. This is a recurrent theme in the military annals of the two countries from the time when General Braddock's officers were rather choleric because Washington and his Virginians skulked behind trees when fighting Indians.

During the American Revolution a Lieutenant Hale of the British 45th Regiment of Foot described the chief qualification of Americans as "agility in running from fence to fence and thence keeping up an irregular, but galling fire on troops who advance with the same pace as at their exercises." This somewhat unsportsmanlike conduct of Americans during the Revolutionary War was still being indulged in at the time of the Second World War. General Truscott has observed that the reaction of the American troops to their defeat at the Kasserine Pass was not to adopt the sporting attitude which often characterized the British with respect to their German enemy. They knew that they had taken a beating but didn't relish it. Defeat did not unnerve them, nor change their natural self-respect. Rather a determined anger possessed them.[21] General Matthew B. Ridgway in his informative memoir, *Soldier,* likewise gives the reader many interesting examples of this same American state of mind.

This treatment of war as a deadly serious business and not as a game is probably in part the result of the heritage of the American task in clearing a continent and exploiting its natural resources in a spectacular fashion. In comparing (prophetically) America and Russia, Alexis de Tocqueville wrote one hundred and fifty years ago that "the American struggles against the obstacles that nature opposes to him; the adversaries of the Russian are men." Something of this seems to have passed over into the American character with reference to warfare. Just as conquering a continent was not looked upon as anything but a serious job at hand, so the approach to warfare is a task to be undertaken seriously and to be won. Professor Brogan noted that in America "being a good loser is not thought nearly so important as being a winner, good or bad." Not unjustly, this is the American character in war. Leo Durocher, that scrappy and successful manager of some of America's greatest baseball teams, put it even more succinctly when he said "nice guys finish last."

Some have professed to see in this American heritage of the drive to win, a danger to the conduct of American national policy in an era in which we may well have to fight wars on a limited scale and in which it might be desirable to restrain our well-known victory drive. This is, it must be stressed, a failure to realize the essence of the American drive to win. In the history of our country we have fought many more limited or peripheral wars than we have fought large-scale wars. It is not the magnitude of the operation, but rather the abiding determination that we will eventually gain the victory which is crucial.

Possibly some of the confusion over the whole question of the will to win or the victory theme in the American consciousness has been caused by the Korean War. Before that incident, there was no confusion, there was no doubt. Americans won their wars—no other alternative was considered or accepted. Perhaps if we can get a general agreement that the

Korean War was only a partial victory and that we firmly
intend to end any recriminations about it, we may then go
on to the proposition that we are still confronted with an
over-all struggle of global magnitude of which the Korean
War was a battle. What follows is, it would appear, the
necessary will—for this continuing war is primarily a war of
will—to win. Any attempt to water down the will to win
denies our own birthright and can inevitably be expected
to give the Soviets and their associates the advantages that
no number of orbiting Sputniks will ever confer.

(6) The final thing which stems from the American national character as it affects warfare is our leaning towards
the all-or-nothing-at-all answer to whatever problem arises to
afflict us. We are, as a people, essentially extroverts, and we go
all-out whenever we engage in any activity. Now, this is not
bad in itself. As noted above, we must be careful not to dimin-
ish the will-to-win spirit which is a part of our heritage. Certainly, also, our passion for competition is one of the things
which has made us a great people. The old frontier spirit of
"root, hog, or die" has much to recommend it and is peculiarly germane in countering the present trend towards a
sense of futility in the presence of possible nuclear blackmail.

What stems from this disposition to favor the all-or-nothing-at-all solution is, however, another matter. For we have
come to believe that we must either have the Black of war or
the White of peace and that we must either annihilate our
antagonists as enemies or else we must embrace them as our
dearest friends. In our previous history this was really not so
much a handicap as it has become today, for the rules of
international politics were rather generally subscribed to by

all of the participants. In the age of modern totalitarian states, however, this American predilection has become something of a handicap. This all-or-nothing-at-all tendency can, however, be turned to our advantage rather than our disadvantage through a better understanding of the nature of the enemy we face, as well as through an understanding of the practical techniques which he employs. To redirect this basically positive American characteristic of the all-or-nothing-at-all approach into productive channels, we must study the nature of the enemy who confronts us and we must recognize and comprehend the new kind of warfare which he is waging.

NOTES

1. Maury D. Feld, "The Writing of Military History," *Military Affairs,* Vol. XXII (Spring, 1958), p. 38.

2. William James, *Memories and Studies* (New York: Longmans, Green and Co., 1911), pp. 286-287; from an essay written in 1910.

3. Henry Adams, *History of the United States* (New York: Charles Scribner's Sons, 1891), Vol. IX, p. 226.

4. Homer Lea, *The Valor of Ignorance* (New York: Harper & Brothers, 1942), pp. 40-41.

5. *Ibid.,* p. 41.

6. For a survey of our military history see R. Ernest Dupuy and Trevor N. Dupuy, *Military Heritage of America* (New York: McGraw-Hill Book Company, Inc., 1956).

7. C. J. Bernardo and Eugene H. Bacon, *American Military Policy* (Harrisburg, Pa.: The Military Service Publishing Co., 1955); this is a scholarly history of American military policy.

8. For an extensive treatment of military theories see Edward Mead Earle, ed., *Makers of Modern Strategy* (Princeton, N.J.: Princeton University Press, 1943).

9. William E. Livezey, *Mahan on Sea Power* (Norman, Oklahoma: University of Oklahoma Press, 1947) p. 273.

10. Margaret Tuttle Sprout, "Mahan: Evangelist of Sea Power," in *Makers of Modern Strategy, op. cit.,* p. 415.

11. Air Vice-Marshal E. J. Kingston-McCloughry, *Global Strategy* (London: Jonathan Cape, 1957), p. 43.

12. Rear Admiral I. J. Galantin, "The Future of Nuclear-Powered Submarines," *United States Naval Institute Proceedings,* Vol. 84 (June, 1958), p. 35.

13. See for example James D. Atkinson, "American Military Policy and Communist Unorthodox Warfare," *Marine Corps Gazette,* Vol. 42 (January, 1958), p. 21ff., for some thoughts on the development of military doctrine.

14. Sir George O. Trevelyan, *The American Revolution,* 2nd ed. (New York: Longmans, Green and Co., 1899), Part I, 1766-1776, p. 297.

15. For some thoughtful ideas about the fear of a large standing army see John J. Pullen, *The Twentieth Maine* (Philadelphia: J. B. Lippincott Co., 1957), p. 8ff. This story of a famous Civil War volunteer regiment seems fair to become one of the classic pieces of the ever-growing literature of that conflict.

16. General William T. Sherman to Thomas Ewing Sherman, July 31, 1876, Sherman Papers.

17. Robert Sherwood, *Roosevelt and Hopkins: An Intimate History* (New York: Harper & Brothers, 1948), p. 438.

18. See Letter in the *Bulletin of the Atomic Scientists,* Sept. 1956.

19. Quoted, Arthur Walworth, *Woodrow Wilson* (New York: Longmans, Green and Co., 1958), Vol. II, p. 111.

20. Joseph T. Durkin, S. J., ed., *John Dooley, Confederate Soldier, His War Journal* (Washington, D.C.: Georgetown

University Press, 1945), p. 8; this book gives a very valuable picture of war as seen by the infantryman. Dooley was a private and later a company grade officer who, despite a frail physique, participated in some of the hardest fighting of the Civil War. His story is a must for all Civil War buffs.

21. Lt. General L. K. Truscott, Jr., *Command Missions: A Personal Story* (New York: E. P. Dutton and Company, Inc., 1954), p. 538.

CHAPTER 2

The Communist Approach to War

THE MARXIST-LENINIST VIEW OF WAR

Every age and every society has its own *rationale* of war and its own philosophy of warfare, whether that philosophy is implicit or has been expressly spelled out. We have noted that the American tendency is to approach war as an overt clash of arms and, further, that the emphasis is on the side of materiel much as though war was another but more gigantic form of industrial or commercial enterprise. Only in the years after the Second World War did Americans—and Britons and Europeans as well—begin to perceive, dimly and hesitantly at first, that war and peace were becoming more and more ill-defined and could be less and less labelled and placed in neat classifications.

The Communists, partially because of their predilection for conspiracy and underground warfare, partially because of the as yet unsolved weaknesses in their industrial and, more especially, agricultural systems, tend to approach war in a way attuned to their historical past, to the writings of their

41

major prophets—Marx, Engels, Lenin—and to what they believe to be the vulnerabilities of opposing or opposed societies. The Communists have created, as a part of their over-all philosophy, a philosophy of war. They have given Marxism-Leninism a military as well as an economic, political, and sociological expression.[1]

If we accept Marx's statement that he stood Hegel on his head with reference to the dialectic and the theory of history, we can certainly say with much greater emphasis that the Soviet Union, the embodiment of Marxist-Leninist theory, has been engaged in standing diplomacy and warfare on their collective heads for the past several decades. This has been accomplished not only by taking the traditional forms and trappings—the externals—of diplomacy which have evolved over the centuries and using them for purposes of propaganda and subversion, but still more by blurring the traditional distinction between peace and war.

The Communist philosophical approach to war may be said to have begun to bear fruit with Leon Trotsky's enunciation of the no war, no peace doctrine of 1918. When, on February 10, 1918, Trotsky announced to the German delegation which had met with the Soviet representatives to arrange a treaty of peace between Imperial Germany and the new Russia of the Soviets that the Communists were going to take Russia out of the war, but at the same time would decline to sign a treaty of peace,[2] he figuratively threw a bombshell which exploded the traditional concept that war and peace were distinct and separate entities. So startling was Trotsky's no peace, no war doctrine that the German representatives were utterly confused, and their chief delegate, General Max

Hoffman, kept saying to himself,[3] "unheard of, unheard of."*

More than four decades later many Western diplomatists and political leaders were still crying "unheard of" when they were confronted with some new variation of the Soviet concept of unorthodox warfare. For the Communists have, by design, by preference, and by reason of their theoretical background, used the Western concepts of international law, diplomacy, and peace and war in such a way as to permit them to conduct a new kind of perpetual warfare against all non-Communist states and institutions. This Communist approach to warfare, then, is derived from many decades of practical experience, but it is equally the result of the theoretical concepts of the masters of Communism beginning with Marx and Engels and continuing down to the ideas of Mao Tse-Tung and other Communist ideologues of the present. For it must be emphasized that for the true Marxist-Leninist theory is always a guide to action.

MARX AND ENGELS

That Karl Marx should have been intensely interested in the phenomenon of war is hardly surprising. His basic idea was not only *not* to reform himself—the starting point of the true reformer—but not even to reform the world. Instead, he wanted to change the world completely, and to do so he projected the direct opposite of the Christian idea—a gospel of violent action whereby an unending state of conflict would

---

*The German word is "unerhört." This may be translated as "preposterous"; but the literal meaning, "unheard of," in the circumstances in which General Hoffman reacted to Trotsky's surprise proposal of neither war nor peace, is the translation which captures the essence of Hoffman's reaction at that time.

exist between the proletariat and the bourgeoisie until the dictatorship of the proletariat finally brought about an earthly paradise for mankind. If, in the process, some millions of human beings could not adjust themselves to Marx's apocalyptic vision and had to be forcibly eliminated, that was a mere detail and even a necessary part of the cost of entirely revolutionizing the whole of human society.

In the *Communist Manifesto* Marx affirmed that the entire history of mankind had been a history of class struggles, and Engels was later to repeat this when he wrote that "Marx has shown that all history down to the present day has been the history of class struggles." Such was the emphasis placed by both Marx and Engels on the continuous nature of the conflict between classes, on the necessity for the use of violence in the class struggle, and on the requirement for revolutionary action. It is manifest that neither Marx nor Engels could be classified as pacifists. For Marx, and hence for the Marxist-Leninist, war and peace are inseparable because war will continue, in the form of some kind of combat, so long as capitalism exists in any part of the world. The Marxist does not concern himself with any attempts at the abolition of war except insofar as these are tactical maneuvers to disarm his opponents. To the Marxist war and peace are inseparably linked. Professor T. A. Taracouzio has clearly shown that according to Marx's historical materialism economics governs everything, including the phenomena of peace and war, so that peace and war are simply diverse paths in which the impact of the economic interests of opposing classes find their outward expression.[4]

In this duality of intermingling of war and peace, however,

Marx and Engels placed much greater emphasis on aggressive or warlike techniques than they did on peaceful methods. This was because both Marx and Engels tended to think along military lines and to study the ways in which *all* methods of warfare could be merged into peaceful, or ostensibly peaceful, forms of conquest. Marx was a keen student of military history. When in England in 1857, he wrote to Engels in praise of Machiavelli's *History of Florence* with its military advice, and in 1861 he wrote to Engels of his appreciation of Appian on the civil wars of Rome.[5]

Marx is, of course, well known for his analytical comments on the American Civil War. General Fuller believes it to be highly significant that both Marx and Engels were very much impressed by the importance of the Civil War and of the lessons which could be learned from it, while on the other hand, the great Chief of the Prussian General Staff, the elder von Moltke, viewed that conflict as a contest between two armed mobs and unworthy of study.[6] This is a measure of the military perceptiveness of the two revolutionaries. Engels was, even more than Marx, a life-long student of military affairs and had served in the Prussian artillery. His associates had given him the sobriquet of "general," but they could hardly be expected to foresee that he was to become (along with Marx) a leading figure in the ideological general staff of Communism. Engels has written so extensively in the field of military science—including military articles and analyses of warfare in Europe and Asia which he ghost-wrote for Marx—that Professor Sigmund Neumann believes that if we take cognizance of the basically disciplined and military nature of Marxism-Leninism, the contributions of Engels to present-day doctrine are decidedly more meaningful than those of Marx.[7]

It is small wonder, with this great interest in the study of military affairs, that both Marx and Engels saw great possibilities in the application of warfare to the cause of world revolution. Colonel William R. Kintner, another authority in this field, believes that the intense concern evinced by both Marx and Engels in military matters during their lifetime had an ineluctable effect on the way in which they viewed the revolutionary process.[8] They viewed the lack of success of past revolutions as being caused by the lack of knowledge of military affairs on the part of the revolutionists. They also seem to have anticipated the later Leninist and Stalinist emphasis on conspiratorial organization based on military lines as a means of overcoming past revolutionary failures.

Even more importantly, however, Marx and Engels devote a great deal of attention to the phenomenon of war in their writings from the politico-military point of view. They, like Lenin, were influenced by the idea which Clausewitz held about the interrelation of politics and war, and it is in this area rather than in the area of military strategy and tactics that the theoretical concepts of Marx and Engels were to have so much bearing on the development of a Communist philosophy of warfare. War is sooner evolved to perfection than peace, asserted Marx. Both he and Engels felt that military history illustrated the close connection between production and social conditions, and they enlarged on Leopold von Ranke's idea of the relationship of methods of warfare to the state of society.[9]

Some early evidence of Marx's tendency to visualize warfare along unorthodox lines is supplied by his observations regarding the battle of Novara in 1849. Always alert to the implications of the political element in warfare, Marx thought that a nation need not necessarily adhere strictly to the recognized laws of war. Instead, there could be employed mass insurrections, revolutionary devices, and widespread groups of guerrillas. He believed that these techniques furnished a means by which a weaker force could hold out against an adversary which had greater resources in men and materiel. Marx went so far as to claim that by such unorthodox methods a weaker power could actually defeat a stronger one.[10] One can see here the germination of the theories (later studied and elaborated so carefully by generations of Communists), which were to call attention to the fact that Communism would, for an unforeseeable time, remain technically inferior to the non-Communist world and hence would require a strategy which would make a virtue of such a weakness through neutralizing non-Communist superiority.

Finally, it would seem that Marx and Engels believed that war was to be thought of primarily as an economic, diplomatic, and political struggle and only secondarily as purely military in nature. Such a concept, of course, fits in nicely with the theory of the class struggle, and hence with the idea of the intimate connection between revolution and war. It is noteworthy that the idea of "insurrection . . . an art quite as much as war" is found in their writings. This suggests a long forward look into the development which warfare was to undergo in the future after being subjected to their influence and to that of their disciples. Perhaps, too, the very practical

47

consideration that the revolution predicted by Marx could hardly be expected to have had the aid of the regularly constituted armed forces of the time had a positive influence on the tendency of Marx and Engels to look at warfare along conspiratorial, socio-political, and, very definitely, unorthodox lines. Just as the syndicalist Georges Sorel considered that the general strike might have the possibility of equalling a great military battle, so Marx and Engels were constantly fascinated by the possibilities of the unorthodox in warfare.

LENIN

While Marx and Engels laid a large part of the theoretical foundations for the Communist approach to warfare, it remained for V. I. Lenin to build up a body of doctrine on this theoretical foundation, to enlarge the theoretical base, and to translate, as Stalin was also to do later, theory into practice. There is definite evidence to indicate that Lenin purposively created a Party which was, in effect, a highly disciplined combat formation organized along military lines.[11] Yet while Lenin was greatly influenced by the necessity for a Party formed along military lines (rather than following the pattern of the loosely organized socialist or similar parties of the past), his ideas went well beyond the specific area of military organization. For Lenin's ideas were intimately connected with the Marxian theory of the constant struggle between the proletariat and the bourgeoisie; and, especially as Lenin was to develop it, this struggle could be either an armed battle or a psychological, political, or propaganda battle. Thus Lenin wrote that "the dictatorship of the proletariat is a persistent struggle—sanguinary and bloodless, violent and peaceful, military and economic, educational and administrative. . . ."[12] Lenin's concept of the many-sided nature of the fight against world capitalism is indicated by the appeal for the formation of the Communist International of January 24, 1919 (signed by Lenin and Trotsky among others). This document discloses that the Bolsheviks foresaw the use of a variety of weapons, a wide range of methods of conflict, since it stated specifically that "the basic method of struggle is mass action by the proletariat right up to open armed conflict. . . ."[13]

Flexibility in the methods of struggle and hence the mingling of warlike and peaceful methods in Soviet policy were always in Lenin's thoughts. This flexibility can be seen in numerous expressions. Bolshevism "stands on the point of view of expediency," and "the whole art of conspiratorial organization must consist in utilizing everybody and everything." And again he urges "in war never tie your hands with the considerations of formality." Such thoughts on the nature and conduct of the battle against the non-Communist world are to be found throughout Lenin's writings, and one can leaf through his various works almost at random and find passage after passage which shows how Lenin steered the new Soviet ship of state on a course midway through peace and war, never failing to see the advantages and hazards underlying both.[14]

While Lenin remained throughout his life a student of military affairs in the formal sense, the theory of conspiratorial and unconventional techniques as forms of warfare received much more specific attention as can be seen by his stress on the point that a revolutionary must of necessity be a professional. For Lenin, there could be no such thing as an amateur revolutionist. This concept of the professional revolutionary and of a Communist Party which would be highly disciplined and composed of carefully chosen and limited cadres, but would yet be a *Party* rather than a strictly military formation, gives a rather good insight into that mixture of war and peace which was eventually to evolve as a practical doctrine from the Marxist-Leninist theories. Thus, Lenin stated, "if you say that every strike bears within itself the hydra of revolution and he who fails to understand this is no Socialist, you are right."

He returns to this same theme of flexibility in the techniques of struggle when he says that "it is our duty as Communists to master all forms, to learn how to supplement with the maximum rapidity one form with another, to substitute one for another, and to adapt our tactics to every change. . . ." He refers again and again to the various devices of an irregular or conspiratorial nature which the Communists must use in their battle to establish the world dictatorship of the proletariat. He points out that "to tie one's hands beforehand, openly to tell the enemy, who is at present better armed than we are, whether and when we will fight him is stupidity and not revolutionariness."[15]

Lenin goes on to indicate an important difference in terminology between the Marxist and the non-Marxist, a difference which, after more than four decades, is still not fully appreciated by most non-Communists. For Lenin, as for all Marxist-Leninists, "battle" means *any* form of struggle, whether it involves force or not. One may note, for example, the constant use of the phrase the *struggle for peace* by Communists throughout the world today. Translated from Communist jargon, the "struggle for peace" means the waging of cold war.

Today's Communists were abjured by Lenin that "to accept battle at a time when it is obviously advantageous to the enemy and not to us is a crime: and those political leaders of the revolutionary class who are unable to 'tack, to manoeuvre, to compromise' in order to avoid an obviously disadvantageous battle, are good for nothing." The duality of politics and the military art is also emphasized by his statement that "the time has fully matured when it is absolutely necessary for every Communist party systematically to combine legal with illegal work." He further indicates that no weapon in the entire Communist arsenal of conspiratorial and unconventional methods can be neglected, by sharply reminding his followers that "we have never rejected terror on principle, nor can we do so. Terror is a form of military operation that may be usefully applied, or may even be essential in certain moments. . . ."[16]

Lenin's concept of the mixing of violent and non-violent methods of warfare into an over-all strategy of unorthodox warfare against the non-Communist world is, however, best exemplified by his appreciation that such mixing of warlike and peaceful methods is a long-term process which will involve apparent compromises and periods of simulated peace between the Communist and the non-Communist worlds. He warned all Communists that "the difficulties of revolution are familiar to everybody. Having begun with brilliant success in one country, it may have to pass through painful periods; for final victory is possible only on a world scale, and only as a result of the joint efforts of the workers of all countries."[17]

He went on to underscore the essence of his grand strategy in words that have ever since served as the guide-lines of Soviet and also of Chinese Communist policy: "our task is one of perseverance and caution; we must manoeuvre and if necessary retreat. . . . The adoption of these tactics is inevitable, however much they may be sneered at by people who call themselves revolutionaries but have no inkling of what a revolution means."[18]

The continuity in Lenin's theory of warfare is strikingly illustrated by Party Boss Khrushchev's statement to the East German Communist Party on September 17, 1955. Khrushchev, in laying down the Party line for the benefit of the East German comrades, cautioned them not to be confused about Soviet foreign policy statements on peaceful co-existence, since "we are in favor of a *detente,* but if anybody thinks that for this reason we shall forget about Marx, Engels, and Lenin, he is mistaken. This will happen when shrimps learn to whistle . . . . we are for co-existence because there is in the world a capitalist and a socialist system, but we shall always adhere to the building of socialism."

Lenin's immediate associates, too, were strongly imbued with his theories. The contributions of such men as Trotsky, Chicherin, Radek, Bukharin, and a host of others have been overlooked because of the later pre-eminence of Stalin; yet it would be a mistake not to take note of the way in which some of their ideas have helped to form the total pattern of Leninist theories on warfare. Trotsky's no war, no peace policy has been cited; but Chicherin, Lenin's commissar of foreign affairs, may well have contributed more to the concept of turning war and diplomacy on their heads than did Trotsky. Perhaps nowhere is the Leninist duality of war and peace better illustrated than in Chicherin's wireless message to the British Government concerning the Soviet invasion of Poland during the Russo-Polish War in 1920. Chicherin employed language as a weapon in a way which has since become a familiar technique to two generations of Soviet diplomatists. Since peace was the basic Soviet desire, Chicherin explained, "the war between Russia and Poland is but an episode in the struggle for peace."[19] Thus was George Orwell's ironic reference to Soviet policy, *war is peace, peace is war,* anticipated by several decades.

Lenin had a profound impact on the thinking of future Communist leaders who concerned themselves with the problem of warfare. Both Stalin and Mao Tse-Tung were to be very heavily in his debt, and the new generation of Communists seems to be just as strongly influenced by Lenin's speculative approach to the duality of war and peace. Above all, it can be said that, while Clausewitz had stressed the idea that war was an instrument of policy, it was Lenin's contribution that peace itself could be equally an instrument of policy.

THE INFLUENCE OF CLAUSEWITZ

The development by Lenin of the duality of war and peace in Soviet strategy was the result of a mixture of the ideas of Marx and Engels, the Bolshevik flair for expediency, and Lenin's own baleful genius. It also derived from Lenin's interest in the political side of the writings of the great German philosopher of war, Major General Karl von Clausewitz. Lenin's interest has been transmitted to a long line of Soviet writers and leaders among whom Stalin was not the least. So

53

impressed was Lenin with Clausewitz's massive study, *On War*, that he made notes in parts of twenty-three chapters and these annotations were published in *Pravda* in 1923 and again in 1930. Lenin himself wrote that:

'War is simply the continuation of politics by the other (i.e. violent) *means.'* This formula belongs to Clausewitz, one of the greatest writers on the history of war, whose ideas were fertilized by Hegel. And this was always the standpoint of Marx and Engels, who regarded *every* war as the *continuation* of the politics of the given interested powers—and the *various classes* within these countries—at a given time.[20]

Lenin apparently saw in the theories of Clausewitz the possibility of the exploitation of the political element in warfare for the benefit of Soviet strategy vis-à-vis the non-Communist world. Such a reading of Clausewitz would be quite natural since one continually finds such Clausewitzian expressions as "war is only a part of political intercourse, therefore by no means an independent thing in itself" and "war is nothing but a continuation of political intercourse with an admixture of other means" and "war is never an isolated act." Colonel Vincent Esposito of the United States Military Academy has declared that Marx was overjoyed in discovering that his own concept of political-military relations had been confirmed by the great Prussian authority on war, while Lenin was also an avid reader of Clausewitz and focused his attention especially on the philosophy of war.[21]

Lenin's belief that "the organization of violence in the modern struggle is a military organization" does not at all contradict the fact that his interest in Clausewitz was always directed toward the political rather than the strictly military side of the problem of war. The one supports the other. For to Lenin, and to all Marxists-Leninists, the external form (in this case the adaptation of military organization to the needs of the Communist Party) is not especially important; what *is* important is the inner idea, the core, the root, the essence. And the inner idea which Lenin distilled from his study of the writings of Clausewitz was that war is at the core politics. This deeper or inner understanding of the duality of war and peace as related to society is well illustrated by Lenin's comment on an observation of Clausewitz's idea that a conqueror loved peace and "would like to make his entry into our state unopposed." Lenin emphasized Clausewitz's statement and then wrote alongside it, "Ha! Ha! Pretty good!"[22] This is quite typical of Lenin, for he apparently believed (and he was right) that the non-Communist world did not understand his strategy. He once remarked to the British Foreign Office representative R. H. Bruce Lockhart, regarding the war then going on (1918), that "like all your countrymen you are thinking in concrete military terms. You ignore the psychological factors. This war will be settled in the rear and not in the trenches."

The psychological factors—and the political as well—were very definitely not ignored by Lenin nor by later Soviet writers and thinkers on warfare from Frunze (one of the proponents of a strictly Marxist military theory and the father of the Red Army)* and Marshal Mikhail N. Tukhachevskii

---

*During Stalin's ascendancy the "father" of the Red Army—and of all else—was the *Vozhd* ("Boss"), J. V. Stalin.

down to the long-time Soviet Chief of Staff Marshal Boris Shaposhnikov. All of these Soviet officers were influenced by the teachings of Clausewitz to some degree, as were the great majority of Russian officers of higher rank, because Clausewitz was standard material in Soviet military schools between the two great wars. Marshal Shaposhnikov, faithful servant and military advisor to Stalin, must certainly have been so influenced. For example, he used Clausewitz's idea of war as a continuation of politics to put the case for a constant mixture of peace and war in Soviet policy by stating that "peace is a continuation of struggle only by other means."[23]

More importantly, Stalin was also a student of Clausewitz; and although towards the end of his life the Red dictator revised the estimate of Clausewitz' influence as a military authority, it is significant that he did not change the emphasis on the importance of the political or philosophical side of Clausewitz which had been placed there by Marx, Engels, and Lenin. Actually, Stalin's corrections of Clausewitz as a strictly military authority seem to have been the result of the megalomania which affected him more heavily in his later years, and even this revisionism was largely couched in Clausewitzian terms. Furthermore, it must not be forgotten that the Sixth Congress of the Communist International in 1928, dominated by Stalin, gave its approval to the concept of war as defined by Clausewitz, and this action has so far not been repudiated.

STALIN

It is notable that while Khrushchev criticized J. V. Stalin at the Twentieth Party Congress of the Russian Communist

Party in February of 1956, such criticism has extended only to certain aspects of Stalin's career. Furthermore, there has been a definite tendency during 1957 and 1958 down to the present to emphasize certain positive accomplishments of Stalin.* Whether, however, Stalin is downgraded one day and resurrected the next (a common enough practice among Communists as regards their stock heroes and villains), it would be difficult to avoid mention of Stalin's contributions to the duality of the Soviet doctrine of peace and war.

Stalin himself said that "during the civil war Lenin required us young Comrades of the Central Committee, as we were then, to study deeply the art of war."[24] Yet Stalin's contribution to the Soviet philosophy of warfare had begun long before. Not only had he had much practical experience in the conduct of irregular warfare, but he had also made a significant addition to the Soviet idea of the duality of war and peace in his essay entitled *Marxism and the National Question*. While this work was certainly not an addition to scholarship, it is of interest to the student of warfare, primarily because it contains the germ for later Soviet ideas for the mobilization of colonial peoples against the capitalist Powers. Lenin had, of course, seen in the East a huge part of the globe which constituted a soft underbelly for Communist

---

*In 1957 the editor and most of the editorial board of *Voprosy Istorii* (*Questions of History*) thought it was safe to criticize Stalin in detail. They found that they had gone much too far and all but four members of the editorial board were dismissed. E. N. Burdzhalov, first deputy editor, was especially singled out for having "blackened" Stalin. The purged editors—and all other Soviet citizens—were reminded that while Stalin might have been guilty of certain errors, he remained "a great Marxist, a great fighter for communism." Western analysts who have hailed Khrushchev's "liberalism" would do well to study this case.

penetration. It remained for Stalin to develop and extend both the theory and practice of the exploitation of the peoples of the East for the advancement of the Communist cause.

It is portentous that as early as February 22, 1919, Stalin wrote an article for *Izvestia* in which he conceived the theory of the "two camps." According to Stalin's thesis the world was divided into the camp of imperialism (the United States, Great Britain, Japan, and other capitalist countries) and the camp of socialism which was headed, of course, by the U.S.S.R. Stalin argued that there was an irreconcilable conflict between these two camps. He predicted that the camp of socialism would finally triumph largely because it would enlist the support of the masses of people in the colonial areas of the East—and for Stalin the East included, as it does for the present rulers of the Kremlin, everything from Africa through the Philippines to Hawaii. Indeed, some students of Soviet policy have suggested that Latin America is also included, since the East is more a theoretical category (of non-industrialized countries) than a geographical division. In any event, the two-camps theory has played an important role in Soviet political and psychological warfare from the post World War II period onward. The emphasis placed on the importance of the East by Stalin was also to remain a key part of Soviet strategy.

It is true that Stalin undoubtedly derived many of his ideas regarding the soft underbelly of the East from Lenin, but it must be remembered that Stalin himself was always psychologically an Easterner. It was probably more than mere propaganda when the Red dictator, embracing Foreign Minister Yosuke Matsuoka at the time of the signing of the Soviet-

Japanese Pact in 1941, said that he was also an Oriental. Certainly his well-known article *Do Not Forget the East,* which was published late in 1918, bears this out. This tract affirms that the Soviets should infiltrate the colonial areas and aid any local movements against the imperialists. It is merely one in a succession of Stalin's writings over a period of years in which he returns again and again to the idea that the East offers a most opportune area for the conduct of Communist unorthodox warfare against the forces of the non-Communist world.

Associated with Stalin's two-camps theory is his theory of the ebb and flow of revolution. This follows the idea of flexibility of tactics enunciated by Lenin, but because of its relation to the over-all Soviet concept of the duality of war and peace, it deserves to be treated separately and in some detail. While Stalin himself may have been somewhat downgraded, his theory of the ebb and flow of the whole revolutionary process has remained an enduring part of Soviet strategy. This thesis was first put forth in a report on the international situation to the Fourteenth Congress of the Communist Party of the Soviet Union on May 9, 1925, when Stalin stated:

One thing that has emerged recently, and which has left its mark on the international situation, is that in Europe the revolutionary tide has begun to ebb, a certain calm has set in, what we call the temporary stabilization of capitalism, while at the same time the economic development and political power of the Soviet Union have grown. What is this ebb of revolution, this calm? Is it not the beginning of the end of the world revolution, the beginning of the liquidation of the world proletarian revolution? Lenin said that with the victory of the proletariat in our country a new epoch had begun, an epoch of world revolution, an epoch filled with conflicts and wars, of advances and retreats, of victories and defeats, an epoch leading to the victory of the proletariat in the chief capitalist countries. If the revolution in Europe has begun to ebb, does it not mean that Lenin's thesis in regard to this new epoch, the epoch of world revolution, loses its force? Does it not mean that the proletarian revolution in the West is set aside?[25]

Stalin then went on to emphasize that such things did not mean that Lenin's thesis with reference to the great epoch of world revolution was incorrect but, rather, that this epoch of world revolution was a prolonged period which would be spread over a long span of years. It was a counsel of caution and of patience, and it illustrates very well the Soviet philosophy of the continuing struggle—an advance here, a retreat there, a bluff here, a threat there, but always a reluctance to risk everything on the throw of the dice of a war in the old-fashioned sense of *a state of declared or formal war.* This was clearly indicated by Stalin:

The epoch of world revolution is a new stage of revolution, *an entire strategic period, covering a number of years, perhaps even a number of decades.** In the course of that period there may and must be ebbs and flows in the revolutionary tide. . . . Since the victory of October we have entered the third strategical period, the third stage of the revolution,

*Emphasis supplied.

which has as its goal the overthrow of the bourgeoisie on a world scale. How long this period will last it is difficult to say. In any case it will be long, just as there is no doubt that it will have its ebbs and flows. The world revolutionary movement has now entered a phase when the revolution is receding, but for a number of reasons of which I shall speak later it will give place to a period of advance which may end with the victory of the proletariat but may not end in such a victory, but give way to a new ebb which in its turn will give way to a new revolutionary advance. . . .[26]

Stalin then moved on to a reiteration of the two-camps theory (which he had propounded in 1919) and advocated the necessity for a long-range Soviet policy to be constructed with this theory as an operative factor. He also raised the question of the eventual triumph of one system over the other and of the enduring opposition between the Communist and the non-Communist worlds. But he did not indicate that such opposition would necessarily bring about a formal state of war in the sense in which the Western world has traditionally viewed war. Whether or not obeisance is paid to the memory of Stalin, theories such as these have remained influential in guiding Soviet policy.

Above all, the concept of flexibility in policy stressed by Lenin and constantly reiterated in Stalin's theoretical writing can, in the Communist lexicon, be taken to mean anything from the cold war moves during a period of peaceful coexistence to the more serious clashes of guerrilla warfare as in Greece or the limited peripheral warfare in Korea. This plasticity, as well as the idea of what may be done to advance the

Communist world goal during periods of the ebb and flow of the revolution, is well illustrated by one of the measures of "peaceful" struggle which can be read in the pages of the official *Great Soviet Encyclopaedia (Bol'shaya Sovetskaya Entsiklopedia)*. This publication states, with reference to the operations of the Communist Party of Great Britain, that there should be brought about in Britain the formation of a government which would:

Put into effect a peaceful foreign policy, and would destroy the political power of the capitalist class. . . . The most important condition for establishing such a popular authority is the formation of a broad popular coalition or alliance of all strata of workers on the basis of a unified labor class.[27]

The article in the *Encyclopaedia* goes on to point out that the British Communist Party is the vehicle which will bring about this unity. It then clearly indicates the nature of Soviet strategy and its long-range aim in securing a Communist-dictated British foreign policy:

The Communist Party, the avant garde of the labor class of Great Britain, is the only active defender of the interests of the British people's fight for friendship with the Soviet Union, the Chinese People's Republic, and the countries of peoples democracy.[28]

Stalin's long-range politico-military theory of ebb and flow, advance and retreat, through the use of seemingly peaceful penetration, propaganda, and diplomatic maneuvering stands out in contrast to Hitler's emphasis on *blitzkrieg* (lightning war). Hitler was a fanatic who took risks often without any apparent attempt at calculating the effect of them.* General Geyr von Schweppenburg has pointed out that the Nazi dictator in his handling of broad diplomatic and political affairs took chances in the conduct of foreign policy which were almost unfathomable to the normal person.[29] Stalin was very much more cautious, and his theory was to advance the world revolution by the Marxist-Leninist mixing of peace and war. One of Stalin's biographers has said that Stalin had a real dread of risk-taking and that he believed that there were struggles—political, diplomatic, and psychological—which were more significant than the ones involved in actual clashes of arms on a field of battle.[30] It must be said, therefore, that the philosophy of warfare which involved the mixing of peace and war, war and peace, into an over all grand strategy was foreshadowed by the writings of Marx and Engels, developed into something approaching doctrinal form by Lenin, and reached maturity under a combination of the theoretical writings, the revolutionary experience, and, perhaps, the native cunning and caution of Stalin.

Lenin had made it axiomatic that, for a Marxist, theory was ever to be a guide to practice. In addition to Stalin's theories regarding the mixture of peace and war in Soviet policy, Stalin's very definite contribution to the development of a new mode of warfare was his translating the experience of conspiratorial and revolutionary action into doctrine which could then be once more redistilled into action on the various

*The remilitarization of the Rhineland in 1936 is perhaps the exception to the rule.

63

fronts around the world. Thus the philosophical approach to the study of war by Marx, Engels, and Lenin, the more indirect influence of Clausewitz, and the later theories of Stalin all have had great influence on the development of Communist techniques of conflict. But it would seem that the actual experience of Lenin and, even more importantly, that of Stalin and his pupils (both in the Soviet Union and elsewhere—Mao Tse-Tung, for example), have had an equally meaningful role in the development of a definite concept of warfare waged along unorthodox lines. While Lenin with his own revolutionary experience charted the course which later Communists would follow, it was Stalin and his associates who made important additions to the doctrine based on further hard, practical revolutionary action.

Stalin's life, from the very beginning, furnishes us with example after example of the way in which he was influenced by the practical apprenticeship which he served in the conspiratorial trade of irregular warfare. Stalin began his preoccupation with unorthodox war at the very start of his career as a revolutionary in the Caucasus Mountains of his native Georgia. It was there that he planned or took part in—more commonly, both—assassinations, terrorism, robbery, strikes, street demonstrations, and the carrying on of propaganda against the existing Czarist order. Trotsky, in writing about this period of unrest in pre-revolutionary Russia, illustrates graphically the course of the Communist methods of struggle of the future when he writes, with reference to Stalin, that "well-organized violence seems to him the shortest distance between two points—he is a kind of opportunist with a bomb. . . ."

Following the success of the Bolshevik seizure of power in

the second, or October, Revolution of 1917 and the beginning of the period of civil war in Russia, Stalin had an even better opportunity for displaying his unorthodox views regarding warfare. Here he came into conflict with Leon Trotsky not only personally, but also on the plane of theory with regard to the conduct of war. Trotsky believed that the internal conflict then going on in Russia was a war which ought to be definitely systematized and centralized according to the known rules and procedures of war as they had been developed by European armies. Stalin, on the other hand, could not be brought to listen to the idea of regulations of war or of any rigid organization since his convictions about the importance of irregular methods led him to maintain that the war between the Red and White forces was above all else a guerrilla war.[31]

In the years 1921-1922, immediately following the civil war period, there arose an interesting controversy between Frunze, who is usually looked upon as the founder of the Red Army, and Trotsky, who had headed the Commissariat of War since 1918, and who was trying to transform the ragged formations of the Red Army into something approaching the regularized units of the European armies of that time. It is not insignificant, incidentally, that Mikhail V. Frunze was to become something of a protegé of Stalin because of his disagreement with Trotsky over theories of warfare. Trotsky argued that not all problems could be solved by the system of historic materialism. Even though it were agreed that there was such a thing as a military science, it would not be correct to hold that such a science could be constructed along Marxist lines, since historical materialism was not a universal system for all sciences. To try to make military affairs a special kind of military Marxism would be utterly wrong.[32]

Frunze and a number of the younger Communist military leaders in the newly developing Red Army, however, argued that all new problems including the military one could be solved by applying the doctrines of Marxism and that there was, in effect, a Marxist-Communist science of war.[33] While these arguments turned chiefly on the role to be played by the Red Army in the future, it is obvious that there is a direct connection between the theories of Frunze and his associates and the general development of a Communist philosophical approach to warfare which would be different from that of the older and more traditional concepts.

Of Frunze's associates none was more inclined towards the revolutionary than Mikhail Tukhachevskii. He had been an officer in the Imperial Russian Army, was captured by the Germans during World War I, and later entered the Red Army, where he soon rose to high rank and was given command of the Soviet army (under the supreme armed forces command of Sergei Kamenev) facing the Poles in 1920. Tukhachevskii ultimately became a Field Marshal and Commander in Chief of the Soviet armed forces. He was executed during Stalin's purge of the Russian military machine in 1937.

But it is not Tukhachevskii's military career so much as his philosophy of war and of revolution that is of interest to the student of Communism. He believed strongly in the Marxist concept of the class struggle and thought that the Red Army would get assistance from the mass of the people in capitalist nations.[34] His ideas, however, reflected not only the ruthless driving force in bolshevism and the quasi-reli-

gious nature of Marxism-Leninism but also the paganism of a
much older Russia. One of his pronouncements indicates
both his own grasp of the changing nature of warfare and
the appeal of Communism to all those who want to fragment
and disintegrate Western civilization. Speaking to a French
army officer, he said: "If Lenin is capable of removing Russia
from the old irons of prejudice, of de-Europeanizing her, I
will follow him. But it will be necessary for him to wipe the
slate clean and deliberately throw us into barbarism. What
a bright prospect! *With the Marxist formulas mixed with
your democratic slogans** we can revolutionize the world.
The right of peoples to order their own affairs! Here is a
magic key which opens to Russia the doors of the East, and
which closes them to the English."[35]

Tukhachevskii then went on to say that what was needed
in order to carry out this grand design and to expand Soviet
influence far beyond the borders of Russia was a new ideology. In fact, "a new religion is indispensable to us." And
for himself, Tukhachevskii clearly indicated that "between
Marxism and Christianity, I choose Marxism."[36] Seldom has
the world conflict of the twentieth century been put so succinctly. Unlike Frunze and Tukhachevskii, Trotsky, perhaps
because he had an essentially European rather than Russian
mentality or perhaps because of his experience in trying to
put together a cohesive military force as Commissar of War,
came into controversy with those Bolsheviks who inclined to
the idea of unorthodoxy as a means to win the struggle to
gain the world. It was not that Trotsky failed to be a revolutionary, but rather that he was less wedded to the idea of

*Emphasis supplied. How prophetic Tukhachevskii was is evident in
the daily events of our own times.

irregular forms of warfare which were bound to gain in importance if one were to accept the idea that there was a new Marxist-Communist science of war. Certainly Trotsky's espousal of the idea that there was *no* strictly Marxian science of war would tend to make Stalin even more obdurate in his belief that unorthodox methods of warfare were the only correct ones.

Stalin's supremacy in the world Communist movement was heralded by the Fourteenth Congress of the Communist Party of the Soviet Union in 1925, but his victory over Trotsky in the field of military affairs had already been established beyond peradventure when Frunze became Trotsky's deputy in February of 1924.* From this period down to his death in 1953, Stalin's leadership was characterized by the same mixture of theory and practical experimentation in the field of irregular methods of conflict that had marked his approach to the subject earlier in his career. Whether fighting an undeclared war under the guise of "border incidents," as with Japan along the Mongolian-Manchurian frontier in the latter part of the 1930's, or waging war by propaganda, Stalin steadily adhered to unorthodox methods in an unrelenting struggle against the non-Communist world. This did not mean that he neglected the regular land, sea, and air forces. As he said in an order of the day issued in the immediate post World War II period:

While expanding peaceful socialist construction we must not forget even for a minute the intrigues of the international

*Frunze became Commissar for War in January of 1925. For an interesting account of the circumstances surrounding his death—he was apparently one more of the many victims of the nihilistic element so pervasive in Communism—see Leon Trotsky, *Stalin, op. cit.*

reaction, which is hatching the plans of a new war. It is necessary to bear in mind the instructions of the great Lenin that having passed to peaceful labor, it is necessary to continue being on the alert, and to guard like the apple of one's eye the armed forces and defense potential of our country.[37]

Yet while building vast military power, Stalin preferred to advance the world revolution by the Marxist-Leninist mixing of peace and war. And in this it was not, perhaps, that he was so adept as that it was difficult for the Western mentality, with its view of the sharp distinctions between a state of peace and a state of war, to grasp the new kind of warfare being waged by the Soviets. Stalin's theory as to the employment of the doctrine of peaceful coexistence is illustrative of his general approach to the value of propaganda as a means of unorthodox warfare. Thus, in his famous interview with Mr. Harold Stassen on April 9, 1947, Stalin stated that "there was not a single party congress or plenary session of the Central Committee of the CPSU at which I did or could have said that cooperation between the two systems was impossible." His other statements (as well as his pronouncements in Communist Party publications) in the years after the Second World War show that he intended to pursue the long view of the ebb and flow of the world revolution, and measures of conflict short of declared war fitted precisely into this long view.

At first glance, the Korean War in 1950 would seem to be a contradiction in Stalin's development of the Marxist-Leninist philosophy of warfare towards maturity. Yet actually the Korean War supports Stalin's record of consistency, since it was a peripheral war waged with Soviet support, but without direct Soviet participation. Mr. Denis Healey, a prominent Laborite member of the British Parliament, has observed that the Korean attack "is the exception which proves the rule, since in this case Russia must have considered America's announcement that Korea was not a vital strategic interest of the United States as giving her *carte blanche* to intervene without the risk of world war. . . . Soviet Russia has always been ready to use force or the threat of force in order to make local advances where this does not appear to involve a serious risk of world war." Mr. Healey argues convincingly that this is the real meaning of the Korean aggression.[38]

Although it is true that Stalin had become somewhat less resilient in his unorthodox warfare maneuvering as old age approached—and as the steady glorification of Stalin as demigod proceeded in the Soviet Union*—this rigidity was more a matter of degree than of kind. Actually, for about a year preceding Stalin's death there was definite evidence of a return to the earlier softening-up tactics of the continuous struggle which he had pursued so successfully during most of his life. Thus, on July 14, 1952, Stalin launched a new English-language propaganda journal entitled *News,* and a lead editorial of this new vehicle of Soviet psychological warfare argued that all countries could cooperate peacefully without any regard to their political or social systems. It went on to state that "we do not believe that war is inevitable. We are firmly convinced that peaceful international cooperation is possible and indeed essential."[39]

*Poets compared Stalin to the sun and the moon (apparently unconscious of the irony of linking the name of the dictator with the heavenly constellations); painters and sculptors reproduced his features endlessly; and musicians hymned his praise from the conquered Baltic republics to Vladivostok on the Pacific.

That this propaganda appeal—addressed especially to the United States and the British Commonwealth—was proceeding from the over-all basis of the Soviet theory of the new warfare was shown by the reports and proceedings of the Nineteenth Congress of the Communist Party of the Soviet Union held in October of 1952. This was the last Congress during Stalin's lifetime, and the theories enunciated there can, of course, be said to represent his views. At that time, Georgii M. Malenkov, delivering the Report of the Central Committee of the Party, stated:

We are confident that in peaceful competition with capitalism, the socialist system of economy will prove its superiority over the capitalist system more and more vividly year by year. We have no intention, however, of forcing our ideology or our economic system on anybody. . . .[40]

He then emphasized the peaceful coexistence line in words which left no doubt that Stalin, even towards the end of his life, still preferred to rely on the cautious and careful approach of the mixture of peace and war rather than on the gamble of an overt war against the West. Said Malenkov:

The Soviet Union has always stood, and stands today, for the development of trade and cooperation with other countries notwithstanding differences in social systems. The Party will pursue this policy in the future as well, on the basis of mutual advantage. . . .[41]

It is interesting also, and hardly a coincidence, that this insistence on the possibility of peaceful coexistence was accompanied by the publication of Stalin's *Economic Problems of Socialism in the U.S.S.R.* In this book, destined to be Stalin's last work on Marxist-Leninist theory and published at the time of the Nineteenth Party Congress in order to draw special attention to its importance, Stalin advanced the thesis (not exactly new) that a war between the Soviet Union and capitalist countries was actually less likely to occur than a war among the capitalistic countries themselves. He also warned that the struggle for peace (a Communist phrase—couched in the Aesopian language they employ so effectively—meaning struggle against the West by unorthodox means) could eventually proceed to the actual overthrow of capitalism, but that to bring about a final stage of (Communist) peace it was necessary to eliminate imperialism— that is, the so-called imperialist powers led by the United States. The concept thus expressed has been a constant element in Communist thought from Lenin to Khrushchev; hence Stalin's words should be carefully examined. He paid particular attention to the unorthodox warfare theme, saying:

It is most probable that the present peace movement, as a movement for the preservation of peace, will, should it be successful, result in prevention of a *given* war, in its postponement, a temporary preservation of a *given* peace, to the resignation of a belligerent government and its replacement by another government, ready to preserve peace for the time being. This is good, of course. Even very good. But this, however, is still insufficient to eliminate altogether the inevitability of wars among capitalist countries. It is insufficient since with all these successes of the peace movement imperialism still remains and remains in power, and consequently the inevitability of wars also remains. In order to eliminate the inevitability of wars imperialism must be destroyed.[42]

Significantly, Stalin's successors, although they have softened the concept of the inevitability of war, have made no basic changes in the idea that final world *peace* must wait for the triumph of world Communism.

Hitler once referred to Stalin as an "intelligent ice-cold blackmailer." This characterization of one blackmailer by another is a measure of the changes in the conduct of world politics in the twentieth century. Stalin's ideas of the mixing of war and peace have, no less than Lenin's, contributed to those changes.

STALIN'S SUCCESSORS

Although Stalin's successors in Russia have continued to carry on a campaign of no peace, no war against the so-called "imperialist" powers, none of them have as yet made so important a contribution to the theoretical side of Marxism-Leninism as did Stalin. On this basis—although not necessarily on the basis of ruthlessness—he still towers over them, and it is ironical that Nikita S. Khrushchev in downgrading Stalin should have made use of a chief tenet of Stalinist psychological warfare. For it was Stalin who, in seeming to denounce Trotsky's "world revolution now" theory, apparently called a halt to that world revolution and reassured many of the leaders of the Western democracies in the 1930's that the revolution had been tamed and that he, Stalin, was concerned only with socialism in one country. Malenkov very slowly and then Khrushchev boldly and with great emphasis sought to convince the non-Communist world that all of the crimes and brutality of Communism were simply due to Stalin and that these bad old days were a thing of the past now that Stalin was dead. Once again the swan song of You Can Do Business with the Soviets was the propaganda line emanating from Moscow.

Khrushchev's audacious scrapping of the Stalin myth, however, was a far more important point of departure in Soviet policy than anything which occurred in the short time during which Malenkov held pride of place in the Soviet Union. The new line ushered in by Khrushchev represents a stroke of daring such as Stalin himself might have used. While it does not herald a new philosophy, it does reveal the acceptance of the idea which was inherent in Stalin's *Economic Problems of Socialism in the U.S.S.R.* This was the concept of the general crisis of world capitalism and the belief that the steadily increasing disintegration of the world economic system of capitalism has now been reached. From this premise, the trained Marxist readily concludes that it may be possible to carry on the Marxist-Leninist mixture of war and peace in a more vigorous fashion.

Khrushchev has updated Stalin's ideas on the general crisis of world capitalism so that the Communists now apparently believe that the balance of power inclines to the Soviet side. They now hold that the era of "capitalist encirclement" is over and that a new era of the encirclement of *capitalism* is beginning.[43]

74

Khrushchev used the Twentieth Party Congress of the Communist Party of the Soviet Union in February of 1956 to announce the downgrading of Stalin, but the Congress was itself a measure of the extent to which Communist mixing of peace and war has become even more flexible than during the latter years of Stalin's life and yet how much it also adheres to so many of the basic tenets of unorthodox warfare theory established under Stalinism. Thus, in a speech at the Congress, Khrushchev pointed out that "the use or non-use of violence in the transition to socialism depends on the resistance of the exploiters." He was even more specific in his adherence to the Marxist-Leninist mixing of peace and war when he indicated that all forms and types of struggle would be necessary, since "in the countries where capitalism is still strong and has a huge military and police apparatus at its disposal, the reactionary forces will, of course, offer serious resistance."[44] It is interesting to compare this with Lenin's idea that "the Party does not tie its hands, it does not restrict its activities to some preconceived . . . method of political struggle; it recognizes all methods of struggle as long as they . . . facilitate the achievement of the best possible results under the given conditions." Even more clearly, Stalin once told H. G. Wells that the Communists would be glad to abjure the use of force if only the bourgeoisie would surrender peacefully!

M. A. Suslov underscored the point made by Khrushchev by stating that "Communists and the working class naturally prefer more painless forms of transition . . . [but] whether the methods are more peaceful or more violent depends . . .

on the degree of resistance offered. . . ." Anastas I. Mikoyan, that canny Old Bolshevik who has survived purges and upheavals in Russia from the rule of Lenin to the days of Khrushchev, reminded his fellow comrades that irregular warfare methods had worked out very well in Czechoslovakia. He hinted at the future application of such a philosophy of warfare when he said "Communists came into power [i.e., in Czechoslovakia] after having allied themselves not only with the parties of the working people which were close to them but also with the bourgeois parties which supported the common national front." The Soviet deputy premier drove home the idea of victory through such methods when he concluded by saying "the Czechoslovak people won by way of a peaceful development of revolution."

The most specific ideas about the application of the Marxist-Leninist philosophy of warfare, however, seem to have been those found in a speech by the former editor of *Pravda,* Dmitrii Shepilov. He warned members of the Russian Communist Party as well as those of the other Communist parties throughout the world that "only formalists and dogmatists of Marxism can believe that such profound upheavals as the transition from one social regime to another can be carried out by a single pattern, by a single mold, say, in Denmark in the same way as in Brazil, and in Sweden in the same way as in Malaya. This is a distortion of the essence of Marxism, of its creative spirit." He then continued in words which are so reminiscent of the theories of Lenin and Stalin and yet so typical of the continuity of thought of *all* Bolshevik leaders from 1917 to the present—as regards flexibility in the conduct of unorthodox warfare—that they cannot be too strongly emphasized. Said Shepilov: "History in all its completeness bears out the prediction of the great Lenin that the *development of revolution in different countries proceeds otherwise. Everything depends on the concrete conditions of each country.*"*

Khrushchev emerged as something of a theorist of Marxism-Leninism from the Twentieth Party Congress. Whether he will contribute anything to revolutionary dogma on the scale of Stalin's additions remains to be seen, and it is, of course, difficult to determine (and not necessarily relevant) whether the pronouncements which he made on theory at the Twentieth Party Congress were his own or were those prepared for him. In any event, so long as he remains the visible head of the world Communist movement, it is vital that all those interested in the future course of world politics should understand that he has continued rather than deviated from the pattern of the cautious approach of the Communist mixture of war and peace. For Khrushchev laid down the task, applicable to all Communists, of translating the theory and doctrine of unorthodox warfare into accomplished fact when he stressed the point that "revolutionary theory is not a collection of 'frozen' dogmas and formulas, but a fighting guide for practical activity for the transformation of the world, for the building of Communism."**

---

*Emphasis supplied. Mao Tse-Tung has frequently stressed this same Leninist principle, and although Shepilov fell from his high position, the idea he expressed has frequently been repeated in one form or another.

**Compare "transformation of the world" in this context with some of Khrushchev's statements to Western statesmen and journalists about peaceful cooperation between Communist and non-Communist powers.

The Chinese Communists have not only borrowed heavily from the unorthodox warfare theories of Marx, Engels, Lenin, and Stalin, but have also made distinct additions of their own. Speaking for the Russian Communist Party, Shepilov paid tribute to these contributions at the Twentieth Party Congress when he said that the approach of the Red Chinese to the communization of their country was a masterful application of Marxist dialectics to the concrete conditions of China.

An indication of the Chinese Communist adherence to the idea of the mixing of peace and war is furnished by a Chinese Communist Party document which delineates the various kinds of warfare—such as armed struggle, conflict in the internal and international arena, and other forms of Communist methods of conflict—and notes that the Chinese Communist Party has had experience with all of these varying kinds of revolutionary conflict.[45] Emphasis on the war-is-politics-and-politics-is-war theme of Marxism-Leninism is also supplied by an editorial in the leading Chinese Communist paper, *Jen Min Jih Pao,* which declared: "We as the proletarian vanguards armed with Marxism-Leninism aim at the liberation of the entire human race. We are politically conscious and strictly disciplined and possess the weapons of criticism and self-criticism which old-fashioned revolutionists never had or could have. Therefore, we will not repeat the mistakes of history."[46]

Mao Tse-Tung has been, of course, the leading exponent

of Chinese Communist theory. Since the death of Stalin he must also be recognized as the leading theoretical spokesman for Marxism-Leninism, even though Khrushchev stands pre-eminent as the leader of the motherland of world Communism and hence the Number One of Communism as a world force. Mao Tse-Tung has enunciated the unconventional side of the struggle against the non-Communist world in terms which could cause him to be ranked alongside Lenin and as probably superior to Stalin insofar as a philosophy of warfare is concerned.

An indication of Mao's philosophical propinquity to Lenin is found throughout his writings. In one instance, the Chinese Communist chieftain wrote: "In carrying out propaganda and organization work of the Communist Party . . . we must lie low to prepare ourselves, waiting for the opportune moment. The tactic of the revolution, led by the Communist Party, is always to take advantage of situations permitted by public laws and social customs. By reasonable, profitable, and systematic means, the Communist Party must step by step carry out the revolution."[47]

Mao Tse-Tung has written widely about the problems of war, and his published works are replete with references to the theory of warfare, guerrilla warfare, propaganda, and especially the intermixture of war and politics. He has warned his Chinese followers that there is a grave danger in failing to note that military means are only *one* of the means for accomplishing political tasks; furthermore, the "Chinese Red Army is an armed force for carrying out the political tasks of the revolution rather than a purely military body."[48]

There seems also to be little doubt that Mao's practical experience—the parallel with Stalin is notable—in propaganda, subversion, political activity, and guerrilla warfare have combined to influence his thinking about the changing concepts of warfare. Perspicaciously recalling his own background, he quotes Clausewitz approvingly and agrees with the Prussian general that "wars in every period have independent forms and independent conditions, and therefore every period must have its independent theory of war." Mao Tse-Tung's thinking about the unorthodox approach to warfare based on Marxism-Leninism may best be summed up in a statement which he made to his subordinates in order to spell out for them his own philosophy of war. Succinctly but definitely Mao laid down the law in these words: "There are some militarists who say: 'We are not interested in politics but only in the profession of arms.' *It is vital that these simple minded militarists be made to realize the relationship that exists between politics and military affairs. Military action is but a method used to attain a political goal.*"[49] [Emphasis supplied.]

The continuity between Mao Tse-Tung's philosophical approach to warfare and that of other Chinese Communist leaders is much like the continuity in the Soviet Union from Lenin to Khrushchev. Thus Mao's sharp reminder to his generals about the nature of warfare is echoed in a warning to all Chinese Communist Party members which was issued by Liu Shao-ch'i at the 1954 Plenary Session of the Central Committee of the Chinese Communist Party. Liu advised his audience of Party faithful that "the enemy knows as well as we do the truth that a fortress can most easily be destroyed from within."

With a historical background of centuries of partisan warfare in Montenegro, Bosnia-Herzegovina, Serbia, and Croatia, it is not surprising that Marshal Josip Brosz Tito and the Yugoslav Communist Party have proved to be apt pupils in the Communist school of unorthodox warfare. Although Tito has tended in the past to incline rather more in the direction of the practical side of propaganda, espionage, guerrilla warfare, and other clandestine or semi-clandestine activities, the Yugoslav Communist chief has shown that he is no stranger to the milieu of Marxist theory. This is underscored by the following exchange between Tito and the judge of a Zagreb court. Tito was on trial for conducting revolutionary activity against the state and was asked by the judge what he was guilty of. Tito replied that although he had propagandized and worked for Communism he did not even "recognize the bourgeois Court of Justice" before which he was being tried "because I consider myself responsible only to my Communist Party."[50]

Like Lenin and Stalin and Mao Tse-Tung, Tito has gained extensive first-hand knowledge of the practical as well as the theoretical side of unorthodox warfare. During the 1930's his work for the Comintern provided him with prolonged and valuable on-the-job training in these matters. In 1936-1937 he supervised the recruitment of Communist volunteers for Spain. Later he reorganized the Yugoslav Communist Party

81

which was then still operating as a clandestine organization.[51] His conduct of guerrilla warfare operations during the Second World War and his elimination of General Draza Mihailovic and other anti-Communist leaders after the war are too well known to require comment other than to note Tito's obvious mastery of the political side of warfare. Tito's break with Stalin has likewise been given very extensive treatment in the press and in a number of articles and monographs, although it would appear obvious that some lines are still kept open from Moscow to Belgrade. It should be added also that Tito's exploitation of the neutralist theme even before Stalin's death may be regarded as a contribution to the overall Communist technique of mixing war and peace; and patently it was for Tito a most effective gambit.[52]

The *rapprochement* between Tito and the leaders in the Kremlin which followed the death of Stalin seems to have been made up equally of Tito's opportunism and the Soviet belief in Tito's value in the campaign of peaceful coexistence and united front maneuvers of unorthodox warfare. While Tito has tried to play what seemed to be a middle-ground position between the West and the U.S.S.R., the fact that he and his associates are Marxists-Leninists has always tended to keep them from going very far in the direction of a pro-Western attitude in the cold war. Thus in January, 1954, Tito used the occasion of a rebuke to his former comrade Djilas to say that Western forms of democracy were "going backward."[53] He indicated that he thought the wave of the future was the movement of Communist revolutionary dynamism.

Two years later relations between Moscow and Belgrade

had grown much closer and Tito's place in the combined peaceful-coexistence, neutralist, united-front maneuver of cold war was signalized on the occasion of h'is Moscow visit during June, 1956. At the conclusion of that visit, Marshal Georgii Zhukov, who had been designated to speak at a ceremony in Tito's honor, repeated the usual propaganda line that "Soviet and Yugoslav military forces are struggling to maintain peace," but added the rather interesting thought that in the event of war "we will struggle shoulder to shoulder for the benefit of mankind." Later in the ceremony Tito presented the Marshal with the Yugoslav Order of Freedom, a decoration never before awarded to a non-Yugoslav person.[54]

Such collaboration had, however, previously been hinted at by the Number Two Communist in Yugoslavia, Edward Kardelj, who had written with reference to the new pattern of relations between Yugoslavia and the Soviet bloc that "such a normalization . . . facilitates elementary contact between Yugoslavia and the Soviet Union and other East-European countries, which can have a certain influence upon further socialist development in that part of the world."[55]

The official communiqué issued jointly by the Soviet Union and Yugoslavia following Tito's visit to Moscow in June, 1956, indicated a continued development along the lines suggested by Kardelj. This communiqué stated, in part, that "taking into consideration the concrete conditions under which present-day Socialist movements are developing, and in the spirit of the internationalistic principles of Marxism-Leninism, the delegations of the League of Communists of Yugoslavia and the Communist Party of the Soviet Union

83

have agreed that it is useful and indispensable that the existing contacts between the two parties should continue and
develop with the view of cooperation in the interest of the
further consolidation and progress of our Socialist countries,
with the view of *cooperation in the international workers
movement and in numerous matters of the present-day development of socialism.*"[*56] Translated from the jargon of Communism this would seem to mean very close cooperation between Tito's Yugoslavia and the Moscow-Peiping axis in the
direction indicated by the doctrinal pronouncements of the
Twentieth Party Congress of the Communist Party of the
Soviet Union: namely, the winning of the rest of the globe
for Communism primarily by propaganda, subversion,
united fronts, peace campaigns, and other forms of unorthodox warfare.

While relations between Tito and the Soviet Union have
blown hot and cold in the years both before and after Stalin's
death, they apparently reached a high point at the time of
the June, 1956, Moscow visit. Since that time, and especially
following the execution of Imre Nagy and his associates in
Hungary during the summer of 1958, relations between Yugoslav and Soviet Communists have been more strained. Yet we
would do well not to rule out another tightening-up of the
bonds of Moscow-Belgrade comradeship, since the two Communist systems could expect great gains from close collaboration in the management of Communist conflict. Furthermore
while Tito may conceivably be more of an opportunist than
a Kremlin-dominated Communist, this can hardly be said

*Emphasis supplied.

84

to be true of the Yugoslav Communists who may some day succeed him.

Milovan Djilas, onetime chief theoretician of the Yugoslav Communist Party, has suggested something which is in the nature of gravitation from one system to the other. Djilas, who was ousted from any position of influence and later imprisoned by Tito but who apparently remains a Marxist, has said that sooner or later the tendency is always for Communism to return to its source, the Soviet Union.[57] The affinity of the two systems seems to be borne out by the action of the Yugoslav delegation to the United Nations. The Yugoslavs have supported the Soviet position quite consistently even when relations between Moscow and Belgrade have not been cordial. The general orientation of the Yugoslav Communist regime is illustrated by Tito's quick action in granting recognition to the rebel government of Iraq soon after the Soviet Union had extended recognition.[58] Yugoslavia had not maintained diplomatic relations with the Iraqi government of King Faisal which had been a leading member of the pro-Western and anti-Communist Baghdad Pact.

Whatever the degree of the *rapprochement* between the Soviet Union and Yugoslavia, or the precise relationship between their Communist parties, Tito and the Yugoslav Communists have made their contribution to the Communist concept of the mixing of war and peace. They are well aware of the nature of the struggle between the Communist bloc and the non-Communist powers. That they have the desire really to be neutral in that struggle is hardly indicated by the record of their past or by the ideology to which they adhere. The

Yugoslav Communist world view is a Marxist-Leninist world view. The Yugoslav Communist ideology embraces specific concepts of war and of peace which are sharply at variance with traditional American concepts of war and of peace. In the continuing conflict between the Sino-Soviet bloc and America is it likely that the Yugoslav Communists will incline towards the American view rather than the Soviet view?

A COMMUNIST PHILOSOPHY OF WAR

The Communist approach to war which involves the mixing of war and peace, peace and war, into an over-all grand strategy was foreshadowed by the writings of Marx and Engels. It was developed into something approaching a definite concept through Lenin's own ideas and through his transmutation of Clausewitzian theory. It reached a matured and doctrinal form under a combination of the theoretical writings and the hard revolutionary experience of Lenin's disciples, foremost among them Stalin and Mao Tse-Tung. Yugoslav Communists and the Communists of other lands have made their contributions, and fresh contributions will continue to be made by a new generation of Communist leaders in Russia and in other parts of the world. But so long as Communists remain Communists, their basic philosophy of war, their essential approach towards war, will necessarily be bound up with their view of the world itself. That world view embracing as it does a philosophy of war ruthless in the extreme was laid down most clearly by Lenin:

War is a great disaster. But a social-democrat cannot analyze war apart from its historic importance. For him there can be

86

no such thing as absolute disaster, or absolute welfare and absolute truth. He must analyze and evaluate the importance of war from the point of view of the interests of his class—the proletariat. . . . *He must evaluate war not by the number of its casualties, but by its political consequences.* *59

NOTES

1. F. O. Miksche, *Secret Forces* (London: Faber & Faber, 1950), p. 18ff., for some aspects of the Marxist philosophy of war. See also D. F. White, "Soviet Philosophy of War," *Political Science Quarterly,* Vol. LI (1936), and Stefan T. Possony, *A Century of Conflict* (Chicago: Henry Regnery Co., 1953).

2. Gerald Freund, *Unholy Alliance: Russian-German Relations from the Treaty of Brest-Litovsk to the Treaty of Berlin* (New York: Harcourt, Brace & Co., 1957), p. 6. See also E. H. Carr, *The Bolshevik Revolution, 1917-1923* (London: Macmillan & Co., Ltd., 1953), Vol. III, pp. 33-38.

3. Freund, *ibid.*

4. T. A. Taracouzio, *War and Peace in Soviet Diplomacy* (New York: The Macmillan Company, 1940), p. 22.

5. William R. Kintner, *The Front is Everywhere* (Norman, Oklahoma: University of Oklahoma Press, 1950), p. 24.

6. Major General J. F. C. Fuller, *Armament and History* (New York: Charles Scribner's Sons, 1945), p. 117.

7. Sigmund Neumann, "Engels and Marx: Military Concepts of the Social Revolutionaries," in *Makers of Modern Strategy, op. cit.,* p. 156.

8. Kintner, *op. cit.,* p. 24.

9. Alfred Vagts, *A History of Militarism* (New York: W. W. Norton & Co., Inc., 1937), p. 34.

*Emphasis supplied.

10. Miksche, *op. cit.,* p. 25.

11. Kintner, *op. cit.,* p. 28.

12. Lenin, *Selected Works,* Vol. X, p. 84.

13. Quoted, *Soviet Documents on Foreign Policy,* edited by Jane Degras (London: Oxford University Press, 1951), Vol. I, p. 137.

14. Taracouzio, *op. cit.,* p. 28.

15. Cited, James D. Atkinson, "The Communist Revolution in Warfare," *United States Naval Institute Proceedings,* Vol. 79 (March, 1953), pp. 286-287.

16. *Ibid.*

17. Lenin, *Collected Works,* Vol. XXII, p. 22.

18. *Ibid.*

19. *Soviet Documents on Foreign Policy, op. cit.,* Vol. I, p. 206.

20. Lenin, *Selected Works,* Vol. V, pp. 179-180.

21. Colonel Vincent J. Esposito, "War As a Continuation of Politics," *Military Affairs,* Vol. XVIII (Spring, 1954), p. 22; see also Bryon Dexter, "Clausewitz and Soviet Strategy," *Foreign Affairs,* Vol. 29 (October, 1950), *passim.*

22. Raymond L. Garthoff, *Soviet Military Doctrine* (Glencoe, Ill.: The Free Press, 1953), p. 11; see also Esposito and Dexter.

23. Quoted, Garthoff, *ibid.,* p. 11; Colonel Kintner's interesting comments on the influence of Clausewitz should also be noted, *op. cit.,* p. 170ff.

24. Quoted, General Augustin Guillaume, *Soviet Arms and Soviet Power* (Washington, D.C.: Infantry Journal Press, 1949), p. 99.

25. *Soviet Documents on Foreign Policy, op. cit.,* Vol. II, p. 25.

26. *Ibid.,* pp. 25-26.

27. *The Great Soviet Encyclopaedia,* Vol. VII, p. 287.

28. *Ibid.*

29. General Baron Geyr von Schweppenburg, *The Critical*

Years (London: Allan Wingate, 1952), p. 170. As the head of the German Navy from 1928 to 1943 has said, "Hitler always leaned by nature towards extreme solutions." See Grand Admiral Raeder, *Struggle for the Sea* (London: William Kimber, 1959).

30. Yves Delbar, *The Real Stalin* (London: George Allen & Unwin, Ltd., 1953), p. 248.

31. Atkinson, "Communist Revolution in Warfare," *loc. cit.*, pp. 287-288; for related aspects of the Trotsky-Stalin argument about military policy see Essad-Bey's biography of Stalin, Bertram D. Wolfe's *Three Who Made a Revolution,* and *Makers of Modern Strategy, op. cit.*, ch. 14. Trotsky's account is given in his *Stalin,* ed. and trans. by Charles Malamuth (New York: Harper, 1941).

32. D. Fedotoff White, *The Growth of the Red Army* (Princeton, N.J.: Princeton University Press, 1944), p. 167.

33. *Ibid.,* pp. 167-169; Leonard Schapiro, *The Origin of the Communist Autocracy* (Cambridge, Mass.: Harvard University Press, 1955), pp. 247-252. For a general discussion of the theoretical controversy as well as related matters see D. Fedotoff White, "Soviet Philosophy of War," *Political Science Quarterly,* Vol. LI (1936). This entire question has been a continuing one in the Soviet armed forces. Whether it could be the cause of any divisive feeling among "professional" *vs.* "Party" military men is a moot point today.

34. White, *op. cit.*, p. 171; see also the extensive discussion of Tukhachevskii's military thought in Possony, *op. cit.*, p. 110ff.

35. Quoted, Pierre Fervacque, *Le Chef De L'Armée Rouge* (Paris: Bibliotheque-Charpentier, 1928), p. 58.

36. *Ibid.,* p. 59.

37. Stalin's Order No. 7 issued as Minister of the Soviet Armed Forces on the occasion of May Day celebrations in 1946 and printed in *Pravda,* May 1, 1946.

38. Denis Healey, "When Shrimps Learn to Whistle:

Thoughts after Geneva," *International Affairs,* Vol. 32 (January, 1956), p. 4.

39. Quoted, the *New York Times,* July 16, 1952.

40. *Pravda,* October 6, 1952.

41. *Ibid.*

42. *Special Supplement, The Current Digest of the Soviet Press,* October 18, 1952, p. 8.

43. Frank S. Meyer, "Principles and Heresies," *National Review,* July 11, 1956, p. 16; this penetrating article should be required reading not only for students of Marxism-Leninism but also for American policy makers.

44. For the full text of Khrushchev's remarks, as well as for the speeches of the other important participants in the Twentieth Party Congress, see the *New York Times,* 16-26 February, 1956. The *Times* has an excellent coverage of the speeches as well as additional stories and comments about the Congress. Leo Gruliow, ed., *Current Soviet Policies* (New York: Frederick A. Praeger, Inc., 1957), contains an even more extensive documentary record of the Congress. It is a compilation based on the *Current Digest of the Soviet Press.*

45. Boyd Compton, *Mao's China, Party Reform Documents, 1942-1944* (Seattle, Washington: University of Washington Press, 1952), p. 171.

46. Quoted, Robert C. North, *Moscow and Chinese Communists* (Stanford, Calif.: Stanford University Press, 1953), p. 262. Professor North points up the intimate nature of the integration of strategy between the U.S.S.R. and the Chinese Communist regime.

47. Quoted, Richard E. Johnson, "Soviet Russia and the Chinese Kuomintang Party, 1918-1925," unpublished M.A. thesis, Georgetown University Graduate School, Washington, D.C.: Georgetown University Library, 1953.

48. Mao Tse-Tung, *Selected Works,* Vol. I, p. 106.

49. Quoted, Atkinson, "Communist Revolution in Warfare," *loc. cit.,* p. 288.

50. Vladimir Dedijer, *Tito* (New York: Simon and Schuster, 1953), p. 71.

51. *Ibid.,* pp. 101-127.

52. See, for example, the survey by Dr. Robert Strausz-Hupé in the *Yale Review,* (December, 1955).

53. *New York Times,* January 18, 1954.

54. *Ibid.,* June 21, 1956.

55. Edward Kardelj, "On Some Problems of Yugoslavia's Domestic and Foreign Policy," *Kommunist,* Belgrade, March 2, 1955.

56. *New York Times,* June 21, 1956.

57. See the thought-provoking analysis by Milovan Djilas, *The New Class* (New York: Frederick A. Praeger, 1957).

58. See the Washington *Evening Star,* July 17, 1958.

59. Lenin, *Collected Works,* Vol. VI, p. 457.

CHAPTER 3

The Evolution of Warfare: Attempts to Eliminate War and Two World Wars

LEGALISM AND WAR

Reflecting the Communist world view is the Communist concept of law (and of morality). This is—in essence—that legality is determined by political expediency. An illustration is supplied from Soviet official sources. During the period in which the well-to-do peasant farmers (the *kulaks*) in Russia were being "collectivized" by murder, transportation to Siberia, and starvation, a Soviet official in the Smolensk area gave a graphic example of Communist legality. He issued orders that "when you are attacking, there is no place for mercy; don't think of the kulak's hungry children; in the class struggle philanthropy is evil."[1]

Equally revealing is the Soviet legal concept of "revolutionary consciousness of right," which justifies any form of arbitrary action against the individual person. This, along with other practices, helps to explain why the Communist concept of "law" is so totally different from Anglo-American theories of law. Some idea of the vast gulf between the

92

thought underlying "revolutionary consciousness of right" and Western legal concepts is supplied by the Soviet revelation in 1959 of hitherto undisclosed circumstances surrounding the fate of Fanya Kaplan, the young Jewess who made an attempt on Lenin's life. The secret police official who had carried out the order to execute this young lady was given prominence in the literary journal *Moskva* in an apparent attempt to refute rumors that Lenin had spared Miss Kaplan's life. The executioner, one Malkov, was quoted as having said that no orders ever came from Lenin to spare Miss Kaplan. He further boasted that he personally had supervised the execution and that he would do it again "if history repeated itself, or repeated itself ten times, or a hundred times or a thousand times."[2] The official praise of such ruthless and arbitrary action speaks more loudly than many volumes devoted to an abstract discussion of Soviet "law."

As in internal affairs, so with external affairs. The Communist views international law in the same light as internal law: it is what serves to advance the cause of Communism, which, not surprisingly, coincides with the interests of the Sino-Soviet bloc. A Soviet professor of international law puts it bluntly: "Those institutions of international law which can facilitate the accomplishment of the stated tasks are recognized and applied in the USSR; those which contradict these aims in any way are rejected. . . ."[3]

The Communists understand, however, the esteem in which law is held by many nations and especially by the United States. The Soviet Union and other Communist states have, therefore, become quite adept in exploiting this regard for the law and nowhere more than in matters of disarma-

The Edge of War

ment and of the elimination of war. The Communists regard disarmament as a technique of political warfare rather than as a real goal. They conceive of the elimination of war as attainable only in a totally Communist world order. They realize quite well, however, that disarmament and the elimination of war are often viewed as legal questions in the Western world.

The Soviet Union, the motherland of world Communism, has in the years since the First World War taken full advantage of the vulnerability of the Western nations which arises from their reliance on the sanctity of law and of treaties. And few nations have placed so much reliance in the law as has the United States.

The American tendency to see either the black of war or the white of peace results in large measure from an attitude toward law which, despite its Anglo-Saxon roots, is specially American. To a far greater extent than the British, Americans have been almost obsessed with the idea that particular problems—small or great—can be dealt with satisfactorily by legislation. That noble experiment, national prohibition of alcoholic beverages, stands as a monument to the American great though fallacious passion for reducing all social, moral, and philosophical questions to legal terms. In the particular instance of prohibition it took us fifteen years to come to a realization that it is impossible to change social customs by legislative fiat. This American penchant for thinking along strict legalistic lines is also the way in which we as a people have often viewed the phenomenon of war.

Although many Americans had long believed that law could be used to control and regulate warfare, it was not until

94

the period following the First World War that our grand design of actually outlawing war was conceived. The Great War and the crusading zeal it had produced among Americans had been followed by an equally strong reaction that the idealism evoked by the war had somehow become tarnished along the way. Not only were Americans appalled by the mass suffering, the vast casualties, and the human tragedy of the first global war of modern times, they were also deeply disturbed that the war to end all wars seemed only to have prepared the ground for a new series of conflicts. If, then, the great crusade to make the world safe for democracy had failed, could not some method be found to place a *legal* ban on war? Was not war a criminal act? Could it not, therefore, be outlawed? The answers to these questions were supplied by the Kellogg-Briand-Multi-Lateral Treaty for the Renunciation of War, which is in many ways a classic example of our passion for legalism as applied to warfare.

This concept of the 1920's—largely based on American thought—came about when M. Aristide Briand, the French Minister of Foreign Affairs, proposed that France and the United States should subscribe "to any mutual engagement tending, as between those two countries, to 'outlaw war,' to use an American expression."[4] The American Secretary of State, Frank B. Kellogg, used M. Briand's suggestion as the basis of a proposal for the conclusion of a multi-lateral treaty among the principal world powers which would condemn war and renounce it as an instrument of national policy. American legalistic thinking was well illustrated the following year in a note sent by the Secretary of State to the French, British, German, Italian, and Japanese foreign offices: Mr.

Kellogg stated that "from the broad standpoint of humanity and civilization, all war is an assault upon the stability of human society, and should be suppressed in the common interest. The Government of the United States desires to see the institution of war abolished. . . ."[5]

Like the attempt to abolish the Demon Rum by law, this was a noble gesture, and we must not be so cynical as to believe that it was attempted from any but the highest motives. Unfortunately, "outlawing" war proved to be devoid of meaning—and it is likely to remain so, unless the concept is based on careful thinking about the problem of war itself and the means whereby some efficient control devices could be developed.

The indispensable conditions for supra-national law—or so-called "world law"—consist primarily in a consensus of people *everywhere* about the law, judicial bodies which have established a reputation for justice, and a workable police force. Not only are all of these things lacking in the world, but—even more importantly—over one-third of the globe is ruled by a system, Communism, which aims to overturn all present law and rule by a mixture of naked force and propaganda.

The Kellogg-Briand Treaty for the Renunciation of War was signed at Paris on August 27, 1928, and ratification was advised by the United States on January 15, 1929. Fifteen nations were original signatories of the pact, and the treaty also went into effect for an additional thirty-one countries on July 24, 1929. Eventually, all but a few of the independent nations of the world gave their adherence to the treaty which was to outlaw war.

Among the nations which solemnly pledged to condemn recourse to war and to carry on relations with one another only by peaceful and friendly means was the Union of Soviet Socialist Republics, which became a party to the Kellogg-Briand treaty on September 27, 1928. It is a melancholy fact that within less than seventeen years the Soviet Union had swallowed up three of its fellow-signatories, made satellites of six other states, and taken territory from a further three. More prophetic for the evolution of warfare, however, was the Soviet note of August 31, 1928, to the French Ambassador in Russia—an indication of the nature of developments in Soviet psychological warfare that deserves to be better known. In the note the Acting Commissar for Foreign Affairs solemnly affirmed that "aiming to bring into effect its policy of peace, the Soviet Government, besides its systematic defense of the cause of disarmament, had also addressed the other governments, long before the idea of the Pact recently signed at Paris had arisen, with the proposal to renounce through bi-lateral pacts not only the wars foreseen in the Pact of Paris but any mutual aggression and any armed conflict whatsoever. . . ."[6] The Commissar then went on to sound a propaganda theme as typical of today as of 1928: "the facts hereinabove stated afford unquestionable proof that the idea of eliminating wars and armed conflicts from the fields of international politics is the predominant idea of the foreign policy of the Soviets."[7]

So little had the study of the phenomenon of warfare been undertaken in the United States that, thirty years after the signing of the Kellogg-Briand Treaty, many Americans were once more seriously proposing law as the key to world peace.

Law, to these people, is a panacea; it is seen as the all-encompassing answer for the control of nuclear weapons, the abolition of the hydrogen bomb, and the solving of all problems which beset mankind. It is interesting, however, that former Secretary of State Dean Acheson was inclined to proceed much more cautiously. Speaking before the fifty-first annual meeting of the American Association of Law Libraries, Mr. Acheson pointed out that laws alone could not be counted on to settle international differences and that "the law has followed rather than preceded authority and has withered without the support of the state."[8]

It is likewise significant that another Secretary of State, John Foster Dulles, on numerous occasions during his tenure of office warned that the United States must maintain an adequate defense establishment and cannot, for its very life, trust in signatures to what may become legally binding on America, but of little moment to a country which does not possess the legal traditions which we have built up over the years and which we inherited from the common law of England. Because of their unflinching realism, Mr. Dulles and Mr. Acheson, probably more than any other Americans, have been the targets of malicious propaganda emanating from the Soviet Union. Perhaps only the late Senator Joseph McCarthy has been more viciously assailed by the Soviet smearbund.

The Soviets were especially incensed in the case of Mr. Dulles with what they termed his "position of strength" diplomacy. They were quite aware that his refusal to commit the signature of the United States to legal documents—honored by Moscow more in the breach than in the observance—had been responsible for checkmating Communist political warfare in many instances.[9]

The legalistic approach has had a long background of historical experience; nor is it a distinctly American quality. What might be said to be the peculiarly American contribution is the idea that war itself can be *outlawed*. A host of thinkers from Roman times on have attempted to adopt legal concepts to the conduct of war. The scholastic philosophers and theologians of the Middle Ages centuries ago dealt with the question of war, and Grotius in his treatise *On the Law of War and Peace* (1623-1624) devoted at least five chapters of this great work to the problem of limiting and moderating war. But while Cicero, Saint Augustine, Saint Thomas Aquinas, Grotius, and even such American thinkers as James Madison and John C. Calhoun would all have agreed that war should only be engaged in as a means to get a better and more durable peace, and while they would have also more or less generally agreed that there was a distinction between a just war and an unjust war,[10] they would hardly have subscribed to the utopian idea that war could be eliminated by statute.

The terrible destructiveness of the First World War coincided with the full flowering of the eighteenth-century concept of the innate perfectibility of man and man's uninterrupted march of progress—twin ideas which had been unashamedly embraced by many intellectuals. This would seem to be the proximate cause which led Americans—and many others as well—to believe in an absolute cure for war without first having completely understood the disease. It is not without significance that, in the decade 1950-1960, there has been a return (with exceptions previously noted) to the older concepts that war cannot be banned by legislative fiat, but that it may be possible to confine it within maintainable bounds. The increasingly large volume of both popular and scholarly works being published in the United States and in many other countries offers hope that war will now be subjected to intensive study from which some kind of effective control devices may eventually result. Such a development would mark a return to reason. It would augur well for a future avoidance of the well-intentioned but specious reliance on the magic formula of a rule of law calculated to end—in a seductively easy way—the gravest questions confronting our civilization. It would mean that we have at last come to the inescapable conclusion that we cannot wish evil away or solve problems by recourse to the emotions alone.

THE PROBLEM OF WAR

Philosophers, theologians, and jurists of the fourth through the seventeenth centuries as well as the later thinkers who sought to outlaw war would, however, have found themselves on fairly common ground if they had approached the problem of the distinctions between war and peace. For war and peace were for long quite sharply distinguished, and even the forms of war were subjected to an appreciable amount of study. Then, too, an actual body of law relating to the conduct of war had been built up through the centuries. Although the regulations for the treatment of prisoners of war and for the protection of non-combatants and similar widely accepted precepts were sometimes ruthlessly ignored, there was, nevertheless, a definite body of rules to which

100

civilized nations paid much more than lip service. During the War of 1812, for example, when the U.S.S. *Hornet,* Captain James Lawrence commanding, sank the British brig H.M.S. *Peacock,* the survivors were treated with such chivalry that the British officers later inscribed a letter of appreciation to Captain Lawrence in which they stated that "we ceased to consider ourselves prisoners." Several wars later Brigadier Desmond Young of the British army in his book, *Rommel: The Desert Fox,* pays tribute to the way in which Field Marshal Erwin Rommel observed the rules of war in the campaigning in the western desert. Rommel completely ignored Hitler's order to liquidate prisoners taken from commando or other special-force-type raiders. It should be remembered that the German officer corps—with some exceptions—did what it could to ameliorate the brutality of the Nazis.*

All of this, of course, was with reference to situations in which a state of war actually existed. It represented a view which assumed also that war was an activity carried on between regularized forces of one kind or another. Diplomats and military men alike looked with a mixture of horror and disdain on irregular forms of warfare and, while at times giving such things a partial sanction, refused to think of them as other than aberrations and as aberrations which could, at that, be controlled.

During the Napoleonic wars the Duke of Wellington was extremely sensitive about stirring up what we would today

*As a prisoner of war in German prison hospitals and camps during World War II, I had rather more than academic knowledge of the rules and laws of war.

call resistance movements in the countries occupied by Napoleon. The Duke's attitude seems to have been much the same as Napoleon's, who forbore to raise a revolt of the Ukrainians against the Czar. These great leaders thought that war was to be conducted by regularized forces of one kind or another, and by such forces alone. Clausewitz, the great Prussian philosopher of war, does discuss the *levée en masse* or people's war, and thus has a very modern ring, but even Clausewitz indicates that he limits himself to a discussion of such warfare on "military grounds" and does not want to consider the broader, political side of such a movement. During the Franco-Prusisan War of 1870 when Leon Gambetta after the fall of Napoleon III employed the people's war against the Prussian armies, Helmuth von Moltke, Chief of the Prussian General Staff, believed that this was a throwback to an uncivilized era, since war was a matter of fighting between duly constituted forces. The strong German aversion to *franctireurs* seems to have become such a fixation from this time on that even during the Second World War the German forces were reluctant to do much in the way of experimentation with commando or other special service troops. A notable exception is to be found in the activities of Colonel Otto Skorzeny and of certain special units which operated against the Russians.

That the professional soldier or sailor thought of war as an operation involving the employment of force in the hands of duly recognized combatants is not at all surprising. Statesmen, philosophers, writers who had studied the question of war, and ordinary folk alike held much the same view. Had not war been the trade of the military man for centuries?

And was not this trade something that all recognized as quite different from the quiet ways of peace? Definite distinctions between peace and war had been the common property of people's mental processes for centuries; and while war and peace occasionally spilled over from one compartment into the other, this was hardly regarded as the normal order of things.

During the French Revolution the National Convention in Paris on August 23, 1793, promulgated a decree which was a measure of total war that involved an entire people in warfare. This "total war" order really did not differentiate between combatants and non-combatants, between soldiers and civilians. It was a radical departure from the usual lines drawn between peace and war. But although this ukase did introduce mass conscription into the modern era and although it left its mark on the conduct of warfare, Napoleon soon tamed the Revolution and again regularized war. The traditional distinctions between war and peace soon became meaningful once more. Unlike the impact of the later Communist revolution in the mode of warfare, the French Revolutionary impulse, while it contained the germ of the later Communist fragmentation of both peace and war, did not have the opportunity to flower. It did furnish a quick glimpse into a dreadful future. Edmund Burke wrote of the French Revolution, in words that are prophetic for our own times, that "it is not with a nation that we are at war, it is with an armed doctrine that we are at war." But in the sunny days of the *Pax Britannica,* which followed the moderate peace settlement of the Congress of Vienna and which seemed to promise an almost endless period of stability in world politics,

Burke's challenging words were, not unnaturally, hardly remembered.

In the one hundred years from 1814 to 1914 there existed a general peace broken by wars which were limited not only in geographical extent but also in aim. This was made possible by the system of balance of power among the Great Powers, but the viability of the balance of power rested in large part on what historians have called the *Pax Britannica*. This was the dominant world position held by Great Britain by virtue of the fact that, from the end of the Napoleonic wars almost down to 1914, she possessed in greater measure than any other Great Power, or even two Great Powers, the combination of industrial strength, trained personnel, and machine capacity for warfare (in the form of the Royal Navy) which added up to supremacy in the employment of force— and the legitimate maximization of force had ever been the other side of the coin of diplomacy.

The hundred-year era from the Congress of Vienna to the First World War was thus a period in which wars were limited and there was a semblance of the working of the rule of law in world politics. This long interval of general world stability was rendered possible through the operations of the Concert of Europe and the working of the balance of power system. But these factors in turn were largely feasible because a single Great Power held a dominant role in the employment of force in its then most efficient form—sea power. Precisely because there was the *appearance* of some kind of rule of law at work in world politics and because wars were kept limited in this era, the distinction between a state of peace and a state of war was apt to appear even sharper than it actually was. It should not be forgotten that the German Army was not alone in having a horror of *franc-tireurs* and anything else smacking of irregularity in warfare—or, in other words, of anything which tended to blur the distinction between war and peace, and between the soldier and the civil authority.

In the British and French armed forces in this hundred-year period (and in the American and other armies and navies as well) the idea that peace and war were in separate, water-tight compartments was no less true than it was among the civilian leaders, publicists, writers, and general public. A study of the fiction dealing with espionage during the latter part of the nineteenth century and during the twentieth down almost to the Second World War—and the analysis of fiction often reveals more about the national mind than an analysis of factual writing—shows that the novelists were concerned with *military* affairs rather than political matters. It is only after the Second World War that we have the novelist turning, generally, to such themes as the subversion of people, the creation of dissent, and the infiltration of political parties, institutions, and governments. The heroes—or villains—of the older fiction attempted to discover the blueprints for a new cruiser or airship or make drawings of fortifications or steal the enemy order of battle. Only rarely were they concerned with anything which could even remotely be called political or psychological warfare. Factually, the realities were remarkably like the fictional themes of the period. Colonel Redl, a high Austrian Army staff officer in the pay of Russia, for example, betrayed the Austrian war plan of maneuver to the Russian secret service some years before the First World War, but his motives were not at all ideological.

THE FIRST WORLD WAR AND ITS AFTERMATH

The First World War was the first true total war. It raised for the first time the possibilities inherent in arousing entire peoples in an effective effort to wage all-out war. And it came to a world which had not only been enjoying the relative quiet of a century free from general war, but also to a world in which man's forward progress seemed inevitable. Whether in early Wilsonian America, Edwardian England, Wilhelm's Germany, France at the height of the rule of the bourgeoisie, or even the Czarist Russia from which Lenin and Trotsky had been escorted over the border instead of receiving a bullet in the back of the neck (as later was the rule under the Soviets), it was a world which possessed a deep-rooted feeling of confidence, of order, and of security. Never after August 1914 were people to be quite so sure of themselves.

Yet not all of this was apparent in the early days of the war. World War I began as a gentleman's war. Thus *The Ilustrated London News* for August 22, 1914, pictured the arrival of the German Emperor on the Rhine and commented placidly that "the truth is that his Majesty is still a very dark horse of the military kind, and has his reputation as a soldier still to make." Such forbearance did not last long. The war soon became a struggle between entire peoples on a scale never before witnessed. We sometimes forget, at this distance in time, that the First World War introduced many of the things with which we were to become all too familiar during 1939–1945. Economic warfare, armored fighting vehicles, the submarine, aerial bombardment of cities, propaganda—all were gradually perfected in the years after 1914.

Developments in the field of public opinion and propaganda during the First World War were especially noteworthy. In a war in which vast conscript masses took the field and were in turn supported by millions of workers in munitions and supply industries, in a war in which for the first time it became possible to communicate with these millions on a mass basis, the total morale of a nation became of prime importance. British and American leaders grasped this fact much more quickly than did the authorities of other countries. President Wilson emerged as probably the first authentic master of psychological warfare. Even though the Germans were more skillful in the marshalling of weapons and in the purely military side of the struggle, it availed them little, since their opponents, although blundering a great deal *militarily,* employed *all* devices, especially the psychological ones, much more effectively. As Field Marshal Erich Ludendorff was to write in his memoirs, "Germany failed in the fight against the *moral* [morale] of the enemy peoples."

Yet despite the introduction of mass propaganda, thoroughgoing devices of economic warfare, and other new forms of warfare, few people saw such things as other than auxiliary weapons brought into play *during a war* in support of strictly military objectives. Ludendorff, for example, appreciated the vast development both of propaganda and economic warfare, but he saw these things simply as additional tools of war which should be placed under the control of the supreme military commander. While he anticipated Hitler in regard to the mobilization of all facets of the life of the nation for war, Ludendorff still thought in terms of a distinct difference between war and peace. He does not even seem to have gone so far as to consider, as did Hitler, a psychological warfare campaign to be used as a softening-up process in the period immediately *preceding* a declaration of war. In short, Ludendorff, while appreciating the rise of other than military factors, nevertheless continued to think about distinctions between peace and war based on traditional lines.

Most leaders—military as well as political—in Great Britain and the United States held views approximating those of Ludendorff on this subject. The Committee on Public Information (CPI), set up by President Wilson under an executive order of April 13, 1917, rendered an effective propaganda service at home and abroad during the war, but it was quickly disbanded in the post-war period. The British were even more skillful in the conduct of propaganda during World War I (they distributed leaflets by balloon as early as 1918, for example), and the British campaign of 1914-1917 to enlist the sympathy of American public opinion is a classic one in the annals of public relations and propaganda; yet the British Government also disbanded its extensive psychological warfare apparatus after the war and did not attempt to reconstruct it until the eve of World War II.

In the years after 1918 it was only here and there (except in the Soviet Union in which both doctrine and practice of conspiratorial warfare were evolving) that writers and thinkers speculated that war of the future might be of an altered nature and that it would eventually envisage extensive operations in peace no less than following a declared state of war. Oswald Spengler, a German philosopher who wrote on the philosophy of history, realized something of the nature of the coming changes in warfare when he perceived the connection between changes in weapons and corresponding changes in communications.[11] And also in Germany, Colonel Nicolai, Chief of the Intelligence Department of the German General Staff throughout the greater part of the war, wrote in his memoirs "only that State the political, economic, and military leaders of which cooperate in the work of the intelligence service, can be assured regarding the future . . . . in future the intelligence service will gain an importance far exceeding that which it had in peace-times before the War."[12]

In the West, however, in the years between the two world wars, reflections such as these, and the writings of Major General J. F. C. Fuller, Captain B. H. Liddell Hart, and others in Great Britain and elsewhere, are hardly to be considered as indicating a broad stream of thought about the possibility of less conventional warfare in future years. Most writers and thinkers, including military ones, continued to concern themselves with the traditional distinctions between peace and war rather than about some of the changes which now began to muddle the differentiation between the two. To this end many things contributed. There was the illusion that the comfortable world of pre-1914 could be resumed and with it man's steady forward progress in the material world. There was the idea, especially strong in the United States, that such activities as espionage and intelligence work were excusable and even acceptable during a state of declared war but that they were not quite the sort of thing that nice people did when the shooting was all over. Thus an American Secretary of State is alleged to have discontinued our efforts (during the 1920's) in decoding the cable and wireless traffic of other countries with the statement that "gentlemen don't read other gentlemen's mail." Very importantly there was, too, the reassertion of the old diplomacy which had been temporarily disturbed by the impact of President Woodrow Wilson's open covenants, openly arrived at.

The Wilsonian idea of appealing directly to the people over the heads of their governments and its utilization of the emerging techniques of public relations and propaganda in the conduct of international politics had been a sharp blow to the older concept of diplomacy. The professional diplomat, whether European or American, had largely been immune from the sweeping changes brought about in the nineteenth and early twentieth centuries by the effects of mass education, mass communications, and the levelling process of the rise in the living standard of the great bulk of the population. Unlike the other professions, including the military, diplomacy—even after the First World War—remained something of a closed corporation through the continuance (or even the further adoption) of rather esoteric entrance procedures and requirements. An observant Englishman has indicated that becoming a member of the diplomatic profession was somewhat on the order of becoming a Vestal Virgin in the ancient days of Rome—for a male an impossibility, and for a female a difficult feat. While this may not have been entirely true in the United States, even here the diplomatic profession had many of the overtones of the aristocratic nature which it retained in Europe long after 1918. Some idea of the extent to which diplomacy retained its knightly character is given in Sir Ernest Satow's 1922 edition of that authoritative work, *A Guide to Diplomatic Practice*. Speaking about the necessary qualifications for the individual who wished to embark on a diplomatic career, Sir Ernest summarized all of the important characteristics by stating that "in short, the candidate must be *an educated gentleman.*" So that there can be no mistaking the Edwardian and Georgian concept of the aristocratic nature of the gentleman, Sir Ernest italicized the phrase "an educated gentleman."

It might be expected that many—if not most—of the products of such a climate of opinion would find it hard, if not impossible, to perceive that the Communists were already in the process of turning diplomacy upside down. Likewise they might reasonably be expected to have difficulty in fully comprehending that in the emerging era of the rise of the total state, the carefully worked out distinctions between peace and war of former days would become less and less meaningful—that the traditional forms and trappings of diplomacy as well as the externals of other institutions might, in future, be retained but that the content would often be perverted.

Between the two world wars, then, the diplomatists were influenced by their desire to return to the old, well-ordered diplomacy of pre-Wilson days in which the dividing line between peace and war was sharply defined and in which wars themselves had been of a limited nature. For this they can hardly be blamed. The relative stability of pre-1914 world politics was in sharp contrast to the period of general unrest— or armed truce—from 1919 onwards. Yet whether President Wilson be praised or blamed, he must be recognized as having not only hastened the rise of the influence of public opinion and the use of propaganda in world affairs but also to have been well in advance of his time in understanding the effectiveness of these and other new forces at work in international relations.

It may be desirable to try to turn back the clock of history, but it is normally impossible to do so. Those statesmen, diplomatists, and other leaders who thought that the employment of propaganda and the conduct of extensive intelligence operations in peacetime might smack of warlike activities were eventually to find that the chiefs of totalitarian regimes were not merely going to do these things but, far worse, were going to do them without much concern for any of the moral or human values involved and in a way calculated to blur the older ideas of peace and war. Under the hammer blows of the new barbarians—Communists and Nazis alike—the luxury-mentality of an illusory picture of the world as a pleasant sort of gentlemen's club to which the ill-mannered and uncouth could not be admitted would inevitably give way.

THE SECOND WORLD WAR AND THE DEVELOPMENT OF NUCLEAR WEAPONS

That the distinction between a state of peace and a state of war continued to be a generally accepted one by all those in the realm of Christian civilization was hardly to be denied. From the dawn of military history men had not only sought answers to the phenomenon of war, but had, in an almost continuous chain of thought, viewed the traditional pattern of war as an overt clash of arms. This was not less true during the Second World War than it had been when General Sherman pronounced war to be hell. Thus, Professor Cyril Falls, the distinguished British military historian

112

and critic, wrote in 1943 that "war in its simplest definition is a quarrel between nations or sometimes between two parties of the same nation, decided by force of arms."[13] And in the previous year one of the ablest of American military historians, Hoffman Nickerson, stated in answer to the question "What is war?" that war "is the use of organized force between human groups pursuing contradictory policies."[14] It can be seen that these definitions are not very far away from the definition offered more than a century earlier by the German philosopher of war Clausewitz. While Clausewitz speaks of war as the continuation of politics by other means, in the very beginning of his great work *On War* he simply says that "war is thus an act of force to compel our adversary to do our will."

As the Second World War progressed, the vastness of the struggle as engaged in by conventional military forces—land, sea, and air—tended to support the traditional views of war as an act of pure military force. True, extensive guerrilla warfare operations took place in many theatres of the war, and propaganda as well as political and psychological pressures nourished them more than anything else. There was the growth and development of widespread "resistance" movements in the enemy-occupied countries. Psychological and economic warfare was conducted on a scale far greater than during the First World War.[15]

At the time, however, these phenomena appeared to be, as they had been in the earlier Great War, merely further manifestations of the purely military operations of the war. They did not seem—except to a few—to mark out a pattern for an entirely new approach towards the conduct of warfare.

113

Thus as the war drew to a close in 1945, it was only dimly perceived that para-military, semi-military, and non-military operations such as guerrilla warfare, underground or resistance movements, propaganda, and economic devices might some day be, at the national policy level, on a par with specifically military operations. More, such techniques might even be adopted and used *in place of* orthodox military methods. That propaganda, psychological, political, and economic warfare could hardly be seen as anything but auxiliary to regular military operations is not in the least surprising. The massive military campaigns of this greatest of wars tended to obscure these techniques. And in August, 1945, in the war's closing days, the dropping of the world's first atomic bombs was such a display of pure force that there seemed to be little future in any lesser weapons or in measures of the subtlety involved in the mixing of violent and non-violent methods.

The appearance of nuclear weapons in warfare seemed at first glance to supply further evidence that war was now, more than ever before, a matter solely of armed force. The atomic bombs dropped on Hiroshima and Nagasaki, raising as they did the possibility of ever-mightier air bombardment in future wars, appeared to cast the future of war in more strictly military terms than in the past with the seeming—and in the strict military sense, relatively unimportant—exception that such a military future would be almost wholly that of the air arm. Indeed, the massive destructive power of nuclear weapons seemed to reduce war to the apparent simplicity of delivering a few quick blows against an enemy and then accepting his submission. Reflecting this early view, Sir

114

William Beveridge wrote that "the atomic bomb has almost certainly relegated all other weapons of modern war—tanks, battleships, guns, rifles, and trained conscript masses—to the museum."[16]

Some warnings against exclusive reliance on A-bombs were, however, sounded by the atomic scientists themselves. Dr. Vannevar Bush, Director of the Office of Scientific Research and Development, pointed out early in 1947 that "if, as Heaven forbid, this Nation ever has to engage in another major conflict, we may be sure that it will have to exert the unified strength of all three arms—land, sea and air—that no one arm will do all the fighting, and, by the same token, that by no means all the fighting will be done by pushing buttons."[17]

In one sense the atomic-destruction, single-weapon idea was a military nostrum, as Dr. Bush and others have implied, since it would be used only in an all-out war. But in another sense the development of the atomic bomb affected total war of the future in a way which was truly revolutionary. The sudden, smashing, knockout blow about which strategists had long speculated now seemed to be a distinct possibility, and it seemed an even greater likelihood with the later development of the thermonuclear bomb. Thus as early as 1949 the possible development of a thermonuclear device was thought of as creating a "super weapon," the ultimate in sheer force, and hence as opening the way towards unparalleled destruction against an enemy if it were used in a war.[18]

The actual development of the thermonuclear bomb in the period 1949-1954 gave greater impetus to speculation concerning massive attack in the event of an all-out war, and little doubt about the tremendous destructive power of thermonuclear weapons remained. Some indication of this enormous power was furnished by Air Force General Nathan F. Twining's statement in 1954 that "the Strategic Air Command in one mission can deliver more explosive power on a target than the combined Allied Air Forces of World Wars I and II."[19]

Certainly the possible employment of nuclear bombs in war tended to overturn previous military concepts. Admiral Arthur W. Radford (then Chairman of the Joint Chiefs of Staff) indicated as much when in 1955 he said that atomic weapons represented "a technological advance that is without precedent in military history."[20] And only a year later, in testifying on the necessity for effective strategic striking power, General Curtis LeMay, head of the Strategic Air Command, pointed up the devastating effects of thermonuclear bombs. General LeMay said that "there are no adjectives which can adequately describe the destruction and desolation which would result from a war in 1960."[21]

Thus the discovery of atomic fusion and the later development of the fusion/fission process which led to the thermonuclear bomb made possible a destructiveness dwarfing that caused by high explosives, artillery shells, and aircraft bombs during World Wars I and II. Atomic weapons and the thermonuclear bomb also vastly increased the advantages which might be gained from a sudden surprise attack. The official policy of the United States was, however, completely to rule out any surprise attack initiated by Americans. Secretary of Defense Charles E. Wilson underscored this policy in 1955 when he defined preventive war as "the initiation of war because you think you have a reason to prevent something worse later. That would be my definition of the term. Our country has been traditionally opposed to such an idea."[22] There is no evidence to suggest that official policy of the U.S.S.R. similarly rules out a surprise attack. One American analyst of Russian affairs believes that, on the contrary, Soviet bloc leadership thinks that there might be some situations in which it would suit their purpose to deliver a sudden surprise thermonuclear attack and that they therefore are in process of developing capabilities which would make such a surprise attack possible.[23]

There can be little doubt but that Soviet leaders would not hesitate to launch a surprise nuclear attack against the United States if they believed it to be feasible. The British historian Sir Arthur Bryant accurately assessed the cold and calculating policy of the Communists when he wrote that "to fail to destroy a capitalist State when it was within the power of the Communist rulers of Russia to do so safely, would be, in their eyes, a betrayal of the workers of that country, of the Marxist creed, and of the cause of world Communism."[24] The emphasis here should be placed on the idea of safety. From Lenin down through Stalin to the present leaders of the U.S.S.R. there has been a careful calculation of the risks inherent in any military or foreign policy move. Whereas Hitler and the Nazis were gamblers in the arena of world politics, the Communists—because of the idea of the historic inevitability of Marxism-Leninism—and by reason of their own hard experience in revolutionary war-

117

fare, have been cautious in the extreme. Hitler's description of Stalin as an "ice-cold blackmailer" is worth repeating as applicable generally to the Kremlin's grand strategy. The cold calculation of the Communist leadership has been reinforced by their deadly fear of being provoked into premature action. Warnings about *provokatsiya* (provocation—being enticed into untimely or precipitate action) abound in Soviet doctrine. So long, therefore, as the United States has the capability of absorbing a Soviet surprise attack and is still able to deliver a crushing return blow it is unlikely that the Soviet bloc leadership will consider the risk worth the game. Furthermore, it can be assumed that the Communists would much prefer to take over a going concern in preference to a burnt-out shell. They appreciate even more than some Americans that the massive productive capacity of the United States is the world's greatest industrial/agricultural complex.

Yet while the atomic bomb, and still more the thermonuclear bomb, have revolutionized the conduct of large-scale war as the world has known it in the past, these awesome weapons have had an even greater effect on the ways in which warfare can be waged under the guise of peace—that is, on what may be called cold war or unconventional warfare.

In the years between the world wars there was, as has been noted, a strong impulse towards the abolition of war. There developed also during these years various ideas and practical measures which were aimed at making it possible to achieve desired goals by actions short of outright war. In India Mahatma Gandhi and his followers perfected the techniques of non-violent resistance which had much earlier been sug-

118

gested by an American, Henry David Thoreau. In other countries men speculated about, or actually experimented with,
the sit-down strike, propaganda, sabotage, and other techniques of an unorthodox nature. In the Soviet Union these
and many other forms of attack against existing institutions,
societies, or governments were brought to a fine art. But the
introduction of the atomic bomb at the close of the Second
World War and the development of the thermonuclear bomb
in the years after the Second World War brought refinements
in techniques of an unorthodox kind and introduced a new
—and major—weapon of political warfare: nuclear-missile
blackmail.

The Soviet leadership was keenly aware of its vulnerable
position in the years immediately after World War II. They
did not have the A-bomb. They saw quite well, nevertheless,
that the United States hesitated not only to use this powerful
weapon, but hesitated even to threaten its use. Unorthodox
forms of warfare could, therefore, give the Soviet bloc the
possibility of continuing to wage war under the guise of peace,
and could help—through massive propaganda and diplomatic
maneuvering—to stay the hand of America. Finally, when the
U.S.S.R. at last came to possess nuclear weapons, these same
weapons could be turned around and used—not by dropping
them on America and the other non-Communist nations—
but as reserves in a worldwide campaign of nuclear blackmail,
and the creation of a fear psychosis about nuclear fallout
and atmospheric poisoning. The development of the intercontinental ballistic missile (ICBM) has heightened the effect
of an already powerful weapon of unconventional warfare.
Perhaps, then, the ultimate significance of nuclear weapons

119

may be the background which they furnish to a vast symphony of unconventional warfare.

NOTES

1. Quoted from a document in the Smolensk Archive, Merle Fainsod, *Smolensk Under Soviet Rule* (Cambridge, Mass.: Harvard University Press, 1958), p. 241.

2. *New York Times,* January 25, 1959.

3. *Soviet Affairs Notes,* No. 233, August 10, 1959, p. 1.

4. *Papers Relating to the Foreign Relations of the United States 1927* (Washington, D.C.: U.S. Government Printing Office, 1942), Vol. II, p. 612.

5. *Ibid.,* 1928, Vol. I, p. 11.

6. *Ibid.,* p. 171.

7. *Ibid.,* p. 172.

8. Washington *Evening Star,* July 4, 1958.

9. Robert M. Slusser and Jan F. Triska, *A Calendar of Soviet Treaties, 1917-1957* (Stanford: Stanford University Press, 1959), list international agreements entered into by the U.S.S.R. including the secret Soviet-German military agreements of 1921-1933. *Soviet Political Treaties and Violations,* Committee on the Judiciary, U.S. Senate, 84th Cong., 1st Sess. (Washington, D.C.: U.S. Government Printing Office, 1955), documents the long list of treaties and agreements broken or evaded by the Soviet Union.

10. One may well imagine the delight they would have taken in demolishing the sophistry in the Marxist-Leninist definition of just and unjust wars whereby a "just war" is any war waged by a Marxist-Leninist state against an "imperialist" state.

11. See the massive two-volume work, Oswald Spengler,

The Decline of the West: Perspectives of World-History,
trans. and with notes by Charles Francis Atkinson (New
York: Alfred A. Knopf, 1928).

12. Colonel W. Nicolai, *The German Secret Service* (London: Stanley Paul & Co., Ltd., 1924), p. 267.

13. Cyril Falls, *Ordeal by Battle* (New York: Oxford University Press, 1943), p. 9.

14. Hoffman Nickerson, *The Armed Horde,* 2nd ed. (New York: G. P. Putnam's Sons, 1942), p. 3.

15. For some interesting ideas about guerrilla warfare see
Christopher Sykes, *Orde Wingate* (New York: World Publishing Co., 1959), and C. Aubrey Dixon and Otto Heilbrunn,
Communist Guerilla Warfare (New York: Praeger, 1954).
Paul M. A. Linebarger, *Psychological Warfare* (Washington:
Combat Forces Press, 2nd ed., 1954), is very good with reference to World War II propaganda. Peter Kemp's *No Colours
or Crest* (London: Cassell, 1958), illustrates the use of a number of unorthodox techniques. The official British publication, *British War Economy* (London: His Majesty's Stationery Office, 1949), is an excellent study of economic warfare.
Wilhelm Hoettl, *The Secret Front* (New York: Praeger,
1954), Paul Leverkuehn, *German Military Intelligence* (New
York: Praeger, 1954), and Walter Schellenberg, *The Schellenberg Memoirs* (London: Andre Deutsch, 1956), give much
information about German espionage, propaganda and
other irregular operations. For complete coverage see the
outstanding bibliographic guide published quarterly in
Military Affairs, Washington 4, D.C.

16. London *Times,* August 14, 1945.

17. Washington *Post,* January 15, 1947.

18. See, for example, U.S. Atomic Energy Commission,
In the Matter of J. Robert Oppenheimer (Washington: Government Printing Office, 1954), pp. 682-683, p. 752ff. and
passim.

19. U.S. Congress, *Hearings, Subcommittee of the Com-*

mittee on Appropriations, House of Representatives, 83d Cong., 2nd Sess. (Washington: Government Printing Office, 1954), p. 91; General Twining testified about "the frightful damage that can be caused by even a few Soviet weapons of modern type" and went on to say that the "strategic air offensive is designed to deliver a sudden, massive blow against the will and ability to wage war. Our ability to react immediately, and with tremendous force, is the principal deterrent to aggression," p. 75, p. 77.

20. U.S. Congress, *Hearings, Subcommittee on Appropriations, U.S. Senate,* 83d Cong., 2nd Sess. (Washington: Government Printing Office, 1954), p. 165.

21. *Ibid.,* 84th Cong., 2nd Sess., 1956 (Fiscal 1957), p. 1225; General LeMay went on to say that "we must have a force strong enough in size, so deployed and in such a condition of readiness to guarantee to him that the inevitable consequences of any attack they might launch will be devastation of his own homeland. Should they be so foolhardy as to miscalculate our capability, this force must be capable of insuring the emergence of the United States as the superior power."

22. U.S. Congress, *Hearings, Subcommittee of the Committee on Appropriations,* House of Representatives (Washington: Government Printing Office, 1955), p. 99. Mr. Wilson's definition in full was: " 'Preventive war' means that you initiate the war while you are strong for fear the enemy will get stronger and you will not be able to overcome him at some later date. The theory is while there is still the time to start the war, give the enemy a licking and you have that one over with."

23. H. S. Dinerstein, *War and the Soviet Union* (New York: Praeger, 1959), ch. VII, *passim;* for a discussion of other aspects of preventive war see Bernard Brodie, *Strategy in the Missile Age* (Princeton: Princeton University Press, 1959), Ch. 7.

24. Quoted, Atkinson, *Communist Revolution, loc. cit.,* p. 285.

CHAPTER 4

The Evolution of Warfare:
Unconventional Warfare

THE ANATOMY OF UNCONVENTIONAL WARFARE

Whether or not it has been the shadow of atomic war which induced aggressors to turn even more strongly to means of conquest other than those of an obviously military nature, the introduction of nuclear weapons hastened the maturity of a new pattern of warfare. This unorthodox warfare was not new if each part of it (propaganda, for example) were to be viewed in isolation. Its techniques had been developed through both theory and practice over the course of many decades. But never before the post World War II period had this mode of warfare been carried on so vigorously, with such coordination, and in so many parts of the globe. The utilization of such wide, almost bewildering varieties of semi-warlike methods of aggrandizement as part of a concerted grand strategy *was new*.

In the years after the Second World War this new warfare was brought by the Communists to a near-perfect state. It was called by some "cold war." General William J. Donovan, World War II Chief of the Office of Strategic Services, believed that a more all-embracing term should be used rather than "cold war." Hence he began using the term "unconventional warfare" in order to describe the new pattern of neither peace nor war.

The late Father Edmund A. Walsh, S. J., founder of Georgetown University's pioneering School of Foreign Service, and one of the earliest scholars fully to understand the significance of the Communist seizure of power in Russia, has said that the Bolshevik Revolution constituted the most important event in recorded history since the fall of the Roman Empire. Certainly the transformation of Marxism from a theoretical concept into an armed doctrine made real by its possession of a great permanent land base and by its harnessing to the dynamo of Russian imperialism has had an earth-shaking impact on the conduct of international affairs. It has had an equally profound effect on the development of the multiform possibilities of unconventional warfare and correspondingly on the content and meaning of the terms "war" and "peace." These words were once more or less generally understood in the same way by all persons and all governments throughout the world. Today nowhere is the impact of the Bolshevik Revolution more apparent and nowhere are there greater diversities than in the meaning of the terms "war" and "peace" as they are understood by the Communist world and by the non-Communist world.

Although the realization that "peace" and "war" do blend into a sort of ill-defined grey amorphous state that is partially both and partially neither is a concept which has become rather more familiar to people in the democracies in recent times, it is as yet not fully accepted.[1] The generality of men—and even some specialists—still tend to think in terms of the traditional distinctions between "peace" and "war." Hence they do not always accept the idea of the mixture of the two which is in essence the basis of unconventional warfare.

The Communists have, without specifically using the term, practiced unconventional warfare for more than four decades. Lenin took the Marxian theory of the constant struggle between the proletariat and the bourgeoisie and developed it markedly. He applied it to an all-embracing area of conflict in which cultural, psychological, political, conspiratorial, and economic techniques would not so much *support* armed forces as in the past, but would rather supplement and even supplant armed force used in orthodox ways.[2]

On a highly pragmatic basis, too, unconventional warfare has had a definite appeal to Marxists–Leninists. Unlike orthodox warfare, it has greater possibilities for expansion and contraction. It can be heated up close to the boiling point, as in the case of the Berlin Blockade or Indo-China. It can be cooled down and made to consist only of propaganda efforts, covert intelligence operations, or long-range argumentation and diplomatic maneuvering in support of political warfare. Thus as long ago as the Communist-sponsored World Assembly for Peace in 1955, the ground was prepared for the present intense political warfare and diplomatic pressure in the fields of disarmament and economic and cultural exchanges, and with regard to the so-called German problem.

Unconventional warfare therefore embraces a broad spectrum of conflict. It includes propaganda, economic warfare, sabotage, espionage, subversion, strikes, civil disturbances, terrorism, political warfare, and guerrilla warfare. And all these can, of course, be used singly or in concert for an im-

125

mediate objective or in furtherance of the over-all grand strategy. Peripheral warfare is also included in the concept of unconventional warfare; the Korean War was an example of the employment of almost all the forms of unconventional warfare, including peripheral or limited war. Unconventional warfare thus employs both non-violent and violent techniques, but perhaps its most distinctive characteristic is that it blends the violent and the non-violent into a new synthesis of warfare.

Of course, Marxism-Leninism has not been solely responsible for bringing the techniques of unconventional warfare into the world. Mankind has seen espionage carried on almost from the dawn of history. The makers of the French Revolution experimented with many methods of unorthodox warfare. In the United States Presidents Thomas Jefferson and James Madison pioneered in economic warfare (the Embargo and other acts) as a device short of open war.

Then in the latter part of the nineteenth century and in the early decades of the twentieth developments in the communication of ideas helped in the evolution towards new forms of warfare. The telephone and radio, the typewriter, duplicating machines, printing advances, and high-speed still- and motion-picture photography gradually provided the means that made a wide variety of unconventional warfare techniques feasible.

Most important, the formation of an intelligentsia of numbers (a seeming contradiction) has made possible the sustenance of political movements dedicated to revolutionary change in a manner not previously possible. It is a truism that revolutions are not made by the masses. It follows that the conduct of unconventional warfare with its many-faceted activities can be conducted on a sustained and extensive scale only if there exists an intelligentsia to furnish the cadres for work of this kind. Some light on the importance of the modern intelligentsia may be gathered by Mr. M. R. Masani's cogent observation that the ruling class in Asia is "neither the landed aristocracy nor the capitalists but the articulate urban educated class; this is the class which creates public opinion and makes and unmakes government . . . [and has] a strategic importance out of all proportion to their numerical or economic strength."[3] In this connection it is well to recall Lord Bryce's much earlier dictum that ten men who care are a match for a hundred who do not. This is particularly applicable to revolutionary organizations, resistance movements, and especially to the conspiratorially trained, highly disciplined, para-military parties that made the Soviet, Chinese Communist, and Nazi seizures of power possible.[4]

Scientific achievements have continued to add greatly to the possibilities inherent in the organization, operation, and maintenance of politico-revolutionary parties, guerrillas, and resistance and underground movements. The Second World War experience in the formation or expansion of resistance movements and the continuing cold war from 1946 onward have demonstrated the possibilities for the future conduct of unorthodox operations through the use of conventional aircraft, helicopters (and still more vertical take-off aircraft), radio and wireless telegraphy, photographic equipment, highly compressed foodstuffs and drugs, and weapons of light weight but great firepower. Finally, it would seem that modern complex society is more vulnerable to attack by unconventional methods than was an earlier and somewhat more primitive society. The paralysis which resulted in Singapore from a Communist-inspired general strike in June, 1955, is illustrative of the sensitivity of today's highly organized, closely interlocking society to unconventional warfare.[5]

But the political leaders, the military authorities, the writers and analysts of the non-Communist world have not been entirely unaware of the meaning of new forms of conflict. The history of the resistance movements in German-occupied countries during the Second World War indicates that the democracies possess both extensive assets and the know-how for waging—and waging successfully—this highly specialized version of combat. The latent possibilities of unconventional warfare were earlier demonstrated to the Western democracies during and immediately after the First World War. There was, however, a general failure to study the lessons of the British Colonel T. E. Lawrence's adaptations and innovations in guerrilla warfare in the Middle Eastern desert areas and of the partisan operations of the civil war in Russia. Even less attention was devoted to the operations of the Irish revolutionaries (1916-1921),[6] although a very great deal could have been learned from them.* The Communists, on

*In a memorandum prepared for me by one of the Irish Nationalists who participated in these operations, something of the nature of the Irish genius for unconventional warfare is indicated when it is pointed out that: "Whereas a standup fight was necessary in 1916, and the effort captured the imagination of the Irish people in whom a spirit of nationality lay dormant, a new method of guerrilla warfare was decided upon, which meant a different form of training, and re-equipping with instruments of warfare. All this was very slow work, and the Irish Republican Army as now named following Easter Week 1916 was composed of ordinary citizens who had to do their daily toil in order to live, and therefore could only afford a limited number of hours during the week. . . . The

the other hand, *have* studied the history of unorthodox warfare. As a result of their success with unorthodox methods during the seizure of power in 1917, and even more because of their intense emphasis on political-psychological factors, they have grasped more quickly and more surely than their opponents the concept that unconventional warfare can be waged even more favorably under the cloak of ostensible peace than under conditions of open and declared war.

In the years after World War II the Communists improved, refined, and extended their techniques of unconventional warfare. Under the impact of their refinements and their renewed vigor—stimulated by the prospect of new vistas of conquest—their cold war, which had been waged more cautiously and certainly more clandestinely during the 1920's and 1930's, became an active, flourishing enterprise.

The British military thinker Captain B. H. Liddell Hart foresaw the increased tempo of this creeping aggression. He asserted that aggression would be inclined to follow improved methods, exploiting the opponent's weak points while refraining from direct threats on really vital matters which might precipitate a total war. Liddell Hart believed that the new form of attack would be different from the older kinds with which the world had grown familiar during the rise of Hitler. The new type of warfare would rely on diplomatic

---

Intelligence Service grew with every recruit to the I.R.A. and care had to be taken not to expose the keymen to any of the fighting units or to the enemy. Later as the fight became more intensified, men and women were taken from ordinary occupations to work full time in the Revolutionary Movement. These full time workers were the key links in the various phases of the war. Such key links are not to be confused with the keymen of Intelligence work, but rather as an auxiliary service. Here were the sources of information. . . ."

maneuvering, political warfare, and similar devices, among which infiltration would constitute the primary design. Such infiltration, he felt, would be far more extensive than anything of this kind previously employed. It would likewise be of a more refined and subtle nature.[7]

A survey of Marxist-Leninist techniques of unconventional warfare in general, but with special reference to the period after the Second World War, will therefore be more remunerative than a description of the more sporadic (and often counter-responsive) unconventional warfare activities undertaken by the non-Communist powers.

PROPAGANDA

Propaganda is one of the chief weapons in the Communist arsenal of unconventional warfare, not only because it is a technique in itself, but because it can be employed in conjunction with so many other devices. It serves to support and assist strikes, civil disturbances, economic warfare, and guerrilla warfare. Above all, propaganda is the handmaiden of political warfare. While political warfare is waged against governments, institutions, or well-organized groups, propaganda is directed at the masses and at identifiable but not tightly knit groups such as intellectuals. If, for example, European intellectuals can be persuaded that the testing of nuclear weapons is harmful, the chiefs of state of the European governments may be more inclined to listen to Soviet proposals for the imposition of a ban on nuclear testing by treaty.

The extent and sometimes the skill of Soviet propaganda would, at first glance, incline one to believe that modern propaganda, like much else, was a Russian invention. This is not at all the case. The British employment of propaganda addressed to the neutrals generally and to the United States in particular during the early years of the First World War constitutes the first great—and successful—usage of propaganda as we know it in the modern sense. And the Americans showed themselves to be almost equally adept in the field, with President Wilson displaying a mastery of both political warfare and propaganda to such an extent that Lenin took lessons from Wilson as regards the employment of the principle of national self-determination.

How was it, then, that Communist propaganda was within a few decades to be so all-pervasive and effective while American and other non-Communist efforts were seemingly so meager and impotent? Primarily, it was because the Soviet Union and later the Chinese Communist regime visualized propaganda as an instrument of warfare and one which functioned continuously whether there were any formal declaration of war or not. The Soviet Union early created an extensive propoganda organization on a permanent basis, with its source of authority at the very top level of the Soviet hierarchy: the Agitation and Propaganda Section of the Central Committee of the Communist Party, more commonly referred to as AGITPROP.

The British and American approach was quite different. Tremendous expansion and the creation of an elaborate organization during the shooting war was followed by the dismantling of the vast structure, the scattering of records, the dismissal of personnel and, most of all, little or no attempt at any continuity of men, machinery of organization, or policy.

Soviet policy with reference to propaganda has, on the

other hand, been further characterized by adherence to Lenin's advice that "the task of the Bolsheviks is patiently to explain." Hence the Communists have adopted a number of standardized propaganda themes, such as peace, disarmament, peaceful coexistence, and have steadily adhered to them. While the Western democracies become timid and embarrassed in the face of some minor incident of racial or economic inequality, Communist propaganda majestically continues to ring the changes on peace and peaceful coexistence in the face of such major crimes as the bloody suppression of the Hungarian national fight for freedom and despite the condemnation of a Special Committee of the United Nations.[8] It should also be noted that Communist propaganda is designed to create the conditions for success and is not held to be an end in itself. By contrast, Western statesmen often naively approach the conduct of propaganda as though it were an end in itself.

Since propaganda is one of the important weapons in the Communist arsenal of unconventional warfare and since it is not a technique in itself but can also be employed in connection with other devices such as strikes, economic warfare and, of course, political warfare, a short review of the Soviet approach to propaganda will serve to pinpoint the present-day Soviet propaganda operations in the light of past Communist aims, objectives, and accomplishments.

At the very birth of the Soviet state in 1917 Lenin and his associates indicated their appreciation of the value of propaganda by the creation of a section of the Central Committee of the Party devoted exclusively to agitation and propaganda.[9] Lenin early apprehended the propaganda possibilities inherent in radiotelegraphy (as it was then called) and wrote to Stalin that "we should not spare expense" for its development. He and his associates were also alert to the necessity of combining both open and secret operations for propaganda, and Germany was an early theatre for their work. In fact, many of the Communist propaganda techniques employed against Germany in 1918 have been used, with refinement, down to the present day. The Soviet embassy in Berlin was utilized as a center for propaganda as were the consulates in Stettin and Hamburg; couriers and trained agitators travelled regularly from Moscow to these places.[10]

A significant case illustrating the Soviet grasp of the nature of propaganda was the Petrograd Telegraph Agency. This organization, created ostensibly for commercial activity, was used chiefly as a propaganda medium in Germany, thus establishing a pattern which was to become world-wide by the 1930's. The Petrograd Telegraph Agency was later renamed the Telegraph Agency of the Soviet Union (TASS), the name by which it is known today. Although it is still apparently an effective propaganda medium, TASS today seems to concentrate more heavily on espionage than on other activities. One of the unique accomplishments of Soviet propaganda has been the gaining of diplomatic immunity for TASS representatives. The Soviet Government advanced the claim of diplomatic immunity in the early operations of the Petrograd Telegraph Agency in Germany, and eventually all states accorded TASS such immunity. The ramifications of such protection as regards both the conduct of propaganda and the carrying out of espionage missions may well be imagined, especially when it is evident that the privilege of diplomatic immunity enables the recipients to be free from so many of the restrictions which would hamper the activities of the ordinary citizen living or travelling in a foreign country.

Another recognizable pattern established during the early period of Soviet propaganda operations in Germany was the lavish outlay of money. The Soviet ambassador and his associates in the Reich in 1918 had a large sum of money at their disposal, and it is significant that some of it was supplied by German leftists. Our State Department noted during this same time the transmission of money from Russia to Stockholm, which was to serve as a center for the distribution of funds for propaganda work in Great Britain and the United States.[11]

This early Soviet appreciation that substantial amounts of money are required for propaganda work—whether for bribing writers, subsidizing newspapers, or for the conduct of overt propaganda—has been a continuing feature of the world-wide Communist propaganda effort. As early as February, 1918, the American Minister in Sweden reported that the Bolsheviks had appropriated five million rubles for spreading subversive propaganda in foreign countries. This was certainly a lavish expenditure for a regime which had the support of only a small minority in Russia and was not at all recognized by the international community.[12] Soviet expenditures for propaganda continued to grow steadily over the years, and by 1951 one scholar estimated that the U.S.S.R. alone was spending one and one-half billion dollars yearly for propaganda purposes.[13] The new Chinese Communist regime added to the volume of expenditures for propaganda, and by 1958 the Soviet Union and associated Communist

Powers were spending approximately three billion dollars annually for propaganda activities of all kinds.[14]

Since neither the U.S.S.R. nor the other Communist states publish a breakdown of expenditures of this kind, such figures must, of course, be in the nature of educated guesses. We can assume, however, that since such estimates do not include figures for covert propaganda operations, the actual total is certainly far higher than three billion dollars per year. The Brussels World's Fair of 1958 illustrates the scale of Communist expenditures for propaganda. The Russians spent $55,000,000 for their exhibit; by contrast, the United States spent $11,800,000. Any estimate of funds employed for the conduct of propaganda must also take into account the fact that the indigenous Communist parties as well as front groups in countries throughout the world spend considerable sums for propaganda; so the grand total of moneys earmarked for propaganda by world Communism must be vast indeed. The free world's efforts in the propaganda field are on a decidedly more modest, if not minuscule, scale. In Japan, for example, Moscow pours out millions of dollars for propaganda; but the Free Asia Association, the only spirited anti-Communist group among the Japanese, cannot get enough money to become a really positive force against Communism.

Some idea of the magnitude of the Communist propaganda effort may be gained by brief glances at two widely separated parts of the globe. In France during 1953, for example, the French Communist Party published fifteen daily newspapers, fifty-one weeklies, and fifty-six reviews and magazines of various types. In addition there were other attempts to influence public opinion, such as the distribution of leaflets and posters and the employment of agitators and speakers. The over-all picture, therefore, reveals that prodigious exertions are constantly underway in the Soviet's propaganda struggles. An interesting glimpse at the kind of Russian assistance may be gained by Simon Wolin's expert analysis in his valuable contribution, *Communism's Postwar Decade*. Dr. Wolin states that *L'Humanité* (the leading French Communist newspaper) received a sharp setback during 1954 through "the loss of a law suit against the newspaper *L'Aurore,* which had accused it of living on Soviet subsidies."*

On the other side of the world, the Chinese Communists—in collaboration with their senior partners, the Russians—have a number of organizations which serve as examples of effective propaganda work in Asia. The Chungking Democratic League, formed in 1946 as a federation of leftist groups and now dominated by the Communists, carries out propaganda, and apparently espionage, through student societies, cultural groups, and business firms among the Chinese people living overseas. Its chief work is primarily along the Hongkong-Bangkok-Singapore-Jakarta line which the Communists appropriately designate the "Great Nerve of Asia." The Federation of Democratically Minded Chinese Youth Organizations, in collaboration with the Soviet-dominated World Federation of Democratic Youth, carries out propaganda among young people both at home and abroad. The *Min-Seng-She*

L'Humanité remained an important force in Communist propaganda work in France, however. Statements made at the time of Khrushchev's visit to France in March, 1960, indicated that circulation was flourishing. The work of the Communist press in France during the Khrushchev visit underscores the importance of Communism's world wide propaganda machine.

organization either directly or through affiliated organizations conducts propaganda through the medium of sports, debating, and other recreational-cultural groups in the Far East. These organizations are typical of the propaganda side of unconventional warfare through which the Chinese Communists intend, as they have publicly stated, to bring about the liberation of Asia from the "imperialist and reactionary bourgeois" influence of the United States and of other non-Communist countries.

Not least among the weapons in the Communist arsenal of propaganda have been the stock propaganda programs which have been used to supplement the political warfare carried on at a different level by the Soviet and by the Chinese Communist governments. These include, among others, such standard items as anti-colonialism, peaceful coexistence, nationalities appeals, and disarmament.

The disarmament theme has played a key role in Communist propaganda in support of the Soviet Government's political warfare from the First World War down to the present day. Thus Ludwig Martens, Bolshevik unofficial envoy to the United States, claimed in 1920 that the Soviet Union would immediately disband all its military forces after receiving similar evidence on the part of foreign powers. Students of Soviet affairs were to learn, but only years later, that the skepticism with which the Soviet proposals for disarmament were greeted were fully justified. For, while openly talking about general disarmament and good will and complete mutual confidence, the Soviet Union began as early as 1919 a secret collaboration with the German General Staff and brought this collaboration to full flower in the 1920's and early 1930's. Yet in November, 1927, the Soviet representative, Maxim Litvinov, was still trumpeting the idea of universal disarmament at the Geneva conference of the Preparatory Disarmament Commission—an illustration of the Soviet theory of unconventional warfare which looks with special favor upon any kind of international meeting or conference as a prospective sounding board for propaganda.

Almost three decades later, the U.S.S.R. was using another international body, the United Nations, as a propaganda forum. During the spring-summer session of 1956, for example, Soviet representative Gromyko proposed that all members of the United Nations should undertake a solemn promise to abstain from the employment or the threat of force and especially to refrain from using nuclear weapons, while in the same breath he refused to accept any effective form of arms control and inspection. The Soviet Foreign Minister followed this with a similar propaganda proposal on July 16, 1956, and the then Soviet Ambassador to the United States, G. N. Zarubin, continued the propaganda campaign with an appeal from the Supreme Soviet on July 25, 1956, which put forth a claim of Soviet reductions in armed strength as an argument for an actual Western disarmament.[15]

Soviet disarmament schemes since the propaganda campaign of the summer of 1956 have varied little except that increased emphasis has been placed on the abolition of the testing of nuclear devices. Meaningless though these proposals have been, they have all had definite propaganda value for the U.S.S.R., since they have made the front pages of the press of the free world and have thus had an effect on public opinion which has resulted in an eventual relaxation of the

138

attitude of Western statesmen towards the diplomatic maneuvering of the Soviet Government.

The really remarkable achievement of Communist propaganda, however, has been its success in obscuring the true attitude of the Soviet Union toward disarmament and toward the Soviet's pledged word with respect to truce arrangements, arms inspection, and treaties generally. The hard fact is, as shown by a scholarly study made for the United States Senate, that of the nearly one thousand treaties and agreements, both bilateral and multilateral, which the Russians have been a party to "in the 38 short years since the Soviet Union came into existence, its Government had broken its word to virtually every country to which it ever gave a signed promise." The study goes on to state that the U.S.S.R. "signed treaties of nonaggression with neighboring states and then absorbed those states," and that "it was violating the first agreement it ever signed with the United States at the very moment the Soviet envoy, Litvinov, was putting his signature to that agreement."[16]

THE SOVIET CAMPAIGN AGAINST THE GERMAN FEDERAL REPUBLIC: A CASE HISTORY OF COMMUNIST PROPAGANDA

Communist propaganda is used especially to support Soviet bloc campaigns which aim to divide the free world nations and sow suspicion and hatred among them. Nowhere is this more evident than with reference to the propaganda conducted against West Germany.

The North Atlantic Treaty Organization—despite Soviet attempts to outflank it in the Middle East and on the African continent—remains a truly formidable barrier to the new

Communist imperialism. This is so because of two key positions. (1) Greece and Turkey. These countries not only bar Soviet egress from the Black Sea area but must always constitute a threat to the Soviet hinterland and to lines of communication as regards Communist-controlled expansion in the Middle East and most of Africa. (2) West Germany. Egress from the Baltic and freedom of movement in the entire Baltic area—a zone close to the heart of Russia—is blocked to the Soviet Union so long as the West German Federal Republic remains a partner in NATO. As Vice Admiral Friedrich Ruge has indicated, while the West continues to control the Danish Straits, Soviet submarines from the Baltic Sea will not be a menace to merchant shipping in the Atlantic sea lanes. At the same time six hundred miles of Baltic seacoast now under Communist domination will be susceptible to the unseen but ever present influence of the seapower of the NATO forces.[17] To the geo-strategic factor and to the build-up of West German defense forces must be added the industrial and technological power of the German Federal Republic, largest in NATO with the exception of the United States. It can readily be seen that the U.S.S.R. considers that the task of neutralizing NATO is essentially the task of neutralizing these two key zones of power and that West Germany, the most critical zone, must be dealt with first.

Communist propaganda has been assigned the task of sowing hatred and suspicion of the German Government and people while Soviet political warfare concurrently seeks to use diplomatic pressures, official statements, and "summit" conferences to drive a wedge between the German Federal Republic and her American, British, and French associates in NATO. As long ago as December 30, 1955, *Pravda* reported that Premier Khrushchev had warned Great Britain and France that Germany constituted a threat to them for, "if one were to suppose for a moment that the completely unrealistic dream of militant U.S. leaders for the inclusion of a united Germany in the aggressive bloc were to be realized, the French and British could hardly live in peace. The hands of the German revanchists would then be freed."

Soviet propaganda has continued to hammer away at the theme that West Germany and the German people are a threat to Britain and France. During his 1960 visit to France Khrushchev consistently introduced the "hate Germany" motif. Thus, speaking in Rouen on March 30, 1960, he said: "Over a period of less than a hundred years the citizens of Rouen have thrice experienced the horrors of wars with German invaders, have drunk their fill of sorrow and know the real value of peace."

Closely associated with the "hate Germany" theme have been the Soviet charges of anti-Semitism against the German Federal Republic. There were overtones of this in the Communist propaganda of the early 1950's, which attempted to give the impression that there was a revival of Nazism in West Germany. There was a consistent effort to smear the German Federal Republic and its leaders, especially Chancellor Konrad Adenauer and the Minister of Defense, Dr. Franz Josef Strauss. They were accused of being militarists and of wanting a war of revenge. The real Soviet charge against them was that they had brought stability to a country that would otherwise have been a fertile ground for Communist exploitation of economic discontent and political grievances. As West Germany grew in industrial strength and as the West German armed forces came to constitute an important part of NATO's defensive posture against the Soviet bloc, these attacks grew more vigorous and were extended to include many officials in the West German government. Higher ranking officers in the *Bundeswehr* (Armed Forces of the Federal Republic) have come under especially heavy propaganda attack. This has been because the Kremlin is acutely conscious of the fact that the disciplined, technically excellent and well-staffed West German armed forces represent a military capability that is a definite barrier to Soviet imperialistic expansion on the European continent.

The charges of anti-Semitism were often included as subsidiary themes against West Germany along with the major propaganda charges of militarism, the desire for revenge, and war crimes in an effort to discredit the Federal Republic and to make it appear that the Germans were not fit partners in a Western alliance. Toward the end of 1959 and in the early months of 1960, however, the anti-Semitic charges became the principal vehicle for propaganda against West Germany and seem likely to form a continuing part of Communist propaganda in support of a lengthy Soviet campaign which seeks to create divisive pressures among America, Britain, and France over Germany. The Soviet leadership appreciates—perhaps even more keenly than the West—the significance of the German contribution to NATO and especially the great German *potential*. And the Kremlin realizes that charges of anti-Semitism are apt to pay bigger dividends in stirring up suspicion and hatred than any other form of propaganda.

On Christmas night, 1959, Nazi emblems and anti-Semitic statements were painted on a Jewish synagogue in Cologne. This was rapidly followed by a series of anti-Jewish incidents in other parts of Western Germany and then throughout the free world. Swastikas were painted on Jewish houses of worship, inflammatory statements were scrawled on walls and on public buildings, and the press in the democratic countries was filled with stories which tended to inflate the dimensions of these incidents. The Communist propaganda machine, already implicated in the creation of anti-Semitic incidents in West Germany, went into action throughout the world in order to add fuel to the flames and to expand the incidents out of all proportion to their original size.[18]

The net result was to bring down a flood of condemnation on the West Germans. As United States Senator Thomas J. Dodd has stated: "Overnight, the West German democracy was placed in the pillory, rendered suspect, morally isolated from its Western allies."[19] While responsible Jewish leaders such as Dr. Nahum Goldmann, President of the World Jewish Congress, and Israel's Premier David Ben-Gurion pointed out that the West German Government's record towards the Jews was outstandingly correct, many people around the world fell into the trap which Soviet propaganda had prepared. They forgot about the real and present danger of Communist imperialism and thought only about the propaganda claims of the German revival of Nazism and anti-Semitism. Communist propaganda achieved, in other words, a certain amount of success in forwarding the long-range Soviet goals of weakening the North Atlantic alliance, of softening up Western determination to stand fast against the U.S.S.R., and of isolating the German Federal Republic.[20]

But the Communist propaganda against West Germany, especially the anti-Semitic part of it, seems also to have an additional aim—to serve as a smokescreen or cover for the very real anti-Semitism which has for years been carried on by the Soviet regime itself. It is an old—and very effective—Soviet propaganda technique to conceal Communist crimes by shouting loudly about the alleged crimes of capitalists, imperialists, social democrats, and other non-Communists. Thus for years Soviet propaganda about British, Dutch, and French "colonialism" helped (and still helps) to conceal the new type of colonialism being practiced by the Soviet Union among the subject peoples of Central Asia, in the conquered Baltic states of Latvia, Lithuania, and Estonia, and in the satellite countries of Eastern Europe.[21]

In like fashion the Soviet Union has for a very long time been guilty of the most flagrant anti-Semitism. But the U.S.S.R. has concealed its true aims, through a cloud of propaganda about anti-Semitism elsewhere in the world, and through an iron curtain of censorship which has only now and again been pierced to reveal the true condition of the Jews in the Soviet Union and in the Communist-dominated countries of Eastern Europe. From the time of Lenin the Communist Party of the Soviet Union was antagonistic to Zionism and to the idea of a Jewish national culture. Communism has also been hostile to the Jewish religion, as it has been to all religions. The inevitable long-term trend of Soviet policy toward the Jews was foreshadowed by Lenin's pronouncement that "Jewish national culture is the slogan of rabbis and bourgeois, the slogan of our enemies. . . ."[22]

Stalin's regime was, especially in the post World War II period, much more harsh in its persecution of the Jews than in the earlier years of his rule. Stalin's successors were seemingly less severe in their treatment of the Jews, but this was primarily for propaganda purposes and did not represent any basic policy change. Thus permission was given to the Moscow rabbis to publish three thousand prayer books, but since there are three million Jews in the Soviet Union, this is rather meaningless. Furthermore, as one Jewish scholar has pointed out, "how the books are to be printed is not clear, because the last Jewish printing press has long been closed and the type melted down."[23]

Despite propaganda about de-Stalinization, the Kremlin has continued repressive measures against the Jews in the U.S.S.R. Jews are systematically excluded from positions in the foreign service, from ranks of importance in the armed forces, from the universities, and, indeed, in a general way from positions of any importance throughout the whole of Soviet society. Some few are, of course, kept for window-dressing as a part of the propaganda program. Even more significant, the Jews have been singled out in much the same way as the Nazis singled them out. They are required to have "Jew" stamped on their internal passport. This is the document which each individual in the Soviet Union is required to have, but other groups are not discriminated against in this way. It is hardly surprising that the Anti-Defamation League of B'nai B'rith has stated: "The prospects for Soviet Jewry are dire and gloomy: at best, the extinction of a once flourishing and rich cultural tradition and life; at worst, the completion by the Communists of the heinous work begun by the Nazis—the liquidation by forcible assimilation of this community of 3 million Jews."[24]

Although Soviet propaganda has sought to disguise the latent hatred which the Soviet regime bears toward the Jews, there are occasional insights which indicate the depth of such hatred and the reason for it. Long ago Mikhail Tukhachevskii revealingly said: "The Jews brought us Christianity. This is sufficient to hate them. . . . The Jew is a dog, the son of a dog who plants his fleas in all countries. . . ."[25] This statement goes to the heart of the matter. The new barbarians want to shatter the entire fabric of the existing social order. The great strength still remaining in most areas of that social order in the world is principally that represented by Judaeo-Christian civilization. This the Communist barbarians recognize must be utterly destroyed. But in the meantime, their vast propaganda apparatus confuses those within the fabric of that civilization so that they see the enemy as now colonialists, now exploiters, now the rich, now the Germans; today it is nuclear testing and the dangers of fallout; tomorrow, yet another spectre will be conjured up by Soviet propaganda. And always it is a propaganda which seems so to befuddle the Western mentality that one can find a British journalist referring to the Soviet tyrant Khrushchev as that "amiable chatterbox." Is it surprising, then, that the masses in the Western democracies—and their leaders—seldom see the real enemy: Communist totalitarianism?

ESPIONAGE AND SUBVERSION

Communist espionage operations resemble Communist propaganda methods inasmuch as there is a multitude of official agencies and of front or other auxiliary organizations engaged in a total espionage effort. Quite apart from its activities in the clandestine networks of the satellite countries and of the Chinese Communists, the Soviet Union engages on its own in spying and subversion through the Foreign Branch of the secret police, the Intelligence Division of the Army General Staff, the Foreign Ministry, the Central Committee of the Communist Party of the Soviet Union, the Comintern (officially dissolved in 1943, but continuing in another form), and the foreign trade ministry. In addition, the Soviet news agency TASS carries out widespread espionage duties, while in various parts of the globe special sections of the Soviet Navy and of other Soviet governmental agencies perform similar work.[26]

The inter-relations of Soviet espionage-subversion operations and propaganda are also shown by the use made of various Russian trade organizations such as AMTORG. As early as 1927, for example, the British Government found that the Soviet trade organization in the United Kingdom, ARCOS, was being used as a cover for the conduct of both propaganda and espionage. This was revealed by a raid carried out in London by British security personnel on May 12, 1927, and the evidence of this use of foreign trade posts by Soviet agencies has since been duplicated in other countries. There is voluminous testimony on the similar employment of AMTORG in the United States, and it is known that the Soviet Purchasing Commission in Washington during the Second World War was almost blatant in its acquisition of information for the Soviet intelligence apparatus.[27]

The Soviet Government claimed (and received) diplomatic

status for AMTORG in 1921 (following the pattern of TASS) and this has greatly facilitated its ability to conduct espionage under the cloak of diplomatic immunity. Having turned diplomacy as well as warfare on its head, the U.S.S.R. has made every possible subversive use of the diplomatic privileges enjoyed by its representatives. As long ago as November 4, 1926, the U.S. Department of State, in explaining its refusal to grant a transit visa to Madame Kollontai, explained that the lady ambassador was "one of the outstanding members of the Russian Communist Party, a member of the Third Congress of the Communist International and a member of the Soviet Diplomatic Service . . . [and] has been actively associated with the International Communist subversive movement."

As previously noted, the Soviet news agency TASS constitutes still another organization used for a combination of espionage, subversion, and propaganda. It also enjoys the cover of diplomatic immunity. The Report of the Canadian Royal Commission indicated that Nikolai Zheveinov, TASS correspondent in Canada, was engaged in the direction and supervision of a large number of persons who were collecting highly secret information from Canadian Government sources for transmission to Moscow. A similar situation was revealed in Sweden during the years 1951-1952. The Swedish police then discovered that Viktor Anisimov, chief of the Stockholm bureau of TASS, was also the director of a network of spies. As a result of this espionage, the Soviet Union was able to acquire, over a ten-year period, detailed information concerning the state of readiness, armaments, disposition, etc., of the Swedish Navy as well as details relating to air bases, land armaments, and Swedish defense plants. The

148

collection of this wide range of intelligence information was made in great detail and included numbers of photographs of airfields and other pertinent data.

Only a year after the Swedish revelation, L. K. Pissarev, the TASS representative at The Hague, was arrested by Dutch police (December 23, 1952) after he had been discovered in the operation of a plan to subvert an official in a ministry of the Netherlands Government. A situation similar to the Swedish case, though perhaps even more widespread, was discovered in Australia during 1953 when Viktor N. Antonov, chief correspondent of TASS in that country, was shown to be the head of an espionage group there. The International Press Association put the case quite clearly when it stated "only a fraction of the information which TASS correspondents abroad send to their head office in Moscow is ever printed. The greater part of their work consists in the gathering of military, political and economic intelligence material intended for various Soviet ministries and other departments."

In the campaign of the new look launched by the Soviet Union in the years following the death of Stalin, and greatly aided by Khrushchev's hand-washing of the crimes (in which, as in the Ukraine, he had participated) of the Stalin era, a propaganda attempt was made to place the onus for terrorism, espionage, and subversion on the supposed bad old days of Stalinism. Behind the facade, however, Soviet unconventional warfare in these fields continued much as in the time of both Lenin and Stalin albeit with more finesse.

Despite the propaganda that such activities were no more than vestiges of the Stalin era, the march of events steadily disproved such claims. Thus the Government of Iran expelled the Assistant Military Attaché of the Soviet Embassy in Teheran on March 1, 1956, after he had been arrested in company with an officer of the Iranian Air Force while engaged in receiving secret documents relating to air force matters.[28]

A few months later the *New York Times* reported (June 21, 1956) that Michael Shatov, a leader of Russian emigré groups in the United States, had testified concerning repeated attempts by two Soviet officials at the United Nations to induce him to return to the Soviet Union. Failing in this, the Russians tried to get Mr. Shatov to engage in espionage work in America for the U.S.S.R.[29]

Two years later during the summer of 1958, and at a time when Khrushchev's propaganda of peaceful coexistence was near its height, the President of the United Press International reported continuing evidence of world Communist subversion and espionage activity. Mr. Frank H. Bartholomew, after a visit to Switzerland, stated that the Chinese Communists were using Bern, Switzerland, as a headquarters for a massive traffic in narcotics. This was so extensive that it was difficult to say whether they were engaged in such trade to support other activities or to further world-wide moral disintegration.

It also appeared that a good deal of Russian espionage activity was being directed from Bern, and there were indications that the plot to overthrow the pro-Western government of Lebanon was planned in the Swiss city. The volume of Communist clandestine enterprises may be indicated by the fact that an estimated one million dollars per week was sent out of Switzerland to espionage agents, provocateurs, and contraband dealers for their work in the Western countries.[30]

Unfolding events in 1960 revealed that Soviet espionage and subversion continued unabated despite Soviet protestations of disarmament, peace, and peaceful coexistence. The *New York Times* reported that a trial in a West German court brought out information that a former West German naval officer had, along with other Germans, been transmitting naval and military secrets to Soviet intelligence officials in East Berlin. The defendant in the West German case admitted having received $1430 per assignment and further stated that he had been recruited by Soviet agents under the threat that his father, who lived in East Germany, would be arrested by the secret police if there should be a refusal to work for the Soviets.[31]

Perhaps another technique in the Soviet recipe for unconventional warfare is the idea of "making crime pay" both ideologically and pragmatically. There is food for thought in an Associated Press dispatch from Moscow dated July 25, 1956, which stated that "former British Diplomat Guy Burgess is vacationing with his mother at Sochi on the Black Sea." Sochi is the plush vacation area frequented by Stalin, Beria, and other Soviet leaders and, currently, by their successors in the ranks of Russia's ruling caste.

Certainly Soviet efforts in subverting officials of non-Communist governments have continued under Khrushchev and his associates in the same way as during the Stalin regime when British diplomats Burgess and Maclean disappeared behind the Iron Curtain. In March, 1960, a former Royal Air Force officer was charged by a British prosecutor with having given Soviet officials British and American secrets. The officer was apparently persuaded to work for Soviet intelligence agents as a result of having become interested in Russian developments in photography through the Society for Cultural Relations with the U.S.S.R.[32] One might adapt the words of Pyrrhus to this situation and conclude that if there are many more such victories from cultural exchanges we are lost.

The effectiveness of espionage and subversion as weapons of Communist unconventional warfare has been meticulously analyzed by the Report of the Australian Royal Commission on Espionage. This state paper, one of the most thorough and careful documents of its kind, notes that Soviet espionage could not have functioned successfully in Australia without the aid, either witting or unwitting, of Australian citizens. It also indicates that freedom of speech and similar rights which the Anglo-Saxon countries had secured after centuries of striving make the democracies vulnerable to such weapons; for, "above all, the Soviet has in Australia, as in other Western countries, an auxiliary force composed of Communists and like-minded persons, some of whom are ready and willing to further the Soviet cause, some even to the point of the destruction of Australian sovereignty."[33]

The Australian Royal Commission also analyzed the unconventional nature of the struggle between the Communist and non-Communist worlds in a concise paragraph which should be required reading for all those who may still believe that it is possible to remain uncommitted in this conflict. The Report clearly but profoundly stated: *"The use of this phrase 'cold war' as applying to Australia is deprecated by Commu-*

nists as being fanciful, but the reality of it is well understood
in Moscow.* In the Moscow Letters Australia is in several
places referred to as *vrag*—'the enemy.' "[34]

The effectiveness of Soviet espionage as a weapon of no
war, no peace has been well-summarized by Lieut. General
Arthur G. Trudeau, the Army's Chief of Research and Development. Speaking at a meeting of the American Society for
Industrial Security, the Army's principal research head rated
Russia's scientific apparatus as very good. Nevertheless, General Trudeau flatly asserted that espionage and subversion
played a more important role in Soviet technological success than any other factor.[35]

GUERRILLA WARFARE

The amount of physical violence used by the Communists
in their unconventional warfare operations depends on the
concrete situation. This was clearly stated as a Marxist-Leninist principle at the Twentieth Party Congress in February,
1956. Suslov pointed out that "the enemies of Communism
represent Communists as advocates of armed risings, violence,
and civil war always and in all cases." Actually, of course
(as Stalin had said much earlier) the Communists are always
ready to abandon violence if their enemies will only surrender peacefully. Suslov added, in spelling out the traditional Marxist-Leninist doctrine, "Communists . . . prefer
more painless forms of transition from one social system to
another. The form of transition . . . depends on concrete
historical circumstances." Just as the gangster prefers that
his victim deliver up the payroll quietly, so the Soviets and

*Emphasis supplied.

their associates would prefer that the West capitulate with a whine instead of affirming its faith in a positive manner. As previously noted (Chapter II), Suslov minced no words: "The question of whether the methods are more peaceful or more violent depends . . . on the degree of resistance offered by the exploiting classes in the process of being overthrown, [of being] unwilling voluntarily to part with big property, political power, and other privileges in their hands." Al Capone in his Chicago heyday never put it more bluntly.

Guerrilla warfare represents the application of a far greater amount of physical force than the penetration of a political party, the conduct of propaganda, or the carrying out of an espionage operation. There are also actions such as assassination, terrorism, and sabotage, which may be used during guerrilla operations, but which, from the Marxist-Leninist point of view, are a part of the operational spectrum somewhere between propaganda and guerrilla warfare.[36]

Guerrilla warfare itself must not, however, from the Communist viewpoint be thought of as *only* an appeal to physical violence. It represents, rather, a combination of violent methods, ranging from small raids up to the deployment of units on the scale of regimental combat teams, and preceded or accompanied by such things as propaganda and political organization. This is because the Marxist-Leninist views every situation from the classic military principle of economy of force, and the Communists hold that the maximization of political effort tends to minimize the amount of orthodox armed force necessary in a particular instance. Hence guerrilla warfare is an unconventional device which is tailored to a particular situation, and its conduct, in the Communist

154

view, is somewhat more of an art than a science. As Lenin has pointed out, "it was Marx who called uprising nothing but an *art*, who said that uprising must be treated as an art, that one must *gain* the first success and then proceed from success to success without stopping the *offensive* against the enemy and making use of his confusion, etc."[37]

Possibly the best current exemplification of this art of mixing violence and non-violence (which is so typical of a guerrilla struggle) is indicated by statements made by Mikoyan and Khrushchev at the Twentieth Party Congress of the Communist Party. Mikoyan ruled out the use of *only* peaceful methods when he warned the assembled Party leaders that "the reformists and revisionists . . . strove and continue to strive to limit the struggle of the working class to small-scale reform, to concessions." He then coldly told the delegates that this was not the approved version of Marxism-Leninism, for such people "are not revolutionaries but evolutionaries." Khrushchev was even more specific in laying down the line for cold warfare of mixed violent and non-violent techniques. He bluntly reminded his followers, "Leninism teaches us that the ruling classes will not surrender their power voluntarily. And the greater or lesser degree of intensity which the struggle may assume, the use or the non-use of violence . . . depends on the resistance of the exploiters."

Mao Tse-Tung, the Communist leader who has written about, and engaged in the practice of guerrilla warfare more extensively than any other Bolshevik chieftain, illustrates this concept of the mixing of violent and non-violent methods when he states that "without a political goal guerrilla warfare must fail as it must if its political objectives do not coincide

155

with the aspirations of the people and their sympathy, co-operation, and assistance cannot be gained."[38] Implicit in this is the idea, which permeates all Communist unconventional warfare, that guerrilla warfare proceeds from the agitation and propagandizing of the masses, from economic bases, from political-organizational activities, and, in many cases, from stimulation through acts of terrorism. Mao's guerrilla warfare strategy makes use of assassination, sabotage, ambushes, spontaneous or seemingly spontaneous uprisings behind the enemy lines, and similar techniques. Above all, it will be politically oriented in accordance with his general views on war. As he has said: "Military victory in the field is valuable only as it pertains to ultimate political success."[39]

A plethora of evidence suggests that Communist theories are strictly followed in actual situations. Thus Tito, when he launched his partisan warfare campaign in Yugoslavia (following Hitler's invasion of Russia, June 22, 1941), con-centrated on the political side of affairs well before his forces engaged in any real combat against the German occupation troops. For example, a People's Committee was set up as a framework for a shadow government in Serbia, a Communist guerrilla newspaper, *Borba (Fight)*, was prepared to begin publication, and a People's Front for the attraction of Yugoslav nationalists as well as Communist sympathizers and dupes was launched with the idea that it would form the basis for the new Communist regime which Tito and his comrades believed could be forged from the fires of the guerrilla war.

This long-range view of the nature and conduct of guerrilla warfare has been well analyzed by a Greek commander who was faced with a similar problem during the period of guerrilla warfare which the Communists waged against Greece. Field Marshal Alexander Papagos has underscored the fact that, during the Second World War, the Greek ELAS partisan force was brought into being, not in order to assist in the struggle against the Nazis, but to help the Kremlin gain the peace at the war's end. It also had the ultimate and extremely long-range aim of putting Russia in a paramount position in the Mediterranean.[40]

An example of still another method of the application of theory to a concrete situation in guerrilla warfare is furnished by Nikita Khrushchev's use of terrorism in support of Russian partisan operations. During the Second World War Khrushchev was in charge of guerrilla warfare (as a high level political officer) on one large sector of the Eastern front.* In order to get more recruits for the Soviet guerrillas and to inflame the populace he gave orders for the assassination of the milder local puppet rulers set up by the Germans, while the cruel puppet leaders were spared in order better to create hatred for the Germans among the occupied population.

Thus, whether the methods used are People's Fronts for gaining the support of particular segments of the people, the employment of clandestine newspapers and roving agitators to enlist sympathy or command support, or the use of terrorism, the object of Communist guerrilla warfare is to mix

---

*Khrushchev held general officer's rank for these operations, a common Soviet practice. Major General Sidor Kovpak, a guerrilla leader at the tactical level had been, before World War II, a Communist Party official. In still another field of Soviet unconventional warfare, Richard Sorge, a leading director of Soviet espionage and subversion in the Far East was apparently given the rank of Lieutenant General.

violent and non-violent techniques in a blended politico-military effort. Major General Sidor Kovpak, a Soviet Party chief who led guerrillas in the Ukraine, has stressed this idea by indicating that partisan warfare requires the winning of the sympathy of the local population. Everything depends on gaining the support of the people regardless of what methods are used to do so. Kovpak was convinced that guerrilla warfare is unimaginable without popular support.[41]

The Chinese Communists put even more emphasis on the intermixture of political-sociological-military factors in guerrilla warfare. A resolution of the Central Committee of the Chinese Communist Party of September 1, 1942, is a case in point. This document directed that "because of the special nature of the guerrilla areas, the unification of leadership should not merely be limited to mutual relationships; there must also be unification, when necessary, of Party, governmental, military, and mass structures. . . ."

During the Second World War the Communists were able to take advantage of the resistance movements organized against the German forces far out of proportion to the actual number of Communists who fought the occupation troops. This was because the Communists possessed so many leaders who were already skilled in conspiratorial work and guerrilla-type activity while the non-Communist groups had to learn such techniques slowly, painfully, and at the cost of many casualties.

After the fall of Mussolini, partisan warfare began against the Germans in Italy and the Communists took much credit for this activity. In point of fact, however, non-Communist Italian groups did the bulk of the fighting.[42] Once again

Communist propaganda counted for more than did actual military skill.

The Communists in Greece organized a so-called National Liberation Front—the EAM—which posed as a democratic movement aimed at the German-Italian invaders. The EAM later organized a guerrilla force known as ELAS and was able to enlist the support of a number of non-Communist Greeks even though ELAS conducted a minimum of guerrilla operations against the German troops. After the war, ELAS, having hoarded its strength during the conflict, was in an excellent position to carry out guerrilla warfare against the legal Greek Government, and from 1946 to 1950 the Communists were able to conduct operations which for a time threatened the very existence of lawful government in Greece. The effects of this guerrilla war have been felt down to the present time and have produced serious economic, political, and social weaknesses in a nation which the U.S.S.R. considers, along with Turkey, as the key area in the Mediterranean-Near East defense complex.

In the Far East, in addition to the Communist conquest of China, in which guerrilla warfare played an outstanding role, the Communists have waged guerrilla warfare on an extensive scale in Korea, Indo-China, and Malaya. The guerrilla activities in Korea were supplementary to the peripheral warfare being conducted by Communist forces in that unfortunate country, but were, quite apart from the greater war, a large-scale affair. As late as October 30, 1952, the chief of the national police of the Republic of Korea stated that his anti-guerrilla security forces had, with assistance from the army, killed 82,000, taken 26,000 prisoners, and received the submission of 47,000 guerrillas who had surrendered.[43] Considering the mass basis which the Communists often strive for in the conduct of guerrilla campaigns, it is probable that these figures are not at all exaggerated.

The irregular warfare in Malaya, however, is one of the most interesting examples which can be found in the many case histories of guerrilla activity in Communist unconventional warfare. The bandit war, as it was named by the British, has been going on intermittently since World War II and has been fitted into the general pattern of unconventional warfare by means of accompanying strikes, propaganda, and psychological pressure exerted against the large group of Chinese residing in Singapore and other parts of Malaya.[44]

The cadres for the leadership of the guerrilla warfare in Malaya may be said to have been established as far back as 1924, for in that year the Chinese Communist Party sent agents to Malaya. One of the early Communist organizers in Malaya later became a partisan warfare chief in his own right. This was Ho Chi-Minh who came to Singapore in 1930 as a Comintern representative. It was not until the Second World War, however, that the Communists in Malaya had either the strength or the opportunity to engage in guerrilla warfare. This occasion arose with the Japanese occupation and the possibility of acquiring arms sent in by the British for resistance against the Japanese invaders. Most of these arms were retained by the Communists, and they were thus ready to begin the first phase of the guerrilla war in 1947 since civil government had been restored in Malaya the previous year.

Plans for a People's Democratic Republic after the model of the Chinese and other Communist regimes were launched by the Malayan Communist Party on January 25, 1949, and since that time the guerrilla war in Malaya has become almost a copybook model of its kind. The Communist tactics of propaganda and terrorization of the population have alternated with assassination,* quick hit-and-run raids, and occasional operations with larger forces.

Such has been the pattern of Communist guerrilla warfare in Malaya; in addition it has been merged with strikes, political, economic, and psychological pressures to constitute a total attack on the existing society of the area.[45] It is, in microcosm, a pattern in the evolution of warfare.

ECONOMIC WARFARE

Since the Communist seizure of power in 1917 the Russian economy has been a closed economy totally subservient to the will of the Central Committee of the Communist Party of the Soviet Union. In the Soviet economy, therefore, foreign trade has always played a secondary role and has been used primarily for purposes of propaganda, as a cover for espionage and subversion, and as a support for Soviet political warfare. The long-term Soviet approach to foreign trade was laid down by Lenin in 1920. In explaining the question of granting concessions to capitalist business concerns, he pointed out that "our chief interest is political; the economic

*The British High Commissioner, Sir Henry Gurney, was one among many who have been ambushed and murdered. Assassination and terrorism are, of course, employed by the Communists (as they have been employed by other totalitarians) in support of operations other than guerrilla warfare.

importance . . . is but secondary . . . [while] we do not for a moment believe in lasting trade relations with the imperialist powers." The same line was pursued by Mikhail I. Kalinin, head of the All Russian Central Executive Committee* in a note of March 20, 1921, to President Harding and the Congress. The note held out the promise of trade as an argument for the establishment of diplomatic relations between the United States and the U.S.S.R. and stated that there would be "the great advantage . . . of the reestablishment of business relations . . . [while] the Soviet republic entirely absorbed in the work of internal reconstruction and of building up its economic life has not the intention of intervening in the internal affairs of America and the All Russian Central Executive Committee makes herewith a categorical declaration to this effect."[46] At the very moment of the "categorical declaration" the Soviets were actively intervening in the United States through the Comintern and the American Communist Party. Such work was largely clandestine and, in any event, was not in Soviet eyes an "official" act of the U.S.S.R. It was, however, the very essence of unconventional warfare.

The Soviets continued to tie economic questions to the larger issues of diplomacy and political warfare in the succeeding years. When the Genoa Conference met in April, 1922, to deal with European economic and financial problems, the Russian delegation threw a bombshell into the ranks of the staid diplomats and economic experts by suddenly proposing universal disarmament. The Russians could hardly have been very serious about this disarmament proposal, however, since during 1921 the Soviet Union had made

*The title of the ruling body of the Communist Party at that time.

162

a secret *rapprochement* with the German General Staff for the exchange of military advice and information. The Soviet-German talks looked forward to the location of German tank, aircraft, and other training establishments on Soviet territory (such weapons and various types of training and equipment being forbidden in Germany by the Versailles Treaty). The Soviet Union has steadily maintained an extensive propaganda barrage favoring disarmament from that time to this, whether tied to economic questions—as is often the case—or not. Thus Maxim Litvinov, the Soviet representative at the Preparatory Commission of the Geneva Disarmament Conference in 1927, proposed complete and universal disarmament, although the Soviet Foreign Minister, Chicherin, privately told Mr. Louis Fischer that "the whole disarmament business at Geneva is merely designed as slogans for Comintern propaganda and for internal politics. It enables us to say that we are threatened."[47]

Soviet economic warfare during the 1930's and 1940's was largely a continuation of the pattern laid down during the formative years of the Bolshevik state. Propaganda directed especially towards Britain and the United States emphasized the big orders that the U.S.S.R. would place in those countries; but somehow the big orders never materialized. Propaganda for recognition of the Soviet Union by the United States in 1933 was definitely based on the golden flow of dollars that would come to America. Following the exchange of diplomatic missions between the United States and the Soviet Union, on the contrary, American exports to the U.S.S.R. actually did not reach as high a figure as they had in the years prior to recognition.[48] It is significant that then as now the Russians were interested only in the purchase of "hard" goods from the United States. That is, the Soviets bought almost solely those strategic goods that added to their military potential. By contrast the only "hard" goods which the Soviets exported to the United States was manganese. Other Soviet exports were "soft" in that they added little or nothing to the industrial capacity of America.

Soviet economic efforts during the Second World War after the outbreak of the Russo-German war were strictly directed to staving off defeat, and in the postwar period the aim was to rebuild the Soviet Union and extract what could be obtained from the economies of the Eastern European nations that had been absorbed from 1945 through 1948. Furthermore, Soviet thinking long continued to await the impending collapse of Western capitalism. As late as 1954 Old Bolshevik K. E. Voroshilov (a Stalin holdover of Khrushchev) repeated the familiar theme that "the postwar development of the economy of the imperialist states took place principally through the growth of war industry. This artificial development of the economy of these countries cannot long continue. And actually, during the last few months in the USA, and in other capitalist countries, too, clear signs of an impending crisis are making themselves felt. . . ."[49]

While the idea of recurring crises in the capitalist system has not been abandoned in Marxist-Leninist philosophy, at some point in the period 1953-1956 a decision was apparently taken to de-emphasize it, and it has been from this period that there has been a gradual build-up in the Soviet bloc's economic offensive against the non-Communist countries. One of the first moves in this offensive was to strengthen So-

viet agriculture—always a weak facet of the Soviet economy—
and at the same time hold out the promise (as in the past)
of eventual large purchases. Early in 1956 the U.S.S.R. placed
orders for $1,700,000 worth of hybrid seed corn and $1,500-
000 worth of farm machinery and equipment in the United
States. Measured in terms of the vast agricultural problems
faced by the Russians, such an order for farm machinery and
equipment would seem to be on the basis of acquiring models
of the latest machine designs and seed types for purposes of
duplication. The *New York Times* noted that during the
past five years immediately preceding this order "the Russians have been promising orders for farm tractors and other
equipment to West European nations . . . but their actual
purchases have been small."[50]

From the time of Stalin's death in 1953 the Soviets attempted to bolster other sections of their economy, especially
the electric power, atomic production, chemical and light
and specialized metals industries. In 1955, for example, Soviet trade and proposals for trade featured heavy electrical
equipment very prominently, and *Pravda* sharply criticized
the Ministry for Construction of Electric Power Stations
which had the responsibility for building the big Kuibyshev
hydroelectric station on the Volga River.[51] A combination
of industrial faults was holding back Soviet nuclear development, and it has been pointed out that electric-power production deficiencies and shortages in computing, control, and
other electronic equipment placed definite handicaps on
Russian nuclear production.[52] While the Soviet Union has
made many industrial advances in the period 1955-1960,
electric power production—a key item in any modern econ-

omy—remains a problem. Khrushchev indicated something of this when he stated on November 28, 1959, "The long-term 15 or 20-year plan for the country's electrification, the long-term plan for the development of the national economy over the same period of time, must become the main pivot of our Communist construction program."[53]

The over-all strength of a nation's economy is, of course, the determining factor in its ability to wage economic warfare successfully. Soviet capacity has been growing steadily, but it can also be exaggerated. As a highly competent economist, Professor G. Warren Nutter, has testified: "Whatever may be said about the pace of Soviet industrial growth it has not been as rapid as stated in official Soviet claims."[54] In sum, both Soviet bloc efforts and capabilities in the economic warfare field have been increasing since about 1953, but they will remain tied to total Soviet economic capabilities.

Soviet economic warfare for the present and as projected in terms of the current Seven Year Plan to 1965 and beyond would seem to be directed toward four principal targets:

(1) The removal of all export controls on sensitive and strategic goods destined for Soviet and Chinese Communist bloc countries. These controls still hamper the general industrial capacity, and hence the war-making capacity of the Soviet bloc. They can be abandoned only at the deadly peril of the United States and her allies.

(2) Soviet bloc penetration of the newly emerged nations in Africa and Asia, the Middle and Near Eastern nations, and the Latin American countries, largely under the guise of economic or technical assistance.

A United States Government summary has pointed out that Premier Khrushchev has openly admitted that the Soviet

Union places first importance on the value of foreign trade for political rather than economic purposes. This emphasis is especially evident with regard to Soviet bloc trade agreements with the economically less advanced countries.[55] Under-secretary of State C. Douglas Dillon has stated that the Soviet Union has granted about two and one-half billion dollars in military and economic credits to the new countries since 1954 and that one billion of this has been in a one-year period, 1958-1959. At the same time the number of Soviet technical people in these nations has risen to four thousand. Mr. Dillon said that the immediate Russian goal in the underdeveloped nations may be described as a maneuver to become identified with indigenous popular aims and ultra-nationalistic movements when these do not run counter to Soviet objectives. This drive is supported and accompanied by Communist propaganda designed to stir up local feelings, develop latent hostility between such countries and the Western nations, and to create a permanent crisis situation.[56]

Cuba furnishes a nearby case history of Soviet economic penetration in concert with an indigenous nationalistic drive which has been infiltrated by Communists and their willing helpers. The regime of Fidel Castro has made a series of agreements with Soviet bloc countries which have had the effect of orienting Cuba into a pro-Soviet and anti-American position. Cubans themselves have acknowledged that Cuba has become an advance base of Soviet penetration of the Western hemisphere. The Cuban naval attaché in Washington resigned with the statement that the Cuban government was "under the most absolute influence of international Communism."[57]

Trade agreements concluded during February and March,

167

1960, illustrate the pattern of Soviet economic warfare. The Soviet-Cuban pact provides for the U.S.S.R. to purchase (in 1960) 425,000 tons of sugar in addition to 575,000 tons already acquired. One million tons will be bought during 1961-1964. Payment will be mostly by barter. The Soviet Union will pay for the 425,000 tons of sugar in goods and will likewise ship merchandise in exchange for all but 20 per cent of the one million tons in the 1961-1964 period. The agreement also gives Russia the right to get the sugar at world market prices. The United States pays Cuba two cents a pound above the world market price as a prop to the Cuban economy. This practice was begun at a time when Cuban policy was definitely friendly toward the American economy and American business concerns. The U.S. arrangement had the effect of giving Cuba 30 per cent of the entire American sugar market.[58]

On March 31, 1960, Cuba concluded a trade agreement with the Communist-controlled government of Poland. Cuba agreed to give Poland sugar, manganese, nickel and iron ores, and other goods in exchange for aircraft (including helicopters), chemical and power plants, food-processing and textile machinery, ships, tractors, and additional industrial items and equipment. This was blatant economic warfare, since the United States had been supplying Poland (1957-1960) with food-processing and textile machinery since, for example, almost three-fourths of Poland's textile machinery was over fifty years old. Furthermore, the United States had for some time been attempting to stop the shipment of arms and aircraft to Cuba and the Caribbean generally because of the tense situation in that part of the world. The Castro regime was apparently bent on moving in another direction and had

168

in preparation additional agreements with Communist East Germany and Czechoslovakia, while the agreement with Poland, calling for the delivery of nickel and iron ores, presaged the expropriation of American-owned properties. In sum, the net effect of the series of agreements appeared to give the Soviet bloc a remarkably effective base in Latin America for waging economic warfare as well as a beachhead for propaganda, espionage, and subversion.[59]

(3) Propaganda concerning the vast markets for American business in the Communist bloc. The first phase of this program is to secure technical know-how and industrial prototypes and processes—chemical and drugs especially—from American industry. The additional aim is to soften up the general business and financial community in order to prepare the way for the extension of economic aid and long-term credits to the Communist bloc countries. Mr. O. V. Tracy, Vice-President and Director of Esso Standard Oil Company, has issued a warning concerning Soviet blandishments about trade which should be required reading for every thoughtful American. He said: "Both Khrushchev and Mikoyan have asked for technical knowledge and equipment. They want the latest models of our advanced machines and instruments— to serve as prototypes for their own production. . . . The Russians are buying machinery and specialized processes only to copy them—and I don't think too much 'repeat business' can be expected."[60] Mr. Tracy's prescience was remarkable. Less than a year after his cautioning words it was announced that Soviet trade officials had purchased two Sikorsky Model 58 and two Vertol Model 44 helicopters.[61] These machines were much admired by Khrushchev on his American visit and

are apparently much superior to present Soviet types. Needless to say, the Russians are not placing any quantity orders.

The ruthlessness of the Communist bloc in using trade as a weapon is shown by the pirating of U.S.-developed pharmaceuticals and their use as an economic warfare weapon. There is evidence that the Chinese Communists are exporting chloromycetin (an antibiotic originated by the American firm of Parke, Davis) to Asian countries, even while they are purchasing the identical thing in Western Europe. An official of the Lederle Drug Company has stated that the Chinese Communists are also exporting goldmycin, even though they need it for their own people. He added: "It's obvious the Chinese want to show the rest of Asia how far they've come under Communism. This seems to be more important to them than saving a few hundred thousand of their own people."[62]

(4) The eventual granting of economic aid and long-term credits or loans by the United States and other countries of the highly industrialized Western allied powers. Khrushchev's constant exhortations that the Soviet Union must and will "catch up" with the United States indicate that the Communist leadership is quite cognizant of the fact that the only sure way in which this can be accomplished is by massive transfusions from the American and other economies (the West German, for example) into the Communist bloc economic system. The negotiations that the Soviet Union has been conducting with the United States over the settlement of a part of the Lend-Lease debt of the Second World War is indicative of the long-range Communist line. The talks were broken off after the arrogant (but, to students of Com-

munism, not surprising) demand of Soviet Ambassador Menshikov to the State Department that "any settlement [of the Lend Lease debt] would have to be accompanied by the simultaneous conclusion of a trade agreement giving most-favored nation treatment to the Soviet Union and the extension of long-term credits on acceptable terms to the Soviet Union."[63] It can be expected that the Russians will resume the talks in the future and that an extensive and subtle propaganda campaign will accompany such efforts. The *Wall Street Journal* has stated: "The State Department said that Mr. Bohlen made clear that a lend-lease settlement is 'an essential prerequisite' before the Administration would ask Congress to approve the trade and credit provisions Russia wants."[64]

POLITICAL WARFARE

Political warfare is in many ways the synthesis of other techniques of unconventional warfare—propaganda, economic warfare, diplomatic suasion, psychological pressure. It is, however, much more. For it is conducted not only against groups, classes, institutions, and political parties, but also on the broadest possible scale against governments themselves. It embraces the pressures and intimidation of diplomacy (a notable example was the Soviet diplomatic offensive against the Baltic states of Latvia, Lithuania, and Estonia in 1939-1940); cultural propaganda; the stirring up of class, religious, racial, and ethnic tensions and hatreds; threats to governments and their citizens (as in the case of nuclear-missile blackmail); and, above all, the sapping of the will of

171

both the governmental leadership and of the mass of the people to resist.

In the aftermath of the First World War it must have appeared to the ordinary observer that Great Britain with her vast chain of naval bases, her lines of communication stretching around the world, and her still-powerful industrial position, was the real center of strength in the world. Yet there was at that very time another and quite a different empire in ferment, an empire dissimilarly situated but actually of infinitely greater significance to all men in all nations. This was the empire of the U.S.S.R., where the newly founded center of Communism had begun, through the practical application of political warfare, the creation of a series of invisible bases in all parts of the world. Apparently insignificant then, these ideological footholds were destined to be very effective in world politics from the 1930's on. For these bases were even more extensive than those upon which the sun never set, and they were represented by the indigenous Communist parties with all of their sinisterly fecund appendages, fellow-travellers, dupes, secret members, agents, and couriers linking the whole apparatus with Moscow.

To the political warfare possibilities inherent in the invisible bases furnished by the world-wide network of the Communist parties, there were added techniques made possible by the introduction of a new element into diplomacy. This new element was the Soviet usage of the Western concepts of international law and diplomacy as instruments of warfare rather than as methods of international communication and cooperation—the way in which other nations had generally employed them in the past.

172

The combination of these invisible bases and the prostitution of the traditional forms of diplomacy has made it possible for the Soviets and the Chinese Communists to conduct political warfare on a scale never before witnessed.

While the forms of political warfare conducted by the Moscow-Peking Axis have been and continue to be multifarious, three examples which are illustrative of the general pattern will be discussed here. These are: (1) The exploitation of nationalism; (2) peaceful coexistence; and (3) nuclear-missile blackmail.

1. *Communist Exploitation of Nationalism*

National self-determination—the idea of the adjustment of national boundaries along national or ethnic lines, and the re-creation of nations which had disappeared as sovereign states (such as Poland)—was one of the famous Fourteen Points enunciated by President Wilson in a speech before the United States Congress on January 8, 1918. The idea, intimately connected with the slightly larger concept of nationalism, was not new, but President Wilson made the entire world aware of it and helped to insure that it would become one of the principal parts of the peace settlement of 1919.

Ironically, a lawful love of country and a feeling of justifiable national pride, while not wrongful in themselves, were soon being used in an exaggerated and distorted form and were still further exploited by some of the Great Powers in the post World War I period. Above all, however, national self-determination became, in the hands of the Bolshevik leaders, a great vehicle for the disturbance of world peace. It was Lenin with his theories on the employment of nationalism as a force in Asia and other underdeveloped areas and Stalin with his famous thesis on the nationalities problem who were to make national self-determination a device which, instead of bringing people closer together, sets them at one another's throats.

The Bolsheviks developed in the course of the Civil War and Revolution in Russia a strategy for the exploitation of nationalism which they were to use successfully *outside* the Soviet Union from 1920 onwards. Stalin hinted at this strategy in a lecture which he delivered at the University of the Peoples of the East in Moscow on May 18, 1925. On that occasion he said, "Proletarian in content and national in form—such is the universal human culture towards which socialism is marching." And he alerted Communists in all parts of the world to their duty in the exploitation of nationalism when he wrote: "The road to victory of the revolution in the West lies through the revolutionary alliance with the liberation movement of the colonies and dependent countries against imperialism. The national problem is a part of the general problem of the proletarian revolution, a part of the problem of the dictatorship of the proletariat."[65]

Communist interest in the nationalities question as a form of political warfare began as early as the Congress of the Peoples of the East held in Baku in 1920. They correctly saw that their greatest gains were to be made in the colonial and underdeveloped parts of the world, and hence the emphasis on the East* at the Baku Congress. It was in these early days, too, that Eastern recruits to the Communist cause were

---

*To a Marxist the "East" is all the vast area from the Straits of Gibraltar to China and thence onward to the Hawaiian Islands.

developed in Moscow. Thus in 1925 Ho Chi Minh formed the League of Oppressed Peoples in China and several years later organized the group which was to become the Communist Party of Indo-China. Mao Tse-Tung was another Easterner who imbibed Stalin's doctrine of nationalist exploitation and even improved it. Thus Mao wrote as early as January, 1940: "In applying Marxism to China, Chinese Communists must fully and properly unite the universal truth of Marxism with the specific practice of the Chinese revolution; that is to say, the truth of Marxism must be integrated with the characteristics of the nation and given a definite national form before it can be useful. . . . National in form, new-democratic in content—such is our new culture today."[66]

The work of these and many other highly trained Communist leaders was aided by the appeal that anti-colonial or nationalistic movements had to many liberal and humanitarian-minded persons in Europe and America. To mobilize the support of these and similar people, the League to Struggle against Imperialism and Colonial Oppression was created in 1927. Similar non-Communist but highly effective organizations have flourished ever since and have aided, sometimes unwittingly, sometimes consciously, the work of Soviet political warfare in its exploitation of nationalism.

How effective such exploitation has been is shown by Khrushchev's statement on this subject to the Twentieth Party Congress of the Communist Party of the Soviet Union in February of 1956. The Red party boss told the assembled Party functionaries: "We are witnessing a political and economic upsurge of the peoples of Southeast Asia and the Arab East. The awakening of the African peoples has begun. The national liberation movement has gained strength in Brazil, Chile and other Latin American countries. . . ."[67]

Khrushchev indicated further targets for Communist operations by pointing out: "Not all countries have freed themselves from the colonial yoke. A big part of the African continent and some Asian and Central and South American countries continue in colonial or semicolonial dependence."[68]

That these were no idle words is indicated by the Communist efforts to arouse Latin American national sentiments against American business firms in that area and by more direct efforts from Moscow. The Soviet Union has stepped up its economic and cultural offensive in Latin America, and the anti-American riots at the time of Vice-President Richard M. Nixon's visit during May, 1958, simply reflected the growth of Communist strength and the increased effectiveness of Communist and front groups in mobilizing nationalist sentiment under the guise of anti-Americanism. These and similar efforts are part of the program for the exploitation of nationalism which the Communists call the "national liberation struggle." The Communist movement is growing rapidly. Communist Party strength in Venezuela alone jumped from 9,000 in 1956 to 80,000 in 1958, while the total number of open Party members in Latin America had reached 238,725 by 1959. Today Communist Party members plus fellow-travellers number more than 4,000,000 throughout the Latin American countries.

Capitalizing on this expansion and on the over-all force of nationalism, the Soviet Union increased its radio propaganda directed to the countries south of the border by almost 200 per cent from 1955 to 1958. Other unconventional warfare activities were also increased. The training of Latin American Communists at political warfare schools had been carried on for many years. But since 1956 this work has been stepped up in the Soviet Union. The Chinese Communists have also begun training Latin American Communist leaders.

On America's doorstep, Cuba has moved in economic and in political matters into the Soviet camp. The Cuban Communists have shown their ability to penetrate governmental agencies and the Cuban armed forces. They have been even more successful in exercising influence by means of pro-Communists and fellow-travellers who have been named to key positions in the government. The Cuban dictator Fidel Castro has not been identified as a known Communist, but his brother Raul, as well as Fidel's most important adviser, Ernesto (Che) Guevara are definitely acknowledged to be strong friends of the Communist Party.[69] Whether these leaders carried Communist Party cards was not really germane. Aided by the Kremlin's political warfare apparatus, they have created under the cloak of nationalism a regime, perhaps best described by a former Cuban official, Captain Jaime Canosa. Canosa, once Fidel Castro's naval attaché in Mexico, has said that Castro turned a nationalist revolution into a Soviet-style movement so that "in Cuba there exists a dictatorship of Communist inspiration, which has resulted in the negation of all liberties."[70]

Significantly, the Moscow political-literature publishing house brought out as early as January, 1960, a book entitled *Cuba in the Fight for Freedom and Independence.* The publication of this book speaks more loudly concerning the intentions and the future course of Communist political war-

177

fare for both Cuba and for all of Latin America than do hundreds of assurances about the meaning of peaceful competition and peaceful coexistence by Soviet government spokesmen. From Cuba to the Middle East and Africa the geographical distance is vast, but in the ideological context of Communist political warfare the distance is not really perceptible; by changing names and place designations in the text the Soviet propaganda book on Cuba could easily be used in any country in the Middle East or Africa.

As a result of recurring disturbances and crises in Iraq, Lebanon, and Jordan, Communist exploitation of nationalism in the Middle East has become relatively well known to the American people.

Less well known have been the Soviet appeals, both open and secret, to the awakening nationalistic movements in Africa. For example, the U.S.S.R. has for many years maintained a diplomatic mission at Addis Ababa, the capital of Ethiopia, far out of proportion to the minuscule trade and political relations conducted with the Abyssinians. In the Cameroons, terrorism aided and abetted by the Communists seems likely to become as grave as the Mau Mau violence was in Kenya. Soviet activities in Africa seem also to have been stepped up from the time of the Twentieth Party Congress in 1956. In 1957 Moscow announced that the Soviet Ethnographical Institute would begin the publication of fifty-five volumes concerning the movement for independence by African nationalities. On January 19, 1958, *Radio Moscow* started thirty-minute broadcasts in a number of African languages, and propaganda by radio and by other means has increased rapidly since that time.

Trained personnel have been sent from Czechoslovakia to construct and man a broadcasting station in Conakry, the capital of Guinea, and Russian and satellite propagandists and technical advisers are active in that country. The President of Guinea, Sekou Toure, has modeled his political machine (Guinea has a single-party system) along Marxist-Leninist lines. This is because he and other native African leaders apparently believe that the monolithic structure of one-party rule is better suited to their needs than Western-type democracy. Undoubtedly the sense of power which the new African rulers derive from the working of one-party rule also plays a part in their opting for this kind of regime. Americans do not always understand that it is not so much Marxism-Leninism as the power structure and organizational apparatus of Communism which may appeal to the ambitious, often ruthless, and always power-conscious new leaders of national movements in Africa, and in Asia and the Middle East as well.

Soviet propaganda has been accompanied by conferences and congresses (such as the fellow-travelling Afro-Asian meeting held in Cairo, Egypt), visits by Soviet leaders and technical missions, and by infiltration of trade unions and local political parties throughout the African continent. Nationalist movements are encouraged, supported, and penetrated with the ultimate aim of taking them over.

The new state of Ghana illustrates the over-all nationalist ferment at work in Africa. This country, which has only recently made its debut on the stage of international politics, has been challenged by the Togoland Congress which argues that Togoland should itself be independent and that the

Ghana government is suppressing the freedom of the Togolanders who are a distinct ethnic group as compared with the Ghanese.[71]

Nationalism is, of course, being exploited by the Communists from the Far East down through the Near East and across the African bridge to Latin America as a means of sweeping out the influence of the West. Once this is accomplished, the local nationalist movements can themselves be ousted and replaced by Communist regimes in the classic manner prescribed both by Stalin and Mao Tse-Tung. These nationalists can then look forward to the same kind of recognition and treatment accorded all nationalities which have fallen under the Communist heel: exploitation, subjugation, and a strong probability of genocide—as, for example, in the case of Latvia, Lithuania, Estonia, and, more recently, Hungary and Tibet.

2. *Peaceful Coexistence*[72]

As with the exploitation of nationalism, Soviet political warfare has for decades been directed toward exploiting the natural yearnings of mankind for peace. The practitioners of the dark Soviet arts have made language a prime tool in this particular task. They have appropriated words which have had certain meanings in the non-Communist world and have attached new sets of meanings to such traditional words or have distorted the original and long-understood meanings of words. Hence the term "peaceful coexistence" can mean one thing to the non-Communist and something quite different to the Communist. Thus the Communists have made Aesopian language work for them in all parts of the world.

Following the success, surprising even to the Bolsheviks, of the 1917 seizure of power in Russia, Lenin and his associates expected the onward march of Bolshevism in Europe to be followed by success in Asia and then in the rest of the world. When the world revolution ground to a halt in Hungary and Germany in 1919 and when the Soviet invasion of Poland was defeated in the summer of 1920, Lenin, always highly practical, saw the necessity for some kind of temporary arrangement between the world of Communism and the other world. He found it in what he called a breathing space, a *modus vivendi* good only until the final extermination of capitalism. Lenin candidly revealed this on November 23, 1920, when he stated that the Soviets did not believe "in lasting trade relations with the imperialist powers [but] what we shall obtain will be simply a breathing space." This breathing-space concept developed into the strategy of peaceful coexistence; it has remained a constantly operating factor in Communist political warfare from the time of Lenin through the latest pronouncements of Khrushchev and Mao Tse-Tung.

Peaceful coexistence was to be understood by all Communists, however, as a part of the grand strategy of the world revolution and as a propaganda line which non-Communists were expected to swallow. True Marxists—Leninists were to remember that any concessions, treaties, or agreements made with the West in the name of peaceful coexistence were simply measures of expedience. Lenin reminded them of this fact quite bluntly: "As soon as we are strong enough to defeat capitalism as a whole," he said, "we shall immediately take it by the scruff of the neck."

This strategy of the indirect approach was given greater

impetus by Stalin than by Lenin. The crafty Georgian saw in peaceful coexistence a device which could be used to advantage in diplomatic and trade negotiations. In addition, he recognized that it offered even greater benefits as a powerful propaganda vehicle which could be employed to enlist fellow-travellers, dupes, and even sincere believers in the cause of world peace.

Stalin early singled out the United States as a nation which would be especially susceptible to the propaganda of peace. In fact he anticipated Khrushchev's claims of peaceful competition by many years when, in his famous interview in 1936 with Mr. Roy Howard of the United Press, he said: "American democracy and the Soviet system can exist peacefully side by side and compete with each other. . . . We can exist peacefully side by side if we do not find fault with each other over every trifling matter."[73]

Stalin returned to the peaceful coexistence theme after the Second World War when he told both Elliott Roosevelt and Harold Stassen that the Soviet Union could live side by side with the United States on a peaceful basis. Using his favorite propaganda device, the interview, Stalin told Mr. Stassen: "It is not possible that I said that the two economic systems could not cooperate. Cooperation ideas were expressed by Lenin. I might have said that one system was reluctant to cooperate but that concerned only one side."[74] He then reassured Mr. Stassen by saying: "As to the possibility of cooperation I adhere to Lenin, who expressed both the possibility and desire of cooperation. As to the desire of the people to cooperate on the part of the U.S.S.R. and the Party, it is possible. . . ."[75]

Stalin neglected to furnish Mr. Stassen with one of his

most famous statements and one which was reprinted in *Bol-shevik* as late as September 15, 1948. This was his 1924 declaration that "the next task is to make the Western Communist Parties really Bolshevik, to develop in them genuine revolutionary cadres, capable of reorganizing all Party activity in the sense of revolutionary education of the masses, in the sense of actual preparation for the revolution."

Although the peaceful coexistence line was not emphasized during the latter part of the 1940's nor during the early part of the Korean War, it was strongly revived during 1952. The Soviet's newly founded English-language propaganda magazine *News* took a strong propaganda line for peaceful coexistence in a lead editorial on July 4, 1952. This theme was greatly extended at the sessions of the Nineteenth Congress of the Communist Party of the Soviet Union held in October of 1952. As previously noted, this Congress also witnessed the publication of Stalin's last work on Marxist theory, *Economic Problems of Socialism in the U.S.S.R.* It is significant that in this book Stalin propounded the thesis that war between the Soviet Union and capitalist countries was in actuality far less likely than war among the capitalist countries themselves. This definitely strengthened the propaganda possibilities of the peaceful coexistence siren song.

It is, therefore, an error to believe that peaceful coexistence was a policy which was pushed strongly only after Stalin's death. Yet one might be pardoned for thinking that peaceful coexistence was a policy instituted by Stalin's successors, since it was trumpeted so loudly in the period following the dictator's death in March of 1953.

The real master of political warfare was not, however,

Malenkov but Khrushchev. Far better than Malenkov, Khrushchev had a sixth sense as regards the susceptibility of the Western mentality for such catch phrases as "peaceful coexistence," "easing of international tension," and "reduction of armaments." In a speech to the Supreme Soviet in April, 1954, Khrushchev began to hammer out the theme that peaceful coexistence of socialism and capitalism was possible, and he has skillfully implemented this line since that time.

Soviet political warfare, especially since the period 1954-1955, has been geared very strongly to the peaceful coexistence theme in order to neutralize the as-yet-greater industrial and defense assets of the NATO and associated powers. These defense capabilities are especially significant in the area of low-yield nuclear weapons, and Soviet peace and disarmament efforts have been significantly directed toward the prohibition of nuclear weapons of *all* kinds and toward an end to the testing of them.

Although the Soviet political warfare campaign of peaceful coexistence has assumed many forms, it has hardly varied in essentials since the Soviet proposal of May 10, 1955, at the United Nations. This proposal (which deserves to be better known) may be summarized as consisting of six major points:

1. Prohibition of nuclear weapons.

2. Reduction of other armaments.

3. Armament inspection by means of control points. (This control-point gambit was the basis of the Communist scheme in the Korean truce of July 27, 1953. It allowed the Communists to violate the truce agreement consistently.)

4. Increased trade between non-Communist and Communist countries with special reference to relaxation of U.S. trade controls.

184

5. Evacuation of overseas bases by United States armed forces.

6. Unification of Germany on terms favored by the Soviet Union.[76]

The acceptance of such a program by the United States would have amounted to the outright surrender of most of the non-Communist world to the U.S.S.R. Yet the rejection of such surrender terms has failed to deflect the course of Soviet political warfare. If anything, it has been continued with a skill and an intensity which must cause Stalin's ghost chronic and severe pangs of envy. Within a few months after the presentation of the Soviet proposals at the United Nations, Khrushchev used the Geneva Conference of Heads of Governments (July 18-23, 1955) as a world forum to make propaganda for agreements which would disarm the West. He followed this by the old propaganda dodge of "Do you still beat your wife?" using this time the platform of the Twentieth Congress of the Communist Party of the Soviet Union in February of 1956. It was on this occasion that Khrushchev propounded an alleged dichotomy in international affairs. He said that the world had only two choices, "either peaceful coexistence or the most destructive war in history. There is no third way." This alternate use of the carrot and the stick, red hot threats of total destruction and massive doses of the soothing syrup of peaceful coexistence, has since been repeated endlessly in Soviet propaganda. It has had an astounding success and illustrates perhaps more clearly than anything else that the warfare of the latter part of the twentieth century is, above all, a battle of the spirit, of ideas, and of the human will.

With the ousting of G. M. Malenkov, V. M. Molotov, and

The Edge of War

L. M. Kaganovich at the June, 1957, plenum of the Central Committee of the Soviet Communist Party, Khrushchev began to press the themes of disarmament and peaceful coexistence more strongly. He now tied these ideas to a so-called conference at the summit which would be used in an attempt to bring about the disintegration of the North Atlantic Treaty Organization, the withdrawal of American forces from overseas areas, and a cessation of testing of nuclear weapons. The ultimate aim of this grand design of political warfare is, of course, the isolation of the United States and, most of all, America's practical disarmament. Soviet policy was strikingly revealed by a diplomatic note released by the Soviet Foreign Office on February 28, 1958, which outlined these and related points on the basis that: "The peoples demand that effective measures be adopted for preventing the threat of an outbreak of war with the use of atomic and hydrogen weapons, that a sharp break be made in the direction of improving the whole international situation, of the creation of conditions for peaceful collaboration of all states."[77]

Following this propaganda warm-up came the real Soviet reason for a high-level conference: "The immediate cessation of tests of atomic and hydrogen weapons. . . . The conclusion of a non-aggression agreement between states entering into the North Atlantic alliance and states participating in the Warsaw Treaty. The reduction of the numbers of foreign troops on the territory of Germany and within the borders of other European states. . . . Measures for the expansion of international trade ties. . . . Prohibition of the use of cosmic space for military purposes and the liquidation of foreign military bases on foreign territories."[78]

186

A few months later Khrushchev used the disturbed situation in the Near East to hold a much-publicized series of talks in Peiping with Chinese Communist Party boss Mao Tse-Tung. They conferred from July 31 to August 3, 1958, and, reminiscent of the famous stage-managed conferences between Hitler and Mussolini, used the world-wide attention of their meeting to continue the political warfare campaign of peaceful coexistence. As usual, it was "the aggressive imperialist bloc headed by the United States monopoly groups [who] persistently opposes peaceful coexistence and cooperation."[79] The United States and Great Britain were denounced for their action in acceding to the request for protection made by the Lebanese and Jordanian governments, and Khrushchev and Mao demanded that a summit conference should be held, and at once. The cloak of peace was once more drawn over Communist political warfare aims by the two dictators who issued this joint statement: "The primary task at the moment is to bring about an agreement among nations on reduction of armaments, discontinuance of the testing of atomic and hydrogen weapons and prohibition of their use, *elimination of all military blocs and all military bases on foreign soil. . . ."*[80]

It is important to note that Moscow's determination to oust American forces from bases in various parts of the world has been a continuing feature of Soviet political warfare for many years and that it has been closely tied to the banning of nuclear weapons. In the field of nuclear disarmament the Kremlin's political warfare can be discerned by its actions rather than by its words. Thus while Khrushchev publicly

*Emphasis supplied.

spoke about peaceful coexistence and the discontinuance of atomic testing, he quietly assigned a high ranking secret police official (Seyemon K. Tsarapkin) to head the Soviet scientific group which went to Geneva (August, 1958) to discuss an inspection system with the Western Powers.

The stick of nuclear blackmail was also rather crudely, if effectively, added to the coexistence carrot and thrown out to the people of the United States and their allies by Khrushchev and Mao at their August, 1958, conference with this saber-rattling assertion: "The aggressive bloc of Western powers . . . should know that if the imperialist war maniacs should dare to impose war on the people of the world, all countries and people who love peace and freedom will unite closely to wipe out clean the imperialist aggressors and so establish everlasting world peace."[81]

It is a sign of the times in which we live that this magnificent bit of bombast could be featured in a prominent place in the press of the free world and evoke nothing more than polite attention and even, in the case of some news analysts, of respectful awe.

Yet this mixture of blandishments (peaceful coexistence) and threats (the danger of war) by Khrushchev and Mao Tse-Tung was no more than Lenin's earlier strategy of the breathing space, the temporary *detente* with the non-Communist world to be employed as a weapon of political warfare only until the Communists are strong enough to defeat the non-Communist Powers as a whole. When that time comes (to repeat Lenin's promise), "we shall immediately take it [capitalism] by the scruff of the neck."

Khrushchev continued to employ the theme of peaceful

coexistence, reaching a new plateau in effectiveness on his 1959 visit to the United States. From this high-water mark there was a gradual relaxation of the emphasis on peaceful coexistence and a tendency toward a toughening of the Soviet attitude on the Berlin question and on other international issues. There was also a return to the use of nuclear-missile threats as the world entered the new decade of the 1960's.

There had, of course, never been in the minds of the Marxists-Leninists any idea that peaceful coexistence was anything other than Lenin's planned "breathing space." The Party faithful were sharply reminded of the true meaning of peaceful coexistence in the Communist strategy for world domination toward the close of 1959 in a notable speech by Khrushchev. Addressing Soviet leaders in the electric power construction industry, he enunciated the inner meaning of the doctrine and indicated future guidelines when he said: *"As far as relations between socialist and bourgeois ideologies are concerned, there can be no coexistence**** and we do not conceal this. The progressive has been and will be victorious over the moribund and the dying. . . . In social development the juster socialist system is achieving and will achieve victory; the advanced communist ideology will be victorious."***82**

Peaceful coexistence thus remains a weapon of Soviet political warfare and is not a *modus vivendi* whereby countries with different social and political institutions can live in true peace. Unless the entire nature of Marxism-Leninism changes —that is, unless Communists cease to be Communists—it can hardly fail to be anything else. For whether it be Lenin (in

*Emphasis supplied.

1920) or Stalin (in 1952) or Khrushchev and Mao Tse-Tung (in 1958), or some as yet unknown Communist leader (in George Orwell's year of 1984), the pattern has not varied and cannot be expected to vary. The Communist leadership always and in all places ever think in *total* political terms, and warfare is, for them, most political when it is least (traditionally) warlike.

3. *Nuclear-Missile Blackmail*

Linking all of the techniques of political warfare and serving as the negative pole for the positive pole of peaceful coexistence is the political warfare technique of nuclear-missile blackmail. Communist psychological warfare on the horrors of nuclear war, on the power and deadliness of Soviet missiles, and on the development of even newer and deadlier weapons can be expected to rise to a crescendo during the 1960's. The aim is the creation of a climate of opinion of fear and futility and hence to produce a paralysis of the will of the non-Communist countries—but especially that of the United States—to resist. Indeed, a primary purpose of the Soviet rockets fired into the Central Pacific would seem to have been their role in the political warfare of intimidation and the creation of a fear psychosis. The boast that the first rocket "fell less than two kilometers away from the predetermined point"[83] will be used to convey the idea that any American city could be hit with pinpoint accuracy by Soviet missiles. Whether such precise operational capability *actually* existed at that time—and it is doubtful in the extreme—is not essential insofar as the build up of a campaign of fear and nuclear-missile blackmail is concerned. Khrushchev has boastfully declared: "I have told Americans: 'You have no intercontinental ballistic missiles. You have missiles that can send up oranges. We have missiles that can send up tons.' "[84] The relation of threats of this kind to the fear/futility theme of the Communist bloc can be appreciated if one examines the statement of Secretary of Defense Thomas S. Gates, Jr., that "the present Soviet lead in very large rocket *engines* does not alter" the picture of total American strength as represented by "manned bombers, which . . . can deliver a great destructiveness with greater accuracy than the ICBM, together with our deployed carrier attack forces, and our deployed theater forces."[85] Nevertheless the Moscow-Peking Axis will use nuclear-missile blackmail to present us with the false proposition that America faces only *two* alternatives: utter destruction or appeasement. The Axis will not be so crude as to use the term "appeasement," however, but will sugar-coat the pill in terms of an "accommodation" or an "understanding." We are already witnessing the attempt to induce in the Western world a mass neurosis by means of a vast psychological warfare campaign about nuclear annihilation. This seeks to induce public opinion—and this means the vocal elements—in both European countries and the United States, to pressure their respective governments to make concessions on a broad political and military (disarmament and nuclear testing) front.

The leadership of the Communist bloc believes that nuclear-missile blackmail, together with the diplomatic pressures of encirclement and intimidation and the softening-up process of peaceful coexistence, will slowly but surely destroy the Western will—and especially America's will—to resist. Important as scientific and technical advances are in today's world, it may well be that they are overshadowed by politico-psychological developments. The present period of political warfare is a war of will and of intent; it is especially a struggle based on what is believed by the Moscow-Peking Axis to be the intent of the United States either to stand fast or to retreat. Implicit in this is the exercise of the will of both the government and the people of the United States not to flinch even in the face of the gravest risks of foreign policy and the hazard of war. Soviet propagandists have called this "brinkmanship." In an era of political warfare on the grand scale, it may more correctly be termed "survivorship."

PERIPHERAL OR LIMITED WARFARE[86]

Although placing the greatest stress on unconventional operations, the Communists have not hesitated to use orthodox armed force if it suited their purpose. Even so, their employment of orthodox armed force tends to make of it a part of the pattern of their total unconventional warfare. Hence when they have used regular land, sea, or air formations in support of an aggressive action, they have sought to limit the scope of the engagement of the regular armed formations, and, at the same time, to extend the unconventional operations of propaganda, political warfare, and similar devices.

Thus in the Korean War the marching of armies was accompanied by a world-wide campaign of propaganda and by extensive political-diplomatic warfare in the United Nations and in the capitals of the free world. As previously noted, also the Communists made extensive use of guerrilla warfare in the actual theatre of war itself. The Soviet Union took care to limit its participation to observers, technicians, possibly certain rear-area troops, and some aviation personnel; and the Chinese Communists, even when putting armies in the field, maintained the fiction of "volunteers." Despite propaganda threats to the contrary, the Chinese Communists did not wish to enter into a state of affairs in which there would be a declaration of war between the United States and the Peiping regime. This sensitivity was obviously directed towards confining the scope of the actual fighting while simultaneously entering a world-wide arena with a carefully planned propaganda offensive, such as the patently false but crudely effective accusations of germ warfare directed against the United States.

There were, of course, a number of precedents for the waging of this Communist-type peripheral warfare. During 1929 the U.S.S.R. engaged the Chinese Nationalist Government in a series of quarrels which had begun when the Chinese tried to maneuver the Russians out of their hold on the Chinese Eastern Railway. These difficulties came to a head when the Soviets attacked the Chinese with both ground and air forces in Manchuria in November, 1929. These attacks, however, were made on a strictly limited basis by the Russian forces and were followed by the initiation of diplomatic talks between the two countries.

An even greater test of peripheral warfare occurred during the 1930's along the Mongolian frontier. Soviet forces engaged Japanese troops in pitched battles over a period of many months. These battles were at times on a large scale; yet Soviet communiqués spoke only of frontier incidents, and the Japanese were almost equally reticent. Although the Russians committed units of strength up to full army corps

193

with supporting tanks and artillery, their intention was obviously to limit the nature of the hostilities, since they took no action which would have turned the conflict into a broader conflagration.

The period of possible nuclear war actually seems to have increased rather than diminished the possibilities of peripheral warfare, since the Soviet type of piecemeal aggression would hardly be furthered by an all-out nuclear exchange which would reduce the Soviet home base to a burnt-out cinder. This contingency makes it possible that an era of nuclear stalemate may be approaching. The British analyst Rear Admiral Sir Anthony Buzzard concluded that Communist aggression on a global basis or possibly even on a continent-wide scale was unlikely.[87] Another British authority on military affairs, Air Vice-Marshal E. J. Kingston-McCloughry, believes it possible that we will increasingly have to deal with aggression by means of unconventional means and through wars on the periphery.[88]

The consensus of informed military men in the United States seems to be in agreement with the thought of British and Continental experts on military affairs. This is well illustrated by the views expressed by Lieutenant General James M. Gavin, the former Chief of Research and Development, U.S. Army. That officer—with a distinguished record in both combat service and the scientific development of weaponry —believes that the United States will probably not be challenged to an all-out nuclear war by the Soviet Union. Instead, General Gavin predicts that America will be increasingly confronted with limited war. Former Chief of Staff of the

Army General Maxwell D. Taylor takes much the same view.[89]

Since it is unlikely that the Communist leaders will offer the United States a choice of weapons in the struggle which they have, after all, begun on grounds of their own choosing, the most probable course of future aggression will be not the audacious and lightning-like moves of a Hitler, but the subtler erosion of Marxist-Leninist methods. The Moscow-Peiping Axis, by means of unconventional warfare devices ranging all the way from neutralist movements to peripheral warfare, will attempt to pinch off the strategic areas which range around the rimland of the free world. With the vast armory of unconventional techniques at their disposal, the Communists will find no small advantages available in peripheral warfare.

The Red leaders realize quite well that we Americans still tend to see war very much in terms of blacks and whites. We tend to wait until we have a clear-cut case of WAR in a legalistic sense before we fully arm ourselves for *all* methods of warfare. Hence when confronted by the vast grey area of Communist attack, there is a feeling, and it is by no means confined to Americans, that we are still in a state of peace and that it is not quite moral or legal to make use of the wide variety of techniques which we do not hesitate to use in outright war.

Further, peripheral warfare renders even more vulnerable the all-too-common American weakness of military unpreparedness which has so many times brought the United States to the brink of defeat. In the case of limited wars we may conceivably be so alerted to the idea of an atomic Pearl Harbor that we will continue to neglect provisions for the forces needed to defeat the piecemeal type of aggression so favored by the Communists. While we seem to have learned little from the state of our military preparedness before the Korean War, the Communist leaders appear to have studied it carefully and to have decided that their future aggression would be conducted on an even more limited scale than was that action. Americans have tended to be somewhat more complacent about the lessons of Korea and the possibility of the Communist exploitation of limited war. Yet that war was an almost classic case history of peripheral warfare. As Congressman Charles B. Deane stated during the discussion of the appropriations for national defense for the fiscal year 1957, "in the fall of 1949 and the spring of 1950, our principal military experts agreed that any future war would be worldwide in nature and thus they had not plans for partial mobilization." The Moscow-Peiping Axis did not, however, intend to wage Hitler's *blitzkrieg* type of warfare; consequently the United States was faced with a war on the periphery. The result, as Congressman Deane clearly pointed out, was that "on June 23, 1950 . . . with a military budget based upon this total war concept, we were called upon to fight not a short total war with atomic bombs, but a limited war. . . ."

SUMMARY

The weapons of unconventional warfare forged by Lenin and Stalin have been skillfully used by their successors. The world is witnessing the period of fruition of techniques that are not so much unique in themselves but have a uniqueness in the way in which they are employed on a massed and co-ordinated scale. A Communist Party theoretician, writing in *Kommunist* (December, 1953) stated that "Lenin and those who agreed with him fought for a Party functioning as the combat staff of the working class, an organization whole, built as a united and centralized organization working under a single plan." One might well say that this is the principle applied by the world Communist movement to the conduct of unconventional warfare. The Communists have not only a general staff for planning world conquest, but also a combat staff for executing the new techniques of mixed violence and non-violence in today's warfare.

This survey illustrates the multiform possibilities for the application of Marxist-Leninist theories and practices of unconventional warfare in both specific and general situations and in the various geographical areas of this great globe. These techniques extend all the way from propaganda to peripheral war, and they can be employed singly or in manifold combinations.

That these widely ranging forms of unconventional warfare will continue to be refined and extended during the decade of the 1960's is indicated by a significant passage in Khrushchev's speech of November 28, 1959, in which he said: "The U.S.S.R. and all countries of the socialist camp constitute the new world. Over a billion people are marching under the banner of Marxism-Leninism. Socialist countries are successful in their development. Now our forces are mightier than the forces of imperialism. But capitalism is still strong. And we may not ignore its strength."[90] It seems obvious that the Moscow-Peking Axis will assuredly increase the tempo of

197

unconventional warfare in order to reduce the strength that Khrushchev himself admits.

But must the United States continue to allow the Moscow-Peking Axis that most priceless of gifts in the area of strategy, freedom of choice of action? Are we incapable of waging unconventional warfare? The record of the past suggests that Americans are by no means lacking in either the imagination or the assets to carry on a struggle by methods short of all-out war. It also reveals, however, that we have often indulged in wishful thinking about the nature of Communism and the meaning of the new forms of warfare which have been hammered out by the Communists in the crucible of world conflict. Hence it has not been that we lacked the ability to conduct a vigorous, positive policy under the changing conditions of world politics. Rather it has been that we have often lacked the will to do so.

NOTES

1. William R. Kintner's, *The Front Is Everywhere* (Norman: University of Oklahoma Press, 1950), and Stefan T. Possony's, *A Century of Conflict* (Chicago: Henry Regnery Co., 1953), are pioneer studies in the field. Professor Possony's analysis of Soviet conflict management is an outstanding exposition. More recently *Protracted Conflict* by Robert Strausz-Hupé, William R. Kintner, James E. Dougherty, and Alvin J. Cottrell (New York: Harper, 1959), elucidates the warfare of the future in a challenging fashion. Raymond Aron's *The Century of Total War* (Garden City: Doubleday,

1954), and Henry A. Kissinger's *Nuclear Weapons and Foreign Policy* (New York: Harper, 1957), are painted on a somewhat broader canvas and are written with acumen and erudition. Brigadier C. N. Barclay, *The New Warfare* (London: William Clowes & Sons, 1953) is a brief but excellent survey of changing patterns of war by a British Army officer. James Burnham's *Containment or Liberation?* (New York: The John Day Co., 1953), ranges widely over the field of unconventional warfare. Even more valuable have been his regular articles in the *National Review* entitled "The Third World War."

2. James D. Atkinson, "The Impact of Soviet Theory on Warfare as a Continuation of Politics," a paper read at the Annual Meeting of the American Historical Association, Chicago, December 30, 1959.

3. M. R. Masani, "The Mind of Asia," *Foreign Affairs* (July, 1955), p. 548.

4. Lenin was keenly conscious of such factors. Thus he wrote: "Without ten leaders of talent—and talents are not born by the hundred—tested and trained in their task, schooled in it through long years, it is impossible in present-day society for any class to carry on any kind of energetic struggle."

5. See, for example, the *New York Times*, June 13, 1955.

6. Some good accounts are: Sean O'Callaghan, *The Easter Lily: The Story of the I. R. A.* (New York: Roy Publishers, 1958); Ernie O'Malley, *Army Without Banners* (Boston: Houghton Mifflin Co., 1937); Frank O'Connor, *Death in Dublin: Michael Collins and the Irish Revolution* (Garden City, N. Y.: Doubleday, Doran & Co., 1937).

7. B. H. Liddell Hart, *The Revolution in Warfare* (New Haven: Yale University Press, 1947), p. 101ff.; see also his perceptive work *Strategy: The Indirect Approach* (New York: Praeger, 1954).

8. See, for example, *Report of the Special Committee on*

199

the Problem of Hungary, United Nations General Assembly, Official Records: Eleventh Session, Supplement No. 18 (A/3592). (New York, 1957). This excellent study deserves to be more widely known. It is required reading for all those interested in international relations in the modern era.

9. The Communists consider "agitation" as the more informal person-to-person type of mixed lecture and group discussion while "propaganda" is the appeal to larger groups and to special groups by means of the mass media.

10. George G. Bruntz, *Allied Propaganda and the Collapse of the German Empire in 1918* (Stanford, Calif.: Stanford University Press, 1935), pp. 153-4; Major General Max Hoffmann, *The War of Lost Opportunities* (London: Kegan & Paul, 1924), p. 231.

11. *Foreign Relations of the United States, Russia 1918,* Vol. I, p. 722.

12. *Ibid.,* p. 724.

13. Richard L. Brecker, "Truth as a Weapon of the Free World," *The Annals of the American Academy of Political and Social Sciences,* Vol. 278, (Nov. 1951), p. 1.

14. For Chinese Communist propaganda activities see Richard L. Walker, *The Continuing Struggle* (New York: Athene Press, 1958), and Evron M. Kirkpatrick, ed., *Year of Crisis* (New York: Macmillan, 1957), *passim.*

15. See, for example, *Wall Street Journal,* July 25, 1956.

16. U.S. Senate, *Committee on the Judiciary,* 84th Congress, 1st Sess.: *Soviet Political Treaties and Violations,* Washington, D.C.: Government Printing Office, 1955, p. iii.

17. Vice Admiral Friedrich Ruge, *Der Seekrieg,* trans. by Commander M. G. Saunders, R. N. (Annapolis, Md.: United States Naval Institute, 1957), p. 403; see also Commander M. G. Saunders, ed., *The Soviet Navy* (New York: Praeger, 1958), chs. 12, 13, and 14; and Major Henry G. Morgan, Jr., U.S.A., "Soviet Policy in the Baltic," *United States Naval Institute Proceedings,* Vol. 86, (April 1960), p. 83ff.

18. See, for example, the German *White Paper,* "The Anti-

Semitic and Nazi Incidents," published by the Government of the Federal Republic of Germany, Bonn, 1960, p. 30ff.

19. Hon. Thomas J. Dodd, "Anti-Semitism, the Swastika Epidemic and Communism," *Congressional Record*, 86th Congress, 2nd Session, for delivery in the U.S. Senate, March 15, 1960, p. 5.

20. *Ibid.*, p. 6.

21. For the Communist propaganda technique of crying "thief," see the interesting study, "The Technique of Soviet Propaganda" by the French journalist Mme. Suzanne Labin as printed for the Senate Internal Security Sub-committee, Committee on the Judiciary, U.S. Senate, 86th Congress, 2nd Session, (Washington: Government Printing Office, 1960).

22. Quoted, Solomon M. Schwarz, *The Jews in the Soviet Union* (Syracuse: Syracuse University Press, 1951), p. 53.

23. Solomon Goldelman, "The Jews" in *Genocide in the USSR*, ed. by Nikolai K. Deker and Andrei Lebed (New York: The Scarecrow Press, 1958), p. 107.

24. Quoted, *Congressional Record*, March 15, 1960, *loc. cit.*, p. 5.

25. Quoted, Fervacque, *op. cit.*, p. 24.

26. David J. Dallin, *Soviet Espionage* (New Haven: Yale University Press, 1955); J. Edgar Hoover, *Masters of Deceit* (New York: Henry Holt & Co., 1958); E. H. Cookridge, *Soviet Spy Net* (London: Frederick Muller, 1955); Vladimir and Evdokia Petrov, *Empire of Fear* (London: Andre Deutsch, 1956), discuss the myriad agencies and organizations employed by the Sino-Soviet bloc and its world-wide network of Communist parties and followers in intelligence and related activities. These accounts of Communist espionage and subversion are especially worthwhile when read in conjunction with the official reports of the Canadian and Australian Royal Commissions on espionage and the official publications of the U.S. Senate and House of Representatives relating to Communist activities in this field.

27. Victor Kravachenko, *I Chose Freedom* (New York: Scribner's, 1946), *passim.*; George R. Jordan, *From Major Jordan's Diaries* (New York: Harcourt, Brace & Co., 1953), pp. 77-78.

28. *New York Times,* March 2, 1956.

29. *Ibid.,* June 21, 1956.

30. *Ibid.,* July 18, 1958.

31. *Ibid.,* January 26, 1960; East Berlin has long served as a center for Soviet clandestine activity. Lt. Col. S. Dombrowski, a former officer in the intelligence service in the Soviet Zone in Germany, stated that in 1958 about 12,500 agents from the zone were operating in western countries especially in Western Germany.

32. *Ibid.,* March 8, 1960.

33. *Report of the Royal Commission on Espionage,* Commonwealth of Australia, Sydney: A. H. Pettifer, Government Printer for New South Wales, 1955, pp. 98-99; the report was issued by the Australian Government on August 22, 1955.

34. *Ibid.*

35. The Washington *Evening Star,* September 17, 1958; significantly, General Trudeau added that he would have liked to have been able to speak freely about "recent cases" of Soviet industrial espionage.

36. For an informative article on the employment of terrorism, etc., in advancing the revolution see the translation, by Regina Eldor, of Lenin's "Partisan Warfare" in *Orbis,* Vol. II (Summer, 1958), p. 194ff. Dr. Stefan T. Possony has contributed extensive supplementary annotations to the text.

37. Lenin, *Collected Works,* Vol. I, p. 224.

38. See especially Mao Tse-Tung, *Selected Works,* Vol. II, pp. 119-156; for Mao on war generally see Vol. I, pp. 63-253; Vol. II, pp. 157-281; Vol. IV, pp. 98-117. For Mao's thesis of the "Protracted War," Vol. II, p. 157ff.; see also the excellent survey by Dr. Robert Strausz-Hupé in *Orbis,* Vol. II (Spring, 1958), p. 13ff.

39. Edward L. Katzenback, Jr., and Gene Z. Hanrahan, "The Revolutionary Strategy of Mao Tse-Tung," *Political Science Quarterly*, Vol. LXX (Sept. 1955), pp. 321-340; this analysis is a valuable addition to our knowledge of both the tactics and the strategy of the Chinese Communists.

40. Alexander Papagos, "Guerrilla Warfare," *Foreign Affairs*, Vol. 30 (Jan. 1952), pp. 229-230; for an important survey of long range objectives in guerrilla warfare see Colonel Virgil Ney, "Guerrilla War and Modern Strategy," *Orbis*, Vol. II (Spring, 1958), p. 66ff.

41. Major General Sidor A. Kovpak, *Our Partisan Course* (London: Hutchinson & Co., Ltd., 1947); although this book contains a generous portion of Soviet propaganda it has many interesting sidelights on Communist ideas about guerrilla warfare.

42. See, for example, the interesting and perceptive account of Italian resistance by a British officer, Major Gordon Lett, *Rossano* (London: Hodder & Stoughton, 1955).

43. Washington *Evening Star*, October 30, 1952.

44. For an informative account of the guerrilla warfare in Malaya as viewed by a young British officer, see Oliver Crawford, *The Door Marked Malaya* (London: Rupert Hart-Davis, 1958).

45. For an excellent general study, see Lucian W. Pye, *Guerrilla Communism in Malaya* (Princeton: Princeton University Press, 1956).

46. *Foreign Relations of the United States, 1921* (Washington: Government Printing Office, 1936) pp. 763-764.

47. See Louis Fischer's thorough study, *The Soviets in World Affairs* (Princeton, N.J.: Princeton University Press, 1951), Vol. I, p. xiii; for German-Soviet relations as well as for many valuable glimpses of Soviet diplomatic and politico-psychological and economic warfare activities, see especially Lionel Kochan, *Russia and the Weimar Republic* (Cambridge: Bowes & Bowes, 1954); Gustav Hilger and Alfred

G. Meyer, *The Incompatible Allies* (New York: Macmillan, 1953); Yves Delbar, *The Real Stalin* (London: George Allen & Unwin, 1953), chs. XXIX-XXXIV; Walter Gorlitz, *The German General Staff* (London: Hollis & Carter, 1953), chs. IX-XI; and Walter Schellenberg, *The Schellenberg Memoirs* (London: Andre Deutsch, 1956), chs. III and XIII.

48. A few figures are of interest. U.S. exports to Russia in millions of dollars in 1928: 74; 1929: 85; 1930: 114.4; 1931: 103.7; 1932: 12.6. By comparison: 1933: 9.0; 1934: 15.0; 1936: 33.4; 1937: 42.9; 1938: 69.7; and in the last year of peace, 1939: 56.6. During the Second World War the United States supplied the Soviet Union with eleven billion dollars worth of Lend-Lease foodstuffs, weapons, machinery and industrial equipment thus contributing in large measure to the eventual Soviet success on the Eastern Front against Germany.

49. *Pravda,* March 11, 1954.

50. *New York Times,* February 22, 1956.

51. *Ibid.,* June 13, 1955.

52. George G. Rosu, "Atomic Bottlenecks in the Soviet Union," *Fact Forum News,* IV-6 (June, 1955), p. 32; the significance of electric power and nuclear production is apparent from the fact that the AEC took 4% of the 520 billion kilowatt-hours of U.S. power output in 1954. Not much is known about the real facts of Soviet nuclear production since it was—and apparently still is—under the control of the secret police.

53. Speech at the All-Union Conference of Power Industry Construction, November 28, 1959; Soviet electric power output was 142.5 billion kilowatt-hours in 1954. Soviet-announced goals call for 110 to 112 million kilowatts by 1965 and 2,170 kilowatt-hours per capita by the same date. By contrast, U.S. electric power output was 520 billion KW-hours in 1954. The American prediction is for 245 million kilowatts by 1965 and, in per capita terms, 6,410 kilowatt-hours in 1965.

54. U.S. Congress, *Hearings, Joint Economic Committee,* 86th Congress, 1st Session (Nov. 13-20, 1959), Washington: Government Printing Office, 1960, p. 62.

55. *NATO Letter,* Vol. 6 (June, 1958), p. 10.

56. C. Douglas Dillon, "The Challenge of Soviet Russian Economic Expansion," *Free World Forum,* Vol. I, No. 5 (1959), p. 23.

57. *New York Times,* March 18, 1960.

58. The published text of the treaty was carried in *Revolucion* (Castro's mouthpiece) on February 17, 1960; for other details see *Wall Street Journal,* Feb. 23 and 25, 1960.

59. *New York Times,* April 2 and 3, 1960; *Wall Street Journal,* March 22, 1960; *U.S. News & World Report,* April 18, 1960, p. 101.

60. O. V. Tracy, "Doing Business with the Russians," Address before the Manufacturing Chemists' Association, June 11, 1959, pp. 10-12.

61. *Wall Street Journal,* March 11, 1960.

62. *Ibid.,* August 5, 1959.

63. *Ibid.,* January 28, 1960.

64. *Ibid.*: it is interesting to note that the *Journal* stated that "President Eisenhower thought he had an agreement with Soviet Premier Khrushchev at their Camp David meeting in September for the resumption of lend-lease negotiations. But the talks never got off the ground. Messrs. Bohlen and Menshikov met only four times for a total of less than seven hours."

65. Stalin, *Marxism and the National Question,* p. 184.

66. Mao Tse-Tung, *Selected Works,* Vol. III, p. 154.

67. *Pravda,* February 15, 1956.

68. *Ibid.*

69. See the testimony of General C. P. Cabell, Deputy Director of the Central Intelligence Agency, Hearings, Subcommittee on Internal Security, U.S. Senate, Committee on the Judiciary, Part III, 86th Congress, 1st Session, Novem-

ber 5, 1959 (Washington: Government Printing Office, 1960), p. 163 and *passim*.

70. Washington *Evening Star,* March 26, 1960.

71. See the *New York Times,* March 19, 1957; for an interesting picture of Soviet exploitation of nationalism in Africa, see John Hughes, "The Soviets Discover Africa," *The New Leader,* October 6, 1958.

72. For a scholarly, exhaustive study of peaceful coexistence and its role in Communist theory and Soviet foreign policy see Wladyslaw W. Kulski, *Peaceful Coexistence* (Chicago: Henry Regnery Co., 1959).

73. *New York Times,* March 5, 1936.

74. *Ibid.,* May 4, 1947.

75. *Ibid.:* for other remarks by Stalin to Mr. Stassen see Chapter 2, *supra.*

76. *Ibid.,* May 11, 1955.

77. *Ibid.,* March 7, 1958.

78. *Ibid.*

79. Washington *Evening Star,* August 4, 1958.

80. *Ibid.*

81. Washington *Evening Star,* August 4, 1958.

82. N. S. Khrushchev, "The Implementation of Lenin's Ideas on Electrification Is a Sure Road to the Victory of Communism," Speech at the All-Union Conference of Power Industry Construction, November 28, 1959.

83. See the official TASS announcement as published in the *New York Times,* January 22, 1960.

84. *New York Times,* July 17, 1959.

85. Press Release, Statement of the Secretary of Defense before the Senate Armed Services Committee, 19 January 1960, p. 5.

86. Robert Endicott Osgood, *Limited War* (Chicago: The University of Chicago Press, 1957), is a first rate analysis; Kissinger, *op. cit.,* has an excellent discussion of limited war problems in chs. 5, 6, and 7; F. O. Miksche, *The Failure of*

Atomic Strategy (New York: Praeger, 1959), discusses certain aspects of limited war; Oskar Morgenstern's *The Question of National Defense* (New York: Random House, 1959), is a perceptive discussion of the limitation of war and of American defense problems and requirements generally.

87. Rear Adm. Sir Anthony Buzzard, "Massive Retaliation and Graduated Deterrence," *World Affairs,* Vol. 8, 1956.

88. Air Vice-Marshal E. J. Kingston-McCloughry, *op. cit.,* p. 203. This study is illustrative of the informed attention devoted to military affairs in Great Britain.

89. See Lieutenant General James M. Gavin, *War and Peace in the Space Age* (New York: Harper & Brothers, 1958); General Maxwell D. Taylor, *The Uncertain Trumpet* (New York: Harper & Brothers, 1960). General Taylor also discusses the making of American military policy. His description of the way in which the Joint Chiefs of Staff function is an invaluable contribution to our knowledge of the decision making process in our government.

90. Speech, Power Industry Conference, *loc. cit.*

CHAPTER 5

American Experience in Unconventional Warfare

RECOGNITION OF THE COMMUNIST CHALLENGE

While Americans have come only slowly and hesitantly to a realization of the new type of warfare being waged by the Communists, there was a rather early recognition of the fact that the establishment of the first Communist state had made a decisive change in the normal order of political affairs in the world. A Sub-Committee of the United States Senate's Committee on the Judiciary was startlingly prophetic when, as early as 1919, it reported with reference to the Bolshevik regime in Russia that "it is perhaps difficult to realize that it has been possible to perpetuate a dictatorship of such a small minority through the many months which have passed since it came into power. Without some understanding of the nature and character of the actual activities of the Bolsheviki the casual observer would be persuaded that the tyranny of this autocracy would in a short time bring down upon its head the wrath of the majority who, with reasonable effort, would have no difficulty in overthrowing the usurpers. A

208

study of the actual methods and practices of the dictatorship, however, clearly established the helplessness of the great mass of the Russian populace."[1]

While the essential nature of the Soviet Communist system did not change in the years after the issuance of this Senate document that so aptly characterized the Soviet regime as an autocracy of a few people who held all power in their hands and who crushed all opposition by intimidation, terrorism, and naked force, the attitude of the Western democracies did undergo a change. This was partially because the Bolsheviks possessed a keener realization of the importance of propaganda than had any previous revolutionary group—a more acute perception indeed than that of most of the leaders of the Western Powers. One of the earliest Western observers of the Soviets, the British intelligence agent Sir Paul Dukes, has pointed out that although their propaganda was tiresome and hackneyed, it was untiringly hammered out.[2] This constant repetition and the massive nature of the Soviet propaganda campaign caused many people in the West to believe that the excesses of the Bolshevik Revolution were temporary aberrations and that the revolution would eventually be tamed.

Then, too, Lenin and his associates were often pictured as rather pure though perhaps somewhat misguided revolutionaries, and the few early writers who attempted to get at the truth were often put down as alarmists or sensationalists. It has not been until more recent times that able and well-known scholars and writers have been able to present the true but much less flattering picture of Lenin as a thoroughgoing totalitarian who, with his fellow Bolsheviks, created a new and more powerful engine of despotism on the ruins of an autocracy that, by comparison, seems mild indeed.[3]

Finally, many supposedly well-informed people in the Western democracies from the 1920's through the 1950's continued to believe that the Communists were building a new and Utopian civilization and that the brutal excesses of their regime were either exaggerated by unfriendly observers or could be explained away on the principle of necessity. This curious self-delusion on the part of Westerners has perhaps been the greatest strength of the Soviet Union as a force in world politics, for such well-meaning people have often been able to stay the hands of the Western democracies at times when vigorous action against the Soviets or their Chinese Communist associates would otherwise have been possible. More than any other consideration, this factor has conditioned the American response to the Soviet challenge. It was true of our policy *vis-à-vis* the Soviet Union in the early years following the Bolshevik seizure of power, and it has unhappily remained true down to the present time.

American policy, in sharp contrast to that of the Soviet Union, has been curiously ambivalent. During the Second World War we tended to believe that the nature of the beast was really changing and that we had to deal with a nationalist and purely Russian phenomenon. During the early part of the Korean War we attributed everything bad in the Communist system to the influence of Stalinism.

A steadfast view that it is the Marxist-Leninist *system* and its concomitant evils (rather than a temporary phenomenon such as Stalinism) that made a lasting and true peace between

Russia and the West impossible seems, through the years, to have escaped a great many intellectual and political leaders in the European democracies and the United States alike. The reason, perhaps, lies in the cogent statement of the Senate committee of that faraway 1919 (a year when Americans were listening to *A Pretty Girl Is Like a Melody* and the fire of idealism of the Great Crusade of the First World War was burning less brightly than the Ziegfield Follies of 1919) concerning the appeals of Communism. The Committee noted that "many well-disposed persons have been deceived into the belief that they were promoting a social welfare movement in advocating it [Communism]." This illusion, seemingly more than any other consideration, lies at the basis of that strange helplessness of American policy in dealing with the Russian and later with the Chinese Communists. True, there were sporadic flashes of that peculiar American genius for the practical instead of the narrowly legal in international affairs. The Truman Doctrine with reference to Greece and Turkey, and later the Eisenhower Doctrine as applied to Formosa and in the Middle East, gave promise that American statesmen had perceived the true facts of the nature of Communism. But even these forthright measures tended to represent reaction to an aggressive Communist thrust rather than action initiated by the United States.

In general, our reactions to the Communist challenge have been slow and hesitant and distressingly unimaginative. We seem, like the international sleepwalkers of the Hitler appeasement era, to believe that either the Soviet leaders do not quite mean what they say or that some new set of leaders will in some mysterious way prove to be more reasonable. Somehow there are always numbers of experts in the Western democracies who see salvation just around the corner. Bad old Joe Stalin will be replaced by a moderate regime, the "managerial class" will come to the fore, or Zhukov and the "Army" will put things to rights. The most recent manifestation of this curious and apparently chronic delusion is the hope that Khrushchev is ready to reach a thoroughly peaceful settlement with the non-Communist world even though concrete Soviet actions have not matched Khrushchev's words.

It is a modern tragedy that too many of our Western intellectuals have clung to the myth that somehow and in some way something good might come out of the Marxist-Leninist experiment. But many have done so despite the fact that the record of history from 1917 through the United Nations' condemnation of Soviet actions in Hungary in 1956-1957 reveals that Communism is an intrinsically evil force. The result has been that the Western democracies have often been paralyzed when the time for action arrived. Far worse, they have been able to take action in a specific instance but unable to decide whether Communism was indeed an enemy *at all times*. This peculiar equivocation has often been characteristic of American policy and seems to reflect something much larger than the attitude of the particular political party which happened to be in power. The lack of flexibility engendered by this attitude toward the Soviet Union and later Communist China—almost a psychosis of alternate enchantment and revulsion—contrasts with the greater elasticity toward other situations short of outright war which has characterized American policy in the past. A brief review of the American imagination as displayed in the employment of force short of war or combinations of force and persuasion will make this contrast even more vivid.

AMERICAN FLEXIBILITY IN THE GREY AREAS: THE HERITAGE

Like the *Federalist Papers,* the Franklin stove, the Kentucky rifle, Bourbon whiskey, and the Colt revolver, American flexibility in the misty grey areas outside the realm of a state of actual war had its foundation deep in the American character. That most American of Americans, Thomas Jefferson—the President who was always most careful about not exceeding his constitutional authority—was, significantly, the first President to order American forces overseas without first consulting Congress. More importantly he took this action as a measure short of war. It was our first excursion into the area of peripheral warfare, an activity that has been so much a feature of Communist strategy in a later age. Jefferson's keen appreciation of the mixing of force and persuasion without, however, any resort to a full-scale war is shown by his message to Congress in which he stated: "I sent a small squadron of frigates into the Mediterranean, with assurances to that power [i.e., Tripoli] of our sincere desire to remain in peace, but with orders to protect our commerce against the threatened attack. . . ."[4]

Much more ambitious as a measure short of war was Jefferson's program of economic warfare that came to be directed primarily against Great Britain, although it was originally intended as a two-edged sword for use against both Napoleon and the English. Jefferson conceived economic sanctions as capable substitutes for war, measures that would yet be sufficiently powerful to bring about concessions from both France and Britain. In a special message to Congress on December 18, 1807, he recommended an embargo. When this was approved by the Congress it placed a prohibition on all shipping, foreign and domestic, entering and leaving U.S. ports. This was extended in January, 1808, to include fishing and coasting vessels, and on March 12, 1808, to include exports by land. A non-importation act had been passed by Congress on April 23, 1806. This prohibited the importation of some British merchandise, but it was not enforced until December, 1807. Following this, the importation of large quantities of British goods was further restricted by the Act of Congress of December 22, 1807; so the total effect of economic sanctions came to bear very heavily on the merchants and shippers of Great Britain.

Since in this period the mercantile class was the most influential group in the United Kingdom, the pressure on the British Government was considerable. The embargo and other economic sanctions were replaced early in 1809 by much less effective measures; consequently we have no way of estimating the effect on Great Britain had they been continued. But the leading authority on the embargo, Professor Louis M. Sears, has stated that the British encouraged Americans to violate the embargo by granting licenses to American ships—mute but eloquent testimony of the tremendous effectiveness of the measure in denying Britain and especially her colonies, of sorely needed supplies.[5] However the effectiveness of the Jeffersonian economic sanctions be assessed, they remain an outstanding example of American ingenuity and one of the earliest (if not the earliest) usages of economic warfare devices in a situation in which no actual state of war existed.

Abraham Lincoln, unlike Jefferson, was confronted with the far greater and different problem of a civil war in which the Southern States could mobilize both land and naval forces. Nevertheless, Lincoln's actions in the days before battle had actually been joined between the North and the South are an illustration of imaginative measures undertaken by a President in anticipation of a war (a situation somewhat comparable to establishing precedents for the cold war). For example, by Presidential proclamations of April 19 and 27, 1861, Lincoln ordered a blockade of the Southern States. This was certainly a warlike measure; yet it was taken without any formal declaration of war. Nor did the President consult with members of the Congress, since Congress was not in session.

Many of Lincoln's other actions in April, 1861, were of the kind that we would today call "short of war": he closed the Post Office to treasonable correspondence, ordered the State Department to put new passport regulations into effect, "caused persons who were represented to him as being or about to engage in disloyal and treasonable practice to be arrested by special civil as well as military agencies . . . ," increased the strength of the regular Army and the regular Navy (this was plainly in excess of his authority under the Constitution), and authorized the expenditure of public money for military and naval purposes without the consent of Congress.[6]

Important as all of these were for future cold war precedents—if a Chief Executive should care to cite them—they were, it would seem, far overshadowed by the statements made by the Supreme Court in *The Prize Cases* (2 Black 635) that grew out of President Lincoln's proclamation of a blockade. The Court carefully avoided the question of a declaration of war and upheld the President's action by stating that "the Constitution confers on the President the whole Executive power" and that he "must determine what degree of force the crisis demands." Additionally it indicated that the power to declare war, which is vested in the Congress by the Constitution, does not impair the authority of the President, in the absence of a declaration of war, to employ the armed forces for the defense of the United States. Certainly the language used by the Court and the general tenor of the decision provide ample precedent for any President of the United States who, in future, believes that it is necessary to employ firm measures against the onward march of Communist aggression and which will yet use that careful *degree* of force that will be short of all-out war.

In the post Civil War years, American armed forces were on numerous occasions used in actions short of war. In 1871 an American force of naval vessels and marines attacked and captured five Korean forts in the course of a retaliatory expedition. A few years later President Grant ordered American armed forces to protect the government of the Dominican Republic against revolutionists at a time when a treaty between that country and the United States was under negotiation. Senator James Harlan defended the President's action before the Senate and indicated the many occasions on which the United States had acted in the past to employ measures short of war. To support this stand, the Senator argued: "When we were disputing with Great Britain about our northeastern boundary, I remember we arrayed some military forces in that vicinity. When we were engaged in a controversy with the same Government on the northwestern boundary, I remember that the disputed territory was taken possession of by the troops of the United States without any formal declaration of war. I have heard something of the bombardment of Greytown by the Navy of the United States, and I have never seen any declaration of war to justify that act of hostility. I have heard something of the bombardment of the ports of Japan by the combined Navies of the United States, France, and England, which . . . was not condemned . . . yet there was no formal declaration of war to justify it. . . ."[7]

Many of these situations, however, involved the protection of the lives and property of United States citizens, and similar conditions obtained in the numerous cases in which the United States took action in the period from the 1890's to the Second World War. President McKinley ordered an Army and Navy expedition to China during the Boxer Rebellion in 1900; and Presidents Wilson, Harding, and Coolidge employed naval forces and Marines in the Caribbean and in other areas to safeguard Americans or their interests. In this connection it should be remembered that the insistence on the equitable treatment of a country's citizens has always had a most salutary effect on barbaric or totalitarian nations.

Modern totalitarian states, such as Nazi Germany or Soviet Russia, resemble in many ways the barbaric despotisms of ancient times. And not the least among these resemblances is the way they are encouraged, whenever a civilized power permits any affront to one of its helpless travelers or envoys to go unpunished, to commit even greater outrages against the civilized power itself. The state which has the firm purpose of protecting its own citizens, however unimportant in rank or privilege they may be, has gone far toward discouraging the totalitarian state from adopting aggressive policies on a much larger scale.

The evidence seems to indicate that public opinion in a democracy instinctively realizes that the insistence on the equitable treatment of the individual against a totalitarian regime helps, in the long run, to safeguard the general peace. And large numbers of Americans have, in the past, been willing to accept a very strong policy line in committing our armed forces to the defense of the rights of the individual from the violations of the totalitarian state. This was shown on numerous occasions by the intervention of our Government in response to pressure from public opinion to protect persons from acts of the Nazi regime, but was brought out even more sharply in an instance in 1949 which involved the illegal detainment of State Department personnel by the Chinese Communists. At that time George N. Craig, the National Commander of the American Legion, speaking as the representative of a group of more than three million Americans, urged the Government to use armed force to secure the release of Consul General Angus Ward and his staff. He added that "in the interest of the safety of all our people outside the continental limits and to salvage some portion of our dearly won prestige abroad, the American Legion calls upon the Government to serve notice on Communist leaders in China that Consul General Ward and his associates must be released unharmed by an early specified date, or armed forces will be dispatched to obtain their release."[8]

By no means all American actions have been undertaken in the grey area between peace and war simply for the protection of the lives or safety of American citizens. Often the Chief Executive has taken measures which were a part of a larger pattern of cold warfare in order to provide a defense against threats to the national interest or as measures to promote the national interest of the United States. George Washington, our first Chief Executive, ordered General "Mad Anthony" Wayne to push any British forces out of the old Northwest in 1793. And in the period 1816-1818 troops of the United States Army went into Spanish territory in Florida in expeditions against British, Indian, and other elements who were harassing our people in adjacent lands.

Much more important than these earlier examples was one of the bold moves of the "Republican Roosevelt." When President Theodore Roosevelt sent the United States Fleet on a cruise around the world (December 16, 1907—February 22, 1909) he gave a demonstration of political warfare which indicated that Americans—given strong leadership—could act as vigorously and as effectively in the arena of world politics as any people.

The background of the world cruise was a crisis in Japanese-American relations. In the wake of their successful war against Russia in 1904-1905 the Japanese experienced a great upsurge of national fervor. As a result they were quite conscious of anything which seemed an affront to their honor. When, therefore, local authorities in California took certain measures during 1906 which the Japanese looked upon as insulting, a tense situation arose in our previously none too good relations with Japan. President Roosevelt endeavored to get the Californians to modify the regulations relating to the school system which had offended the Japanese. This he considered to be a matter of justice. At the same time he believed that any abject appeasement of the Japanese would not only not mollify them but might very well precipitate a war because appeasement would be looked upon as weakness and would encourage extremist elements in Japan to clamor for war. In short, "Teddy" decided to follow his own adage of "speak softly but carry a big stick."* The President wanted to impress on the Japanese the point that the United States had important interests in the Far East and would defend them. On Japan and on the European powers alike he sought to convey some idea of America's growing naval might. Most of all he believed that the surest way to preserve the peace during this time of strained Japanese-American relations was by a show of force. Theodore Roosevelt's judgment was correct. The world cruise of the American fleet was an overwhelming success. It strengthened the ties of friendship among the English-speaking peoples. It created a vivid picture of America's naval capabilities. And in Japan (where the fleet was cordially greeted at the great seaport of Yokohama) it gave the impression of an America which wanted to be friendly but which had the power to be bellicose. Above all, it used the technique of the show of force as a symbolic act of American imagination in political warfare.[9] Sir George O.

*President Roosevelt said: "I determined on the move without consulting the Cabinet . . . in a crisis the duty of a leader is to lead and not to take refuge behind the generally timid wisdom of a multitude of counselors."

Trevelyan, the noted British historian, probably best summed up the results achieved by the world cruise. Writing to Theodore Roosevelt almost three years after the event he hailed it as an example of "politics at its highest level."[10]

Almost equally challenging was President Woodrow Wilson's action in 1916 when he sent a punitive expedition into Mexico. This was done in order to neutralize the forces of Pancho Villa, the Mexican guerrilla chieftain who had been terrorizing Mexicans and Americans alike along areas of the Mexican-American border. In that instance, the Army had the larger purpose of upholding the general prestige and interest of the United States, and the forces under command of Brigadier General John J. Pershing remained in Mexico eight months. Although the President asked for Congressional sanction only after the expeditionary force was already in Mexico, it is interesting to note that Congress supported Wilson vigorously and that he enjoyed the backing of public opinion.

PRESIDENT FRANKLIN D. ROOSEVELT AND MEASURES
SHORT OF WAR

While actions short of war have not been unusual in the course of American national policy, it was only with the period 1939-1941 that such measures occurred even more often and created precedents that were to become significant for any future cold warfare operations.

Although President Franklin D. Roosevelt had directed certain economic warfare measures to be put into effect against Japan and Germany before the spring of 1940, it was not until June of that year that measures short of war began

221

to be taken in earnest. On June 1, 1940, the President requested the War and Navy Departments to list guns and similar items available for aid to the Allied powers. By June 3 steps had been taken to send sizable numbers of weapons to the embattled British, and delivery of the arms had been accomplished by the end of July. The transfer was made quite simply: an American concern purchased the weapons and at once resold them to the United Kingdom. Their sale was allowable under statutes that related to the disposal of U.S. surplus goods. The possibilities for unconventional action were present but it took imagination, flexibility, and will to realize them.

If this was an audacious move in cold warfare, what followed was much bolder. By means of an executive agreement of September 2, 1940, President Roosevelt gave fifty over-age destroyers to Great Britain in exchange for ninety-nine-year leases on naval and air bases in British possessions in the Western Hemisphere. In upholding the power of the President to do this, Attorney General Robert H. Jackson used language that would furnish later Presidents a standard for intrepidity in cold warfare if they should choose to follow such a positive course. The President of the United States is empowered to take actions of this kind, said the Attorney General. This power emanates from the President's position as Commander in Chief of the Army and Navy of the United States. The Attorney General further held that the Constitution made the Chief Executive Commander in Chief but did not define or limit his authority under this title.[11]

That the President's maneuver in the grey area between peace and war was a daring one is shown by the comment of an observer who has had more than a little experience in statecraft. Sir Winston Churchill characterized President Roosevelt's transfer of the fifty destroyers to the United Kingdom as a distinctly unneutral action on the part of the United States and added that such a maneuver would "according to all standards of history, have justified the German Government in declaring war upon them."[12] Yet as great a figure in world politics as was Churchill, he did not fully understand the mentality of the totalitarian mind. Churchill viewed Roosevelt's action according to the rules of international law relating to neutrality. But for the Nazis—and equally for the Communists—there were *no norms** of law whether domestic or international law. Hitler would have understood (and appreciated) the concept of law expressed by Soviet Attorney General N. V. Krylenko.** When given evidence that certain Mensheviks who had been condemned to death were actually not guilty, he replied: "We must execute not only the guilty. Execution of the innocent will impress the masses even more."[13]

Unfortunately, in the years that have passed many other free world statesmen have also failed to grasp the deeper

---

*The Communist view of law is characterized not only by a state of flux (witness the new "worker's courts") but above all by the highest degree of expediency. Hence it is difficult to argue that there are any norms of law in the Communist ethos.

**Krylenko's fate resembles that of some character from the novels of Dostoevski. He rose to high rank in the Red Army and the Communist Party, became Attorney General, and eventually Commissar for Justice. In his last post he was loaded with decorations by Stalin for his work in many important political "trials" that were, in reality, mockeries of justice. In 1937 Krylenko was himself arrested and was executed in 1938. The new Commissar for Justice wrote in *Pravda* that Krylenko was "a miserable traitor."

meaning of the despotic psyche and have attempted to treat it as though it were a conventional one. To these traditionalists the fact was that President Roosevelt might, according to all standards of history, have been taking something of a risk in such a warlike act. But with the Nazis, as with any other totalitarian regime, *there were no standards of history*. The total state, the absolute government, cannot be provoked; it cannot be hurried; it cannot be angered into precipitate action—it moves *only* when it has decided to do so, and not as a result of some supposed stimulation on the part of another power.

Actually, this is much truer of the Soviet Union and other Communist countries than it was of the Nazis. Since Hitler was something of a gambler, it might have been possible to provoke him in some instances, although the German records reveal that he always refused to be provoked by President Roosevelt's far-reaching deeds.

It is meaningful for America that a sizable portion of Marxist-Leninist writings is devoted to the question of provocation and warns Communists not to be goaded by the capitalist world into making any rash moves. This stolidity is well illustrated by the events along the Mongolian frontier in the period 1937-1939 when the U.S.S.R. refused to be galvanized into any action against the Japanese other than the unpublicized military measures that the Soviet forces took. This is especially interesting since the conflict was essentially a limited war and the Soviets not only employed ground troops but also used 200 to 250 aircraft.

Somewhat similarly with reference to Roosevelt's distinctly

warlike act in the destroyer transfer, Hitler and the Nazis fumed but failed to move. Then in 1941 the President followed this audacious deed with a series of actions that have had no parallel in boldness as measures short of war.

The foremost of these moves was the concept of Lend-Lease as a masterful venture in the grey area between peace and war. President Roosevelt prepared the ground for this enterprise through a press conference on December 17, 1940, by using the comparison of one neighbor helping another put out a fire through the loan of a hose. He drove his point home by a personal radio talk to the American people on December 30. Legislation was soon introduced, and the Lend-Lease Act became a law on March 11, 1941. The powers that this law enabled the President to exercise even though the country was not at war were immense, far-reaching, unprecedented, and effective in the extreme. One noted authority in the field of American foreign policy has asserted that not even in wartime had a President of the United States previously been granted powers such as those contained in this Act.[14]

The Lend-Lease measure enabled the President, in effect, to carry on unconventional warfare without running the risks of a formal war; its ramifications were so vast that they remain even today difficult to assess fully. Many competent military men and political figures have stressed the great importance of Lend-Lease, but one of the most interesting observations about its early effectiveness has been made by a German, General Geyr von Schweppenburg, who based his views on his own experience in Russia in the summer of 1942.

225

General von Schweppenburg has flatly stated that "without the aid furnished by America the Red Army would not have survived the defeats of 1942."[15]

Other measures—equally bold and imaginative as actions short of war—taken by President Roosevelt before Pearl Harbor can be summarized as follows:

1. The occupation of Greenland by American forces as a result of an agreement of April 9, 1941, with the Danish Minister to Washington.

2. A proposed Azores expedition. Admiral Harold R. Stark stated on May 24, 1941, to Admiral Husband E. Kimmel: "Day before yesterday afternoon the President gave me an over-all limit of 30 days to prepare and have ready an expedition of 25,000 men to sail for, and take the Azores."

3. The order to the U. S. Navy of May 27, 1941, to sink on sight any foreign submarines discovered in American defensive waters. American defensive waters were then interpreted as extending so far into the Atlantic Ocean that they reached well beyond Iceland!

4. The sending of a message to the Congress on July 7, 1941, in which he announced that United States forces would occupy Iceland and thus relieve British forces.

5. The delivery of a radio address to the American people on September 11, 1941, in which he stated that American patrols would strike first at Axis forces. He matter-of-factly added, "if German or Italian vessels of war enter the waters, the protection of which is necessary to American defense, they do so at their own peril. The orders which I have given as Commander in Chief to the United States Army and Navy are to carry out that policy at once."

226

6. The decision to supply American transports to carry 20,000 British troops from Halifax, Nova Scotia, to the Middle East. A conference of Admirals Ernest J. King, Harold R. Stark, and Emory S. Land, and Harry Hopkins discussed this matter on September 5, 1941; the final decision was taken in October, 1941.[16]

When to all these things is added the political-warfare and propaganda effects of the famous Atlantic Charter meeting, the total effect of the measures short of war taken by President Roosevelt is vast indeed. And these actions obviously set precedents that can guide some other American President in acting against another totalitarian power or combination of powers. These and other Rooseveltian measures short of war carried within them the seeds of destruction of the Nazis. There is reason to believe that similar unconventional warfare activities would be equally effective against the Communist totalitarians who today menace a durable world peace.

The meeting between Roosevelt and Churchill that took place at sea in Argentia Bay, Newfoundland, in August of 1941, was a forceful psychological dramatization of the great potential power of America in a situation short of war. The United States at that time was not committed to actual hostilities; yet this country could use its position as the chief supplier of war materiel through Lend-Lease and its latent military power for purposes of political warfare. These facts are well illustrated by the propaganda impact generated by the issuance of the Atlantic Charter. This event was made public on August 14, 1941, through what was in reality only a press release, although the announcement had all the power of an official utterance by the Chief Executive of the United States and even the Nazis acknowledged that it was a masterful stroke of psychological warfare.

It is history's irony that President Roosevelt, so adept in devising measures short of outright war, should be duped by that "ice-cold blackmailer" in the trade of unconventional warfare, Stalin. Roosevelt understood Hitler's methods of waging war and moved to counter them with propaganda, economic warfare, and political warfare. Did he understand the Communist concept of conflict? Did he apprehend that in destroying one despotism he might act in such a way as to nourish another equally evil despotism?

As early as January, 1943, War Department planners raised the question of a stiffer policy towards the Soviet Union. They believed that "the United States should continue to furnish Lend-Lease supplies to Russia to the full extent of our capacity, provided—and provided only—that Russia cooperates with us and takes us into her confidence."[17] The Army strategists thought that the United States had no need to appease the Soviets, for "as we grow more powerful (and 1943 will most certainly see the United States far stronger, at least on the sea and in the air, than any other belligerent) we can afford to, and in simple self-interest must start exercising the dominant influence to which such power properly entitles us. The time is appropriate for us to start some straight-from-the-shoulder talk with Mr. Joseph Stalin."[18]

Whether or not the President ever read these words (written in *The Weekly Strategic Resume*), he apparently failed to grasp the idea that the Soviets were quite capable of carrying on unconventional warfare against the United States at the very time that they were receiving massive Lend-Lease aid and every other kind of cooperation from us. The day for straight-from-the-shoulder talk never came.

Roosevelt was not alone, however, in failing to understand the Soviet grand strategy. Field Marshal Lord Alanbrooke (Britain's wartime Chief of the Imperial General Staff) wrote in his diary that the British had got off to a bad start from the very beginning of their wartime efforts at cooperation with Moscow since "we gave everything unconditionally and never asked for anything."[19]

Is it strange, then, that by the end of the Second World War the Communists were preparing for a continuation of the war by other means (that is, by unconventional, or "cold war," methods) while British and American leaders were preparing for a long era of peace? This was to be a peace to be brought about by continued cooperation with their wartime ally, the Soviet Union—a peace to be brought about especially through the creation and operation of the United Nations, a body that—in the rosy dawn of tomorrow—was to guarantee the peace that the Western democracies thought they had won.

THE PERIOD OF COLD WAR

The audacious imagination of Franklin Roosevelt in the murky area between peace and war (or, perhaps, for his opponents, the unscrupulous imagination) appeared in the post World War II period to be matched primarily by the Soviet and Chinese Communists while the Western democracies responded to Soviet thrusts without—seemingly—possessing the vitality to take the initiative in the cold war. The origin of the term "cold war" is itself of interest.

And "cold war" was the term that came into vogue in the uneasy years after the Second World War. The phrase was first used publicly in an address made by Mr. Bernard Baruch in his native State of South Carolina. Speaking to the State Legislature on April 16, 1947, the elder statesman said: "Let us not be deceived—we are today in the midst of a cold war. Our enemies are to be found abroad and at home. . . ." According to a statement made to the press in reference to the expression several years later, Mr. Baruch generously insisted that Mr. Herbert Bayard Swope had originated the term. Mr. Swope had coined the phrase as early as 1946, but Mr. Baruch did not employ it until 1947.[20]

The late Herbert Bayard Swope had been a member of the United States delegation to the United Nations which was headed by Bernard Baruch and which proposed the famous Baruch Plan for control of nuclear materials. Since the Soviet Union had refused to accept the controls proposed by the Baruch group, it is quite likely that both Mr. Swope and Mr. Baruch felt very strongly about the subject of cold war. They were indeed among the first Americans to experience at first hand the onset of Soviet unconventional warfare tactics in the so-called honeymoon period after the Second World War.

Whatever the cause, the phrase used by Mr. Baruch soon became current in describing Communist attempts to take over the world without all-out war or blitzkrieg of the Nazi variety. The expression is apt; it has continued in use to the present time and seems destined to occupy a permanent place in the Western lexicon. It would be idle to argue that it is either more or less descriptive than "unconventional warfare." Both expressions are useful.

The first severe crisis of the cold war came with the Berlin Blockade of June 16, 1948. The Russians staged one of their walkouts from the Allied Control Council in Berlin and then put in effect a blockade of all rail, passenger, and road traffic between the Eastern and Western Zones. The Soviet action was apparently an attempt to force the Allies, especially the Americans, to withdraw from the Berlin area as well as to distract world attention from the Communist conquest of China which was then at its height. The answer of the United States—in cooperation with the United Kingdom—was to begin, on June 26, 1948, an airlift to bring in food, medical supplies, and fuel for the beleaguered Berliners and to impose restrictions on the movement of trade between East and West. After months of haggling in Germany and in the United Nations an agreement was finally arrived at on May 4, 1949, whereby the Soviet Union consented to end the Berlin Blockade. Throughout the period President Harry S. Truman remained steadfast in his determination not to withdraw from Berlin, but on the other hand decided not to adopt more drastic measures.[21] Nevertheless, President Truman's refusal to be overawed by the Soviet fulminations must be considered a positive and courageous step forward.

Little more than a year later, the Korean crisis brought Mr. Truman to the point where he was ready to take much sterner measures. On June 26, 1950, the Chief Executive ordered United States sea and air forces to support South

Korean forces against the North Korean Communists who were attacking the Republic of Korea. He further ordered the United States Seventh Fleet to prevent any attack on Formosa. The President also stated that he had directed that "military assistance to the Philippine Government be accelerated [and that he had likewise ordered] . . . acceleration in the furnishing of military assistance to the forces of France and the Associated States in Indo-China and the dispatch of a military mission to provide close working relations with those forces."[22]

All of these actions were, of course, measures short of war, since no actual declaration of war was ever made nor, indeed, did the President even request Congress to make a declaration of war.

The Korean conflict was waged throughout as a "police action." Yet it must be included in any discussion of the cold war because it was, if not a case of American initiative in the cold war, at least a sharp and bold response that apparently came as a rude shock to the Soviet Union. The Soviets had not, it would seem, believed that the United States would interpose its forces to prevent the conquest of all of Korea by the Communists. Whatever may be said in criticism of the conduct of the war in Korea, it would be difficult to fault the action of President Truman in ordering American troops to the support of the South Korean Republic in the first instance. Although this meant engaging in a peripheral albeit an undeclared war, it would be, on balance, a net gain had *nothing else* been done, because the Soviet Union from that time on could never feel reasonably capable of predicting the American response to a given action.

This fact was recognized by many people at the time, among them responsible leaders in both political parties. Thus Senator Taft was quoted by the *New York Times* as having stated that although President Truman usurped Congressional power in ordering intervention in Korea he (Senator Taft) "supports the policy." Another prominent Republican leader, Senator Styles Bridges of New Hampshire, was even more outspoken in his statement supporting the original action of the President. That these prominent and powerful Senators were reflecting public opinion on the willingness of Americans to take risks in the cold war is indicated by a typical editorial of the day. The Richmond *Times-Dispatch* on July 1, 1950, unequivocally took the stand that "the use of ground troops ordered yesterday by the President as Commander-in-Chief was a step reluctantly taken [but] . . . as the hazy picture of the Korean [situation] comes more clearly into focus it is evident that our own government and the United Nations could not have done otherwise."

The undeclared war in Korea brought a stepped-up economic warfare against the Soviet bloc, although it was hardly so stringent as the economic warfare waged against the Axis powers before Pearl Harbor. Already on the statute books was the Export Control Act of July 2, 1940, which granted the President the power to restrict the shipment of any materials that he considered or decided were essential to our national defense. This legislation had been further supplemented during the course of the Second World War and was available in the postwar period, for the 80th Congress had by an Act of June 30, 1947, extended export controls.

As previously noted, some controls had been levied as a

part of President Truman's cold warfare answer to the Soviet challenge of the Berlin Blockade. On March 1, 1948, for example, destination controls, already in effect, were reinforced by the imposition of export-licensing control over shipments of all commodities to Europe. Their chief purpose was to curtail shipments to Eastern Europe of industrial supplies and equipment having high military value, and there was the additional aim of giving priority to the needs of countries participating in the European Recovery Program (which was itself a partial measure of economic warfare).

The Korean struggle, however, resulted in a re-examination of the question of economic warfare devices, and as a result the existing controls were greatly strengthened and extended by the Mutual Defense Assistance Control Act or, as it is better known, the Battle Act. This statute became effective October 26, 1951, and provided for the termination of aid to countries that intentionally export goods judged by the Administrator of the Act to be of primary strategic significance unless the President should decide that the cessation of aid would clearly be detrimental to the security of the United States. While the Battle Act did not stop all trade with the Soviet bloc—only the trade in strategic goods— it was a strong measure of economic warfare and one that gave the Kremlin some taste of its own *no war, no peace* medicine. Following the Korean armistice agreement, relaxations were made in export controls by the United States in the period August-December 1954, and further relaxations have taken place since that time. These less stringent restrictions apply, however, to the Soviet Union and the satellite Communist states of Eastern Europe, and not thus far to the

Chinese Communist regime. A more realistic policy toward the Red Chinese still obtains.

President Dwight D. Eisenhower, like President Truman, has tended to follow a middle of the road policy with reference to the cold war. Thus gradual relaxations in the economic warfare against the Soviet bloc have been made, but export controls have not been completely abandoned. A more sinuous policy was also apparent in such actions as our participation in the Geneva Summit Conference of 1955, in the signing of a cultural exchange agreement with the Soviet Union in 1958,[23] and in the granting of economic aid to the Polish Communist regime.

On the other hand, the Eisenhower administration wisely prepared a politico-diplomatic offensive in the Far East. Notable in this respect was the request that the President made of the Congress for approval of his policy on Formosa. This must be listed as a positive step in political warfare *vis-à-vis* the Mao Tse-Tung dictatorship.

At the request of the Chief Executive, the 84th Congress approved a Joint Resolution on January 29, 1955, stipulating that the "President of the United States be and he hereby is authorized to employ the Armed Forces of the United States as he deems necessary for the specific purpose of securing and protecting Formosa and the Pescadores . . . and *the taking of such other measures as he judges to be required or appropriate in assuring the defense of Formosa and the Pescadores."** The language thus used by Congress indicated the intention of the legislators to give the President a broad area of discretion in using a mixture of force and persuasion

*Emphasis supplied.

short of war. Peiping Radio had been conducting a large-scale propaganda campaign in which the Chinese Communists threatened to take Formosa by force of arms. But with the passage of the Congressional Joint Resolution and with the President's actions to implement it, the Chinese bellicosity subsided, and the threats to Formosa were abandoned, not to be resumed until the summer of 1958.

On July 31, 1958, Soviet Premier Khrushchev journeyed to Peiping and began a series of conferences with Chinese Communist Party Chief Mao Tse-Tung. These talks lasted for four days and in addition to the usual verbiage of peaceful coexistence, a propaganda attack accusing America and Britain of aggression in the Middle East was opened.[24]

Apparently the two dictators also plotted a war of nerves in the Far East, for on August 23 and 24 an intensive artillery bombardment got underway against the Chinese Nationalist positions on Quemoy. This was followed by heavy aerial attacks and an intensification of the war of nerves on August 27 when the Chinese Communist army command in Fukien Province declared that landings on Quemoy were imminent. The Communist psychological warfare build-up continued until September 8 when a statement by Khrushchev provided concrete evidence as to the chief purpose of the war of nerves. The Soviet leader sent a message to President Eisenhower urging the admission of Communist China to the United Nations and calling on the United States to withdraw its naval forces from the waters around Formosa and to surrender Formosa itself to the Chinese Communists. Simultaneously Mao Tse-Tung laid down a supporting propaganda barrage of threats mixed with vituperation. China's number one Communist accused the United States of world-wide aggression and charged that the American capitalists would eventually "be hanged by the people of the world."[25]

That freedom-loving people in Asia were not deceived by such fulminations, however, was shown by the reaction in Manila. The Foreign Minister of the Philippines, Mr. Felixberto M. Serrano, urged the United States to maintain a posture of "unrelaxed vigilance" before conducting any talks with Communist China.[26]

But the most telling counterstroke in political warfare was that launched by President Eisenhower. Speaking to a nationwide audience by radio and television on the night of September 11, the President gave heart to the friends of liberty throughout the globe. He reminded people everywhere that America would never resort to force of arms except when required to do so by an aggressor. Tellingly, he recalled the tragic Munich era and the utter failure of the policy of appeasement. The President then went on to point out that if Americans were craven enough to give way to Communist bullying, the western half of the Pacific Ocean would come under Soviet and Chinese Communist control with all the grave consequences to the security of the United States which this would entail. After this forthright and powerful presentation of the case against appeasement, President Eisenhower held out the hope of a peaceful settlement for the Far Eastern crisis provided the Chinese Communists would abandon their patent aggression.[27]

Again, as in the 1955 war of nerves, the Chinese Communist belligerence partially abated, although they and their Russian senior partners have continued to claim that Formosa would inevitably be taken by the forces of Mao Tse-Tung.

Whatever the eventual outcome of this Far Eastern encounter may be, the Chief Executive's resolute refusal to take the weaker course of bowing in face of the Soviet and Chinese Communist threats must be accounted a positive gain for freedom-loving people everywhere. Like President Truman's courageous decision to fight Communist aggression in Korea in 1950, its reverberations have echoed throughout the world and have caused the aggressors to pause in an effort to regroup their forces.* President Eisenhower has wisely shown that if we are *willing* to fight to protect Formosa, *we will not have to fight.*

While the Far East remained in turmoil during the latter part of the 1950's, Communist exploitation of nationalism contributed to the *brouhaha* already present in the Near and Middle East and brought about a recurring series of crises in that part of the world.

Here again the President acted as vigorously as seemed feasible in that strife-ridden area. In order to obtain a freer hand to deal with Soviet political and subversive warfare, the President appealed to an extraordinary joint session of Congress on January 6, 1957, for a clear expression of approval in support of his policy. On March 9, 1957, the 85th Congress, after much debate, resolved that "if the President determines the necessity thereof, the United States is prepared to use armed forces to assist any such nation or group of nations [in the Middle East] requesting *assistance against armed aggression*** from any country controlled by interna-

*It is significant that Mr. Truman publicly hailed President Eisenhower's action.

**Emphasis supplied.

tional communism." The Joint Resolution also authorized the President to engage in military assistance programs in concert with any country or combination of countries in the Middle East which wished such friendly cooperation.

The Joint Resolution, while a step in the right direction, left much to be desired. It can be seen at once that the term "armed aggression" does not cover some of the important techniques of Communist unconventional warfare since, for the Soviets, armed aggression is merely one of many aspects of total struggle. Furthermore, the idea that the United States will come to the aid of a Middle Eastern country if that country requests assistance against armed aggression from any country controlled by international Communism leaves several obvious loopholes. Aggression, even though armed, may come from a country not controlled by international Communism but simply acting in concert or in league, overtly or secretly, with the U.S.S.R. Then, too, it may frequently be difficult or impossible to obtain public proof that a country is controlled by the Moscow-Peiping Axis.

Despite these gaps in the Resolution the United States was nevertheless able to take some action at the time of the Baghdad *coup d'état* of July 14, 1958. Although America could not come to the aid of the King of Iraq in time to prevent his murder or the murder of other pro-Western Iraqi government officials, President Eisenhower was able to make use of the Joint Resolution and to send assistance to the besieged government of Lebanon. The President sent more than 5,000 marines and supporting naval and air forces to Lebanon on July 15, 1958, in order to help that country maintain its freedom. Mr. Eisenhower explained his action in a special message to Congress on the same day, and delivered a radio and television talk to the Nation. This force was followed on July 16 by the dispatch of 1,600 U.S. Army airborne troops from Western Germany.[28] American forces were able to end the threat of any *coup de main* against the Lebanese Government. Rebel guerrilla forces, however, remained for some time in active opposition to the legal government in Beirut, and violence continued to flare up in sporadic incidents.

The President's action was a reminder that in the cold war it is as vital to come to the aid of one's friends as it is in a hot war. Senator Hubert Humphrey had previously pointed out that, although Communist agents were active in Lebanon, its government was friendly to the United States and we should make it clear that this government could look forward to definite manifestations of American support.[29]

President Eisenhower's actions during the 1958 crisis in the Middle East and the Congressional Joint Resolution on the Middle East of March 9, 1957, were in many ways extensions of the earlier policy outlined by President Truman in his Greek-Turkish aid program. Policy decisions of the Truman and Eisenhower administrations with reference to the entire Middle Eastern area were aimed at promoting the greatest possible amount of stability in the area and thus countering Soviet cold war activities. Due in large part to the urgings of Secretary of the Navy James V. Forrestal, an American naval force had been sent into the Mediterranean in 1946. This was at first a "show the flag" task force visit to the Eastern Mediterranean, and its announcement in August 1946 brought forth the usual Soviet propaganda statements about American imperialism. It also revealed the value of plain speaking in the cold war. Fleet Admiral William Halsey's comment on Soviet threats was characteristically blunt. Said he: "It is nobody's damned business where we go. We can go anywhere we please."[30] Soviet reaction to American firmness was instructive. The Kremlin apparently feared that the United States intended the naval movements in the Mediterranean as a provocation. This was the tenor of an article in the official Soviet government newspaper *Izvestia* on September 26, 1946. But *Izvestia* indicated that the U.S.S.R. would refuse to be provoked by the American action.[31]

The temporary naval task force in the Mediterranean was soon placed on a permanent basis and in 1950 was designated the Sixth Fleet. Our forces in the Mediterranean have been supplemented by the establishment of a naval Middle East Force in the Persian Gulf area. This force has responsibilities covering the Persian Gulf, the Red Sea, and a goodly part of the Indian Ocean.[32]

But in the cold war politics of the twentieth century the Sixth Fleet and the Middle East Force represent not merely showing the flag nor the gunboat diplomacy of an earlier era. They should be thought of as an ever-present reminder of America's politico-diplomatic determination to support her friends in the entire Mediterranean and Middle Eastern areas. The U.S.S.R. has often indicated that it recognizes the political effectiveness of the deployment of our naval forces in that part of the world. Thus *Radio Moscow* on March 30, 1960, in an attack on the Sixth Fleet stated that "units of this fleet, constantly navigating in the Southeastern Mediterranean, have more than once staged military demonstrations in order to force their will on the independent Arab countries." It can be seen, therefore, that the Kremlin recognizes not only the combat capabilities represented by the air-striking and amphibious forces of our naval power in Mediterranean–Middle Eastern waters, but is also keenly aware of their cold war potential.

The cold war and the unconventional type of aggression carried on by the Sino-Soviet bloc has ranged widely around the world. It has flared up (and can be expected to continue to flare up) in the Formosa Straits, in Laos, and elsewhere in Asia, and in widely separated parts of the Middle East, Africa, and Latin America. Conventional military forces have played and will continue to play a key role in that cold war. But they are often in the background as reserves while the shock troops actually in action in the cold war are represented by unconventional forces. Chief of Naval Operations Admiral Arleigh A. Burke succinctly underscored this when he said: "Military preparedness in itself *is* vital but Communist aggression calls for a lot more than that. . . . The cold war in which we are now engaged will last just as long as we shall live. How we make out in this war will be largely dependent upon what we, as a nation, are willing to do. . . ."[33] To see what we have been willing to do in the unconventional warfare of our times it may be instructive to examine two cold war case histories in which Americans were not only willing to do something but did it rather well.

TWO COLD WAR CASE HISTORIES:

IRAN AND GUATEMALA

1. *Iran*

Soviet policy toward Iran was an outgrowth of Czarist Russian policy but was cast in more long-range terms and within the framework of the Communist view of the world revolution. Failing in their attempt to incite a revolution in Iran in 1920, the Soviets turned toward the slower process of economic penetration and building up ultra-nationalist groups which they hoped eventually to exploit in such a way as to bring about a Communist-dominated government.[34] Their plans were partially assisted and partially frustrated by the Second World War. Red Army troops moved into Iran on August 25, 1941, charging that the 1921 Soviet-Iranian treaty justified such a move in the event a foreign power should threaten the frontiers of the U.S.S.R. and the Iranian government could not prevent such a menace. The Soviet claim was that Hitler's Nazi regime presented a threat by its plans against Iran and through Iran against the Soviet Union. The British Government supported the Soviet decision, but at the same time moved to send a British occupation force into Iran. Thus instead of a Soviet occupation of Iran there was a joint Anglo-Russian occupation.[35]

British troops were withdrawn from Iran after World War II within the time limit agreed upon, but the Red Army forces remained in direct violation of the pledge which the Soviet Union had made on August 25, 1941, when Soviet troops first crossed the Iranian border. Furthermore, the Soviets gave every indication that they had come to stay. They aided the Iranian Communist (Tudeh) Party and attempted to split Iranian Azerbaijan away from Iran. In protest against these activities the Iranian Government appealed to the United Nations on January 19, 1946. The Soviet reaction was the usual one of using the United Nations as a propaganda forum and avoiding any concrete terms for evacuating Soviet troops. While the debate was going on in the United Nations, President Truman acted. After consultation with Secretary of State James F. Byrnes and Fleet Admiral William D. Leahy, he sent a strong protest to Stalin. Then, on April 4 it was announced in Teheran that a draft Soviet-Iranian oil agreement had been drawn up and that the U.S.S.R. would withdraw its troops from Iran. Troop withdrawals were completed in May, 1946, and by December the Iranian Government had reestablished its authority in Iranian Azerbaijan and had greatly reduced the activities of the Communist-inspired Tudeh Party. It has been stated that President Truman's diplomatic note to Stalin was, in essence, an ultimatum.* It has also been said that the Soviet decision to get out of Iran was due to the fact that the Kremlin believed that the Premier of Iran had been won over to the Soviet side, oil concessions were to be received, and that eventually Iran would fall into the Soviet orbit.[36]

Not having access to the Soviet archives,** it is of course difficult to say with precision exactly what factor or factors entered into Stalin's decision. It is suggested, however, that

*Mr. Truman has since stated that he warned Stalin that if the Soviet dictator did not order Soviet troops evacuated from Iran, the President would "move the fleet as far as the Persian Gulf." Mr. Truman added that: "I also told Stalin I would send troops, if he did not get out." See the *New York Times*, April 25, 1960.

**Even this might not be helpful. Soviet archivists and historians have had the amazing ability to "find" documents which are required to fit the current Party line approach to either internal or international questions much as Soviet writers can produce "unpeople." Thus Beria, onetime chief of the secret police was removed from the *Great Soviet Encyclopaedia* and foreign subscribers to it received a substitute article on the Bering Sea.

it was a combination of American firmness in the cold war and the Soviet fear of provocation that led to Stalin's order evacuating Soviet troops from Iran. Supporting this hypothesis are the following facts: (1) The hard-hitting speech on a strong U.S. policy toward Russia made by Secretary of State Byrnes at the Overseas Press Club in New York on February 28, 1946.* (2) The Fulton, Missouri, speech, made in President Truman's presence, on March 5, 1946, in which Sir Winston Churchill attacked Russia's "Iron Curtain" and suggested what amounted to an Anglo-American military alliance. (3) President Truman's stern note to Stalin. (4) Sole possession by the United States of atomic bombs. Soviet espionage had been collecting a mass of information on all aspects of the A-bomb for several years and should have had a good appreciation of its capabilities. (5) Sole possession by the United States and Great Britain of an operational, long-range air striking force. (6) The rather primitive state of Soviet air defenses as of early 1946. For example, even the early types of YAK and MIG jet fighter aircraft were only ready to go into production in quantity during 1946. (7) Overwhelming American sea power at a time when Soviet sea power was still insignificant.

Some of this may seem a recital of the obvious. But interpreted in terms of Marxist-Leninist doctrine the listed facts take on a somewhat different aspect. Sir Winston Churchill's visit to the United States as the special guest of President Truman would have appeared to be for the purpose of planning something dear to the hearts of Communists: an impe-

*The Byrnes get-tough-with-Russia theme was repeated in another speech in New York on March 16, 1946.

rialist provocation. This thought was almost certainly strengthened in Stalin's mind by the Byrnes speech (and the choice of place and audience for delivery) just a few days before Churchill spoke. Through his massive espionage apparatus Stalin must have been very well aware of America's atomic destruction power and the capability of the Air Force to deliver it on target. Additionally, the Red dictator may well not have been too confident that his same espionage net could, at this particular time, have been so efficient in supplying information about American intentions. For on September 6, 1945, Soviet code clerk Igor Gouzenko had walked out of the Soviet embassy in Ottawa, Canada, with a large amount of highly secret information about many of the ramifications of the Soviet intelligence system and its agents, dupes, and fellow-travelling assistants. It is unlikely that the Kremlin could have assessed the full extent of the gaps and weaknesses in its espionage system as early as March, 1946. Nor was Stalin as apt to have been as confident as he had at some times been in the past regarding the possible course of American policy decisions. In sum, then, to the usually suspicious mind of Stalin and the caution characteristic of Soviet policy, there was likely to be called for, at this particular moment in history, a definite manifestation of the Marxist-Leninist tendency to beware of provocation. What better way (in the mind of a Communist) to provoke the world motherland of socialism than by an ultimatum carefully worked out between the two strongholds of imperialism, America and Britain? Soviet doctrine had already assigned to America the role of leader of the camp of imperialism and it must have been gratifying to Stalin to see Churchill hasten to America to do (according to the Soviet view) the bidding of the chief imperialist power. There (as a Communist might well see it) he plotted with Truman the preparation of a provocation. Should the U.S.S.R. be provoked and reject the demand to get out of Iran, Stalin may well have believed that a sudden surprise attack with atomic bombs and massive sea power would be launched by the "imperialists." The course of action open to a disciple of Lenin's *One Step Forward, Two Steps Backward* idea would hardly be difficult. Avoid the provocation, retreat, regroup one's forces for the next round of the battle and, in the meantime, employ propaganda, interminable diplomatic negotiations, and every other device of political warfare to neutralize the enemy's advantage in atomic weapons.

Truman and Churchill, of course, had planned no such thing. A surprise atomic attack following the rejection of a diplomatic note was quite alien to their Western, democratic mentality. But we should remember that Stalin and his associates were thinking in Marxist-Leninist terms. More especially, in view of the Communist emphasis on theory as a guide to practice, they were probably thinking about what *they* would do if the situation had been reversed and they were able to destroy America without fear of retaliation.

In the event, Stalin did agree to get out of Iran.* The Soviet representative in the United Nations, Andrei Gromyko, had issued a tentative announcement of troop withdrawals on March 26, and the official decision was announced in the

---

*Whether Stalin would also have ordered the evacuation of East Germany and Poland at this same time is a moot point. The United States did not exercise the same pressure with reference to these areas as it did over Iran.

capital of Iran on April 4, 1946. All Soviet troops had departed by late May, 1946. But only the troops in uniform returned to the Soviet Union. The troops not in uniform—that is, the agents and aides employed to conduct unconventional warfare in Iran—were left behind. Slowly and patiently the Communists took up once more the task of bringing Iran into the Soviet orbit.

In the years after the Soviet evacuation the Communists in Iran tightened up their organizational apparatus and made use of a number of well-tried techniques. Propaganda and subversive activities were carried on through the subsidization of journalists, the infiltration of labor organizations, and by means of front groups. These included the Leftist Youth Movement, cultural groups, the Partisans of Peace, and the Association to Fight Imperialist Oil Companies. The fronts became especially important since the Communist (Tudeh) Party had been outlawed in February, 1949, after an attempt had been made to assassinate Iran's ruler, Shah Mohammed Riza Pahlavi. Nor were strong-arm methods scorned. The attempt on the Shah's life was only a part of the pattern of civil disturbances and terrorism inspired or directed by Soviet agents. It was not surprising, therefore, that an assassin succeeded in taking the life of General Ali Rasmara March 7, 1951. General Rasmara, loving his country, had worked hard to advance her legitimate interests. He might have been able to work out some kind of an equitable agreement with the Anglo-Iranian Oil Company and thus settled a dispute which was endangering the entire economy of the country. But General Rasmara was not a fanatical nationalist, and this

248

helped to bring about his assassination, which was apparently inspired rather than actually carried out by Soviet agents. For the Communists, fishing in the troubled currents of ultra-nationalism in Iran was as profitable as in many other countries throughout the globe.

The new Prime Minister was Dr. Mohammed Mossadegh. Not a Communist, he was one of those ultra-nationalist fanatics whom the Communists have often exploited. The interest of the Communists is in using any kind of movement if it can be employed to disrupt and fragment the existing social order. The Iranian situation was made to order: an extremely nationalistic party (Mossadegh's National Front) not so interested in the long-range good of the country as in immediate power; a foreign company (Anglo-Iranian Oil) wielding great influence because of its vital role in the country's economy. The result was as might be expected. Dr. Mossadegh took over the great Abadan refinery of the Anglo-Iranian Oil Company (in which Britain owned a controlling interest) in October, 1951, and in the months that followed the British and Iranian governments engaged in an acrimonious argument regarding the seized company. The United States attempted to act as a mediator in the dispute but without success and on September 24, 1952, Anglo-American proposals for a settlement (as put forth in a joint proposal of August 30) were formally rejected. Prime Minister Mossadegh severed diplomatic relations with Great Britain in October and then turned increasingly toward the Soviet Union. This was evidenced especially by the benevolent attitude which the Mossadegh government displayed towards the increasingly active operations of the Communist (Tudeh) Party. Although still officially outlawed, it was obvious that it was not in disfavor with Mossadegh and his associates.

During the summer of 1953 the situation in Iran continued to deteriorate and it seemed as though that country would soon become a captive of the Soviet bloc. Dr. Mossadegh had earlier (May 28) hinted at something in the nature of attempted blackmail when he requested financial aid from the United States. The alternative apparently suggested was close economic and military relations with the Soviet Union. President Eisenhower replied to the Prime Minister in a message on June 29, 1953, in which he indicated that his inability to come to an agreement with the British in the oil controversy "handicapped" the United States in rendering monetary help or in making arrangements to buy Iranian oil. The note was a polite but firm refusal to be blackmailed.

Thereafter events moved with some rapidity. Mossadegh moved still more in the direction of the Soviet Union and engaged in close conversations with a Soviet politico-economic mission in Teheran. It would seem that the United States did not remain idle. Brigadier General H. N. Schwarzkopf, who had been in Iran (1942-1949) assisting in the training of the semi-militarized Iranian constabulary, made a vacation trip to Iran in August to renew old friendships. One of his old friends was General Fazlollah Zahedi, with whom he had been associated in the Iranian national constabulary. It has also been noted that on August 10 Mr. Allen Dulles, the Director of the Central Intelligence Agency, took a vacation in Switzerland and that Mr. Loy Henderson, the highly capable American Ambassador, was also on holiday in that beautiful country. The Swiss Alps apparently had a strong appeal to people from the rather hot Iranian climate, for Princess Ashraf, the Shah of Iran's twin sister, was also spending some time there.

On August 13 it was suddenly announced in the Iranian capital that the Shah had decreed that Dr. Mossadegh must step down as Prime Minister. General Zahedi was designated as his successor. But on August 15 Dr. Mossadegh arrested the officer who had been ordered to give him the official notification of the change in the premiership, and the Shah, accompanied by the Queen of Iran, left the country. Only four days later, in another sudden reversal, rioting broke out in Teheran with numbers of demonstrators everywhere proclaiming their loyalty to the Shah. At the same time and apparently by prearrangement, many officers and men in the armed forces proclaimed themselves for the Shah. Within nine hours it was all over. The army was in control, Mossadegh had been arrested, and his followers were being rounded up. The Shah returned from his very brief exile and proclaimed General Zahedi Prime Minister. As the new head of the government, the General sent an appeal on August 26 to the United States. This was at once answered and on September 5, 1953, it was announced that President Eisenhower had made $45 million available for economic aid to Iran on an emergency basis. General Zahedi's government was solidly established on a firm pro-Western, anti-Communist basis, and vigorous action was taken to enforce the laws (ignored by Dr. Mossadegh) against the Tudeh Party.[37]

The August, 1953, events in Iran had an interesting aftermath. On August 31 it was rumored that the Soviet Ambassador to Iran, Anatoll I. Lavrentiev, had attempted to commit suicide in his summer home near Teheran. In answer to the rumor, a Soviet Embassy spokesman said: "I officially deny that Lavrentiev is a suicide. He is ill, just as any other man can become ill." When an official of the Iranian Foreign Ministry inquired about Mr. Lavrentiev's health, Soviet authorities stated that the Ambassador had suffered a heart attack. On September 8 the chief of protocol of the Iranian Foreign Ministry paid a call on the Soviet Ambassador in order to wish him a speedy recovery. Mr. Lavrentiev personally greeted the Iranian diplomat and told him that he had indeed suffered a heart attack but that he would return to his official duties within a week or ten days.[38]

Certainly the rush of events during mid-August would have contributed to a heart attack to any but the most optimistic man. And if one happened to be the Soviet Ambassador to Iran at a time when that country seemed about to drop neatly into the Soviet orbit only to see the situation suddenly reversed and to find that the Iranian government had suddenly changed direction and was now in the Western camp, what then? Would it not be enough to induce a sudden malaise?

Although General Zahedi's government gradually brought stability back to Iranian affairs, there still remained the problem of the oil dispute between Britain and Iran. American ingenuity played a major role in the settlement of this question. Mr. Herbert Hoover, Jr., special adviser to Secretary of State Dulles on worldwide petroleum affairs, went to Great Britain and to Iran in the latter part of 1953. Quietly and skillfully he talked to the businessmen and government officials involved in the problem and then proceeded to work out a solution which is a model of its kind. The Anglo-Iranian Oil Company relinquished its exclusive position and was replaced by an international consortium of oil companies which took over the task of operating the oil fields and refining facilities and of exporting and selling the refined products. The consortium consisted of Gulf Oil, Socony Vacuum, Standard Oil of New Jersey, Standard Oil of California, the Texas Company (10% each), Royal Dutch Shell (14%), Compagnie Française de Petroles (6%), and Anglo-Iranian Oil (40%). The agreement covered a period of 25 years, with provisions for three 5-year extensions. It also provided for increased revenues for the Iranian government and made oil products available for consumption in Iran through the National Iranian Oil Company at cost. The settlement must be acknowledged as a triumph of American economic diplomacy. It is also an example of the wealth of human resources that America possesses. Mr. Herbert Hoover, Jr. was ably assisted in working out the settlement by an outstanding team of Americans: Mr. Loy Henderson, U. S. Ambassador to Iran, Mr. Torkild Rieber, ex-chairman of the board of the Texas Company (serving as adviser to the Iranian government), and Mr. Orville Harden and Mr. Howard Page of the Standard Oil Company of New Jersey.[39] President Eisenhower's message to the Shah of Iran on August 5, 1954, expressing American gratification over the solution of the long and vexing oil dispute is indicative of the essence of the problem. The President said, in part: "There is concrete evidence of the friendship that exists between our two countries and of our desire that Iran prosper independently in the family of free nations. We have endeavored to be helpful in the form of economic and technical assistance and we are happy to have helped in finding a solution to the oil problem."[40]

Soviet unconventional warfare activities did not cease with the restoration of tranquility in that country. The Kremlin was obviously unhappy about Iran's adherence to the American-oriented Baghdad Pact on October 23, 1955.* Its attitude toward this agreement is, of course, representative of its views toward any attempts to bring stability to the Middle East (and to other parts of the world). A steady stream of propaganda has continued to pour out of Soviet-controlled East Germany and from other Soviet sources directed against the Shah's anti-Communist government. This propaganda has been directed at all pro-Western Iranians and has gone so far as to urge the assassination of the Shah. The Soviet pressure is also felt through official statements of the Soviet Government indicating displeasure with Iran's participation in the Central Treaty Organization (CENTO), as the former Baghdad Pact was renamed. The outlawed Tudeh Party aids the propaganda emanating from the Soviet bloc and carries on infiltration and other activities through front organizations and clandestine groups inside Iran. The Iranian Communists have also been assisted by the resurgent Communist Party of adjoining Iraq.[41]

Thus in microcosm the situation in Iran reveals the pattern

*This was the Pact of Mutual Cooperation between the Kingdom of Iraq, the Republic of Turkey, the United Kingdom, the Dominion of Pakistan, and the Kingdom of Iran. It was first signed in Baghdad by Iraq and Turkey, Feb. 24, 1955. Following the *coup d'état* in Baghdad which resulted in the murder of King Faisal and his pro-Western associates, the new government of Iraq withdrew from the pact.

of unconventional warfare so characteristic of our times. World politics today is unlike that of the eighteenth, nineteenth, and early twentieth centuries, when politico-diplomatic crises arose at irregular intervals. Rather the cold war resembles one of the old serials of silent movie days such as *The Perils of Pauline* in which there is an air of continuing crisis. Perhaps the distinctive nature of the cold war is that it features a climate of permanent unease and unrest. Certainly this has been well illustrated not merely for Iran but for most of the Middle East and for Africa and thence across the South Atlantic to Latin America.

2. *Guatemala*

The exploitation of ultra-nationalistic forces throughout the world has long been a hallmark of Soviet unconventional warfare. Not the least among various areas of the world to experience the pressures stimulated by the Communists has been Latin America. Even during the Second World War the Soviets had been able to devote sufficient attention to Latin America that the then Secretary of the Navy, James V. Forrestal, had noted Soviet infiltration in Brazil.[42]

The events which led up to the Communist seizure of power in Guatemala began also during World War II. It was in 1944 that a revolution took place which brought to power a junta led by Major Francisco Javier Arana, Captain Jacobo Arbenz Guzman, and Senor Jorge Toriello. The Communists had not taken part in the overthrow of the old regime, but they soon began to infiltrate the groups that had made the revolution possible. They brought to the attention of the revolutionaries a Guatemalan professor, Juan Jose Arevalo,

255

who had been exiled from the country. With the support of the junta, Arevalo was elected President in 1945.

It soon became apparent (*after* the election) that Arevalo was not simply an ardent nationalist but a strong supporter of Communism. During his administration he encouraged those forces which sought to turn Guatemala into an advance base of Soviet imperialism in the Western hemisphere. He welcomed Communist agents and fellow-travellers from many different South American countries and encouraged the Communist takeover of various institutions and organizations in Guatemala, not the least of which included key governmental agencies. For example, Virginia Bravo Letilier (in later years identified as a Communist propaganda director in East Berlin) came from Chile as did Pablo Neruda and Cesar Godoy Urrutia. The latter two were active in promoting Communism among Guatemalan intellectuals. Arevalo saw to it that Communists got control posts in the governmental operated mass media, the Department of Education, the social services (an exiled Guatemalan Communist, Alfonso Solorzano returned to take over the Social Security Institute), and the diplomatic corps. The country's diplomatic service largely became a subsidiary of the Kremlin's subversion apparatus with its members being used as messengers, bringing orders from Moscow by way of Russian and Czechoslovak embassies to Guatemala and other nations in Latin America.

Very instructive as an example of Communist control devices was the approach to the workingman. Labor unions had not been allowed under past dictators in Guatemala. The Arevalo regime made a pretense of permitting freedom of association by the workers. But the workingmen soon found that they were controlled far more rigorously and certainly more efficiently than they had ever been under the most dictatorial government of the past. With the help of the chief Communist labor specialist in Latin America, the Mexican Vincente Lombardo Toledano, the workers were soon dragooned into Communist-dominated "unions." A labor law set up labor courts which always ruled in favor of Communist-controlled unions in cases involving jurisdictional differences among unions. Through these and similar measures it became necessary for a workingman to take orders from Communist union bosses if he wanted to keep his job.

Quite naturally, opposition arose against the Communist-dominated Arevalo regime. It found a leader in the army chief of staff, Colonel Arana, who had been one of the leaders of the 1944 revolutionary junta. But Colonel Arana did not live to help his people. The Communists assassinated him in July, 1949, and felt so secure in their control of the country that one of their leaders, Carlos Manuel Pellecer Duran,* publicly acknowledged Communist authorship of the deed. Colonel Arana having been disposed of, the Communists had little difficulty in securing the election (they preferred a stage-managed "free" election) of their candidate, Colonel Jacobo Arbenz Guzman (generally referred to as Arbenz). Arbenz, an extreme leftist-nationalist, took over the Presidential office March 15, 1951, and from this time the Communists

---

*Duran, or Pellecer, as he was usually known, did not follow the ascetic life which Marxists-Leninists often boast about (but infrequently adopt). He spent money lavishly and drove a shiny Cadillac convertible. The Cadillac was not used, however, when he harangued a meeting of workingmen. Then he drove up in front of his audience in an ancient jeep. One is reminded of some of the later leftist leaders in Latin America and their penchant for rough dress and a general air of uncouthness.

257

threw off whatever pretenses they had maintained in the past. In the past, while gradually taking over real power in the country they had preferred to operate behind the scenes. Now they no longer believed this to be necessary.

One of the early manifestations of the Communist new look was emergence of a clearly labelled Communist Party. Previously, the Communists operated under the banner of a Communist-line party called Partido Revolucionario Obrero of Guatemala (PROG), that is, The Revolutionary Workers Party of Guatemala. The founder of this party, Victor Manuel Gutierrez Garbin (styled Gutierrez), visited Moscow in January, 1952. On his return, he merged PROG with the Guatemalan Communist Party. In December of the same year the Communist Party became known as the Guatemalan Labor Party (GLP) and was recognized by the government as a legal political party. It was a faithful copy of the Communist Party of the Soviet Union; and, like its prototype, it emphasized a highly disciplined, elite organization. The number of Guatemalans who were members has been estimated as between 3,000 and 4,000 by early 1954. It can be seen, therefore, that the GLP resembled its master organization in Russia inasmuch as it was interested in the elite. These could control the masses through key positions in governmental agencies and through the direction of front groups, Communist-dominated labor unions, and other mass organizations. It is interesting to note that *The Great Soviet Encyclopaedia* (2nd ed., 1953) in its listing of Communist parties throughout the world quite plainly indicated the real nature of the Guatemalan Labor Party. Thus the entry read: "The Guatemalan Labor Party (GPT) was formed in 1952; prior

258

to that it was called the Communist Party of Guatemala."

During 1953 the Communists in Guatemala continued to extend their control over and their influence in the country. They were greatly assisted by the international unconventional warfare apparatus of the Soviet Union. Propaganda material, for example, was printed for the GPT in Russia for later distribution inside Guatemala. Guatemalan youth leaders and governmental officials were taken on tours of the U.S.S.R. and of the satellite nations, and Russian-made propaganda films were shown in Guatemalan motion-picture theaters. The GPT was not, however, inactive. It not only sought to propagandize the people but more and more tended to terrorize them. Those who spoke out against the Communists were imprisoned, and hundreds of anti-Communists were brutally tortured and then executed by the secret police. By the spring of 1954 the GPT had achieved a position of dominance throughout Guatemala. It had not yet fully penetrated the army, possibly because the armed forces had not been numbered among the opponents of Communism, and possibly because some army officers (such as Colonel Arbenz, the President) had been so favorable to Communism. Perhaps, too, the Guatemalan Communists had developed such grandiose plans of conquest that they neglected to make absolutely certain that the army was thoroughly Communized.*
For in the early months of 1954 subversive activities against other Central American states, notably Nicaragua and Honduras, were begun by the Guatemalan Communists. During March and April an unidentified submarine was reported off

*It would seem that later Communist-controlled movements in Latin America do not intend to make the same mistake.

the Nicaraguan coast following previous reports that an unidentified submarine had refueled in San Jose, Guatemala. Shortly after the submarine was seen off Nicaragua, a supply of small arms and ammunition was discovered in a coastal area, and the Nicaraguan police broke up a plot to assassinate the President of the country. In the first days of May, Communist-inspired strikes broke out in Honduras, and it was obvious that the money and tactics were being supplied from outside Honduras. Then on May 15, 1954, a chartered ship, the *Alfhelm,* made port in Puerto Barrios, Guatemala. This ship, whose destination had originally been Dakar in French West Africa, had loaded what purported to be optical goods in the port of Stettin in Communist-controlled East Germany. The "optical goods" were actually arms and ammunition (including small-caliber artillery pieces), and the destination of the ship had been changed from time to time until it ultimately put in at Puerto Barrios. The fact that the *Alfhelm* was actually carrying munitions and weapons of war was announced in a press statement issued by the U.S. State Department on May 17, 1954. Secretary of State Dulles amplified the news release and indicated the gravity of the situation in a press conference on May 25 when he said: "The important question is whether Guatemala is subject to Communist colonialism, which has already subjected 800 million people to its despotic rule." In a further news conference on June 8 Mr. Dulles indicated that an exchange of views was underway among the members of the Organization of American States with reference to the desirability of taking some kind of action.

Much more direct action soon took place, however. On

June 18, 1954, Colonel Carlos Castillo Armas led a force of 250 anti-Communist troops from Honduras into Guatemala. Colonel Castillo had previously been exiled from his native country because of his opposition to the Communist regime in Guatemala. Now he returned at the head of a liberation force. He also sent two World War II type fighter aircraft to make a demonstration over the capital, Guatemala City. This bit of psychological warfare was accompanied by an uprising inside the Guatemalan armed forces which was led by a patriotic officer, Lt. Colonel Jose Luis Cruz Salazar, who along with other anti-Communist officers played an important role in preventing most of the army from being used against the liberating forces of Colonel Castillo. A secret radio station had already been preparing the ground by broadcasting anti-Communist propaganda, and two young intellectuals, Mario Lopez and Lionel Sisniega Otero, had been the object of an intensive hunt by the Communist secret police for their part in operating the clandestine radio. All of these factors combined to bring about the overthrow of Guatemala's Communist regime by June 30, 1954. The former President, Arbenz,* fled along with the Communist high command and many lesser Communist leaders—not, however, before they had looted the treasury and destroyed most of the official records of the government. Secretary of State Dulles announced on July 8 that he hoped the United States would be able to extend diplomatic recognition to the new Government of Guatemala, and recognition was granted on July 13.[43]

It has been stated that the Central Intelligence Agency

---

*Arbenz eventually took up residence in Communist Czechoslovakia.

played a role in the overthrow of the Communist regime in Guatemala and that, in general, the position of the United States Government was that of encouragement of and support for Colonel Castillo Armas and his anti-Communist forces.* Some persons have seen in the stories about possible American assistance to the anti-Communist Guatemalans a cause for apology or explanation. This seems strange indeed. The real question in Guatemala was not so much that of American intervention in the internal affairs of a Latin American nation. Rather it was whether the United States should remain passive, and thereby aid in its own destruction, for fear that it might offend "world opinion" by aiding anti-Communists who were themselves fighting against an already existing intervention by Soviet imperialism in *their* affairs.[44] It would seem that Abraham Lincoln answered that question long ago when he asked, rhetorically, whether he should give the order to execute a soldier for desertion and yet not harm a hair on the head of the agitator who tempted the soldier to act.

SUMMARY

The case histories of Iran and Guatemala indicate that we Americans have the capabilities and possess the ingenuity to take action in the cold war. It must, of course, also be admitted that they are also examples in which the United States has scored notable successes in the cold war and that other examples could be cited which would indicate something less

---

*James Reston wrote that, "if you want to start a revolution in Guatemala don't visit John Foster Dulles, go see Allen Dulles." *New York Times,* June 20, 1954.

than high marks for our cold war actions. It is also generally true that American measures in the shadowy area of *no war, no peace* in the years 1939-1941, as compared with such measures in the cold war from 1946 to the present time, tended to be somewhat bolder and more imaginative than they have been in the latter years. Admirable and forceful as many of the actions taken during the cold war from 1946 onwards have been, they have remained primarily responses, reflex actions as it were, to the Soviet cold war initiative.

There may be a tendency to proceed with less forcefulness because of the introduction of the nuclear capability into considerations of grand strategy. But it would seem that this tendency is also, in part, because our Presidents, and our elected and appointed officials in high places, are gentlemen, with all that this connotes. They are products of a way of life and of a spiritual-cultural heritage that has slowly and painfully evolved over the centuries. The milieu that they inhabit prescribes a code of conduct utterly alien to the whole pseudo-civilization being forcibly erected by world Communism. The Communist leaders aim at nothing less than the construction of a global Communist civilization conjointly with the establishment of a world dictatorship. This cosmic plan is so vast and so couched in Aesopian language as to be often almost a phantasy to American and European statesmen alike. The concept of the remaking of the universe is one calculated to be least understood by Americans, whose pragmatic genius has ever been almost consciously to avoid abstruse ideas.

Then, too, perhaps because the Communist leaders have followed a policy of avoidance of the *blitzkrieg* strategy of Hitler, the leaders and the people of the West are encouraged

263

to believe that there are *some* generally accepted beliefs or views held by both the Communists and the West and that some workable solution for enduring and truly peaceful relations between the opposed worlds can be found.

Whether it be Soviet Premier Khrushchev's visit to the United States (in September 1959) or the latest cultural exchange featuring the arrival of assorted Soviet musicians or folk dancers, we eagerly look for some sign that the Soviet Union has embarked on a new course in world politics, that Communism has at last been tamed.

Whatever the root cause of Western misunderstanding may be, the melancholy fact is that in the face of the Marxist-Leninist transformation of warfare into a grey and ill-defined area of *no war, no peace,* the response of the United States— the natural leader of the forces of freedom—has often been unimaginative and at times devoid of long-range purpose.

The Kremlin knows how it intends to remake this world; moreover it has no doubt but that America is *vrag*—the enemy. To many Americans the issues are not yet so clear.

We live in an era in which "life adjustment" courses in our schools are often deemed more important than a knowledge of the well-springs of American greatness. "Togetherness" is apt to be accounted of more worth than willingness to stand up for what is right. We tend always to shy at an amorphous thing that has been designated "world opinion." Even such an outspoken American as former Secretary of Defense Wilson has testified before a Congressional committee that "too big a military force on our part might convince most of the people in the world *that we were going to start trouble. They might be afraid we are going to start a war.*"*[45]

*Emphasis supplied.

264

We Americans seem to want, above all, never to offend. We want to be loved.

NOTES

1. U.S. Senate, *Senate Documents,* Document No. 62, 66th Congress, 1st Session, Report and Hearings of the Subcommittee on the Judiciary, Volume 14 (Washington: Government Printing Office, 1919), p. 29.

2. Sir Paul Dukes, *The Story of "ST 25"* (London: Cassell, 1938), is an informative account of some aspects of the early days of Soviet power in Russia, especially as regards internal propaganda.

3. See, for example, I. N. Steinberg, *In the Workshop of the Revolution* (New York: Rinehart & Co., Inc., 1953), Leonard Schapiro, *The Origin of the Communist Autocracy* (London: Bell, 1955, and Cambridge, Mass.: Harvard University Press, 1955), and Alan Moorehead's *The Russian Revolution* (New York: Harper & Brothers, 1958). E. J. Scott, "The Cheka," *St. Anthony's Papers, No. I: Soviet Affairs* (London: Chatto & Windus, 1956), shows how Lenin attempted to deceive (and with much success) people at home and abroad about the real terroristic nature of the Cheka as the Soviet secret police was first called. George Katkov, "The Kronstadt Rising," *St. Anthony's Papers: No. 6: Soviet Affairs* (New York: Praeger, 1959), is a revealing account of a little-known incident. As he says, (p. 65): "At the very moment when the reluctant (Menshevik-influenced) typographers were setting pages depicting the horrors of General Galifé's atrocities, Tukhachevsky's troops were butchering wounded prisoners of war in the streets of Kronstadt. Those who survived filled the Petrograd prisons and some of them were shot by the Cheka many months later. Others were sent

to the concentration camp on the Solovetsky Islands . . . (and) if one can trust the report of a fellow-inmate, they helped to organize the first concentration camp labour force. . . ."

4. *Messages and Papers of the Presidents,* Vol. I, pp. 326-327.

5. See L. M. Sears, *Jefferson and the Embargo* (Durham, N.C.: Duke University Press, 1927).

6. *Messages and Papers of the Presidents,* Vol. VI, pp. 16-19, 78, 102-104.

7. *Congressional Globe,* 42nd Congress, 1st Session, p. 52ff.

8. *New York Times,* November 20, 1949.

9. For the world cruise see Joseph Bucklin Bishop, *Theodore Roosevelt and His Time* (New York: Charles Scribner's Sons, 1920), Vol. II, pp. 64-68; Penelope Babcock, "The World Cruise of the US Navy 1907-1909" in William E. Daugherty and Morris Janowitz, eds., *A Psychological Warfare Casebook* (Baltimore: The Johns Hopkins Press, 1958); Arthur M. Johnson, "Theodore Roosevelt and the Navy," *United States Naval Institute Proceedings,* Vol. 84 (October, 1958), pp. 80-82.

10. Bishop, *op. cit.,* p. 184.

11. *American Journal of International Law,* Vol. 34 (October, 1940), p. 729.

12. Winston S. Churchill, *The Second World War,* Vol. II (Boston: Houghton Mifflin Co., 1949), p. 404.

13. Quoted, Steinberg, *op. cit.,* p. 227.

14. Samuel Flagg Bemis, *A Diplomatic History of the United States* (New York: Henry Holt and Company, 1953), p. 853.

15. Von Schweppenburg, *op. cit.,* p. 40. See also General W. Anders, *Hitler's Defeat in Russia* (Chicago: Henry Regnery Co., 1954), and Major General John R. Deane, *The Strange Alliance* (New York: The Viking Press, 1947), for first hand accounts of the over-riding importance of Lend-

Lease supplies to the Soviet war effort. Richard M. Leighton and Robert W. Coakley, *Global Logistics and Strategy, 1940-1943* (Washington: Government Printing Office, 1954), in the United States Army in World War II series describe military aspects of Lend-Lease from 1941 through mid-1943. A second volume which will carry the study through the war's end is forthcoming. There is no complete official account of Lend-Lease although an important part of the history of Lend-Lease is told in T. H. Vail Motter, *The Persian Corridor and Aid to Russia,* U.S. Army in World War II (Washington: Government Printing Office, 1952).

16. See James D. Atkinson, "Can the President Send Troops Abroad," *Thought,* Vol. XXVI (Spring, 1951), pp. 122-123.

17. Maurice Matloff, *Strategic Planning for Coalition Warfare, 1943-1944,* U.S. Army in World War II, Office of the Chief of Military History, Department of the Army (Washington: Government Printing Office, 1959), p. 282.

18. *Ibid.*

19. Arthur Bryant, *The Turn of the Tide, 1939-1943: A Study Based on the Diaries and Autobiographical Notes of Field Marshal The Viscount Alanbrooke* (London: Collins, 1957), p. 461.

20. *Christian Science Monitor,* May 3, 1950.

21. See for example, the excerpt from President Truman's diary in William Hillman, *Mr. President* (New York: Farrar, Straus and Young, 1952), p. 140; a good detailed study is Walter P. Davison's, *The Berlin Blockade; A Study in Cold War Politics* (Princeton: Princeton University Press, 1958).

22. For official statements by the President as well as for comments by members of Congress and expressions of opinion generally see the *New York Times* for June 26-July 2, 1950.

23. Speaking in New York City on December 14, 1959, Mr. Frederick T. Merrill (who had charge of East-West contacts

in the Department of State) stated that due to a variety of reasons American cultural groups had not been reaching the wide audiences that Soviet entertainers and cultural representatives had been appearing before in the United States. See the *New York Times,* Dec. 15, 1959.

24. For the official communiqué see the *New York Times,* August 4, 1958.

25. *New York Times,* September 9, 1958.

26. *Ibid.*

27. *New York Times,* September 12, 1958.

28. *New York Times,* July 16-17, 1958.

29. *The Middle East and Southern Europe,* Report of Senator Hubert H. Humphrey on a Study Mission, 85th Congress, 1st Session, July 1, 1957 (Washington: Government Printing Office, 1957), pp. 28-29.

30. Dr. Stephen G. Xydis, "The Genesis of the Sixth Fleet," *United States Naval Institute Proceedings,* Vol. 84 (August, 1958), p. 47.

31. *Ibid.,* p. 48.

32. *Ibid.,* pp. 49-50; William H. Hessler, "By the Shores of Araby: The Persian Gulf Command," *United States Naval Institute Proceedings,* Vol. 82 (October, 1956), pp. 1027-1030.

33. Admiral Arleigh A. Burke, lecture delivered at the U. S. Naval War College, December 10, 1958.

34. Alexander Barmine, *One Who Survived* (New York: G. P. Putnam's Sons, 1945), p. 77, pp. 139-152; this account by a former Soviet diplomat is one of the best of the analyses of Soviet policy by former citizens of the U.S.S.R.

35. Bernard Fergusson, ed., *The Business of War: The War Narrative of Major-General Sir John Kennedy* (London: Hutchison, 1957), pp. 137-163; Alvin Z. Rubinstein, ed., *The Foreign Policy of the Soviet Union* (New York: Random House, 1960), pp. 161-162.

36. James F. Byrnes, *All in One Lifetime* (New York: Harper, 1958), pp. 333-343 and ch. 23 *passim.*; H. S. Truman,

Memoirs (Garden City, N.Y.: Doubleday, 1956), Vol. II, ch. 7; Joseph M. Jones, *The Fifteen Weeks* (New York: The Viking Press, 1955), ch. 2; Motter, *op. cit.,* ch. 19; Kulski, *op. cit.,* pp. 364-371; Rubinstein, *op. cit.,* pp. 207-208; W. W. Rostow, *The United States in the World Arena* (New York: Harper, 1960), p. 184.

37. The principal sources used for the Iranian problem were: Department of State, *American Foreign Policy, 1950-1955* (Washington: Government Printing Office, 1957), Vol. II, 2167-2276; *New York Times,* especially the analysis of June 10, 1951; Rear Admiral E. M. Eller, USN (Ret.), "Troubled Oil and Iran," *United States Naval Institute Proceedings,* Vol. 80 (Nov. 1954), p. 1189ff; Richard and Gladys Harkness, "The Mysterious Doings of CIA," a series of three articles in the *Saturday Evening Post,* October 30, Nov. 6 and Nov. 13, 1954; *Events in the Middle East,* Committee on Foreign Relations, U.S. Senate, 85th Congress, 1st Session (Washington: Government Printing Office, 1957), *passim.*; Byrnes, *op. cit.*; Jones, *op. cit.*; Truman, *op. cit.*

38. *New York Times,* Sept. 2 and Sept. 9, 1953.

39. Eller, *loc. cit.,* p. 1196; *Foreign Policy, 1950-1955, op. cit.,* Vol. II, pp. 2273-2274; Cameron Hawley, "The Honored Name I Bear," *Life,* October 11, 1954, p. 171ff.

40. *Foreign Policy, 1950-1955, op. cit.,* Vol. II, p. 2275.

41. Wilfred Ryder, "Incitement in Iran," London *Tablet,* August 23, 1958, pp. 148-149; *Time & Tide,* Feb. 21, 1959, p. 204; the Washington *Evening Star,* September 18, 1958; *Wall Street Journal,* September 4-5 and October 9, 1959.

42. Walter Millis, ed., *The Forrestal Diaries* (New York: Viking Press, 1951), p. 41; Mr. Forrestal also took a keen interest in evidence regarding Soviet clandestine operations in Latin America from a base in the capital of Mexico.

43. The principal sources used in the Guatemalan case history were: *Foreign Policy, 1950-1955, op. cit.,* Vol. I, pp. 1291-1316; *Report of the Subcommittee to Investigate Com-*

munist Aggression in Latin America, House of Representatives, 83d Congress, 2nd Session (Washington: Government Printing Office, 1954), *passim.*; Richard P. Stebbins, ed., *The United States in World Affairs: 1954* (New York: Harper & Brothers, 1956), pp. 367-390.

44. On the question of American involvement in the Guatemalan liberation see Harkness, *loc. cit.,* Oct. 30, 1954, p. 20ff.; Stebbins, *op. cit.,* pp. 382-383; Daniel James, *Red Design for the Americas: Guatemalan Prelude* (New York: John Day Co., 1954), p. 316; Harry Howe Ransom, *Central Intelligence and National Security* (Cambridge, Mass.: Harvard University Press, 1958), p. 89. *Red Design for the Americas* is also very good on a wide variety of matters relating to the Guatemalan question such as the Communist technique of warfare by proxy. Among newspapers see especially the *New York Times,* June 20, 1954, and the *Christian Science Monitor,* June 22, 1954.

45. U. S. Congress, *Hearings, Subcommittee of the Committee on Appropriations,* House of Representatives, 84th Congress, 1st Sess., *op. cit.,* p. 31.

CHAPTER 6

The Fusion of War and Peace

The tendency toward a sheeplike conformity, the desire to please "world opinion," the desire to be loved—these are, after all, not attitudes that are found today exclusively among Americans. They are symptomatic of feelings observable in some degree in Western civilization. They are made manifest by a trend toward the development of a mass mind, a lowering of taste, and an acceptance of (or at least an absence of vigorous protest against) the least common denominator in everything from the mass media of communications to literature and music. As the Spanish philosopher Ortega y Gasset prophetically wrote: *"The characteristic of the hour is that the commonplace mind, knowing itself to be commonplace, has the assurance to proclaim the rights of the commonplace and to impose them wherever it will."*[*][1]

The tendency toward the commonplace, with a concomitant dimunition of the good, the noble (the virtue of patriotism, for example), the just, results in great part from the revolutionary tides of modern times, especially from the revolutions in education, communications, and weapons,

*Emphasis in the original.

and the revolution effected by the politicization of warfare. Additionally, the cult of the commonplace saps the resistance that Western civilization offers to the new barbarism of Communism.

1. *The Revolution in Education*

Beginning rather more than a century ago, the idea of universal education came into vogue. Increasingly since that time, the mass of people in most countries have acquired a basic literacy while multitudes have additionally acquired an elementary or even higher education. The effect of this has been to provide the propagandist of the latter half of the twentieth century a mass audience undreamed of and even impossible in earlier periods of history. In effect, the propagandist today has the *possibility* of reaching almost incredibly large masses of people.

A second result of the revolution in education has been to create a mass intelligentsia. The concept of the intelligentsia may be said to have begun with the Renaissance, but it has not been until the modern era—and through the pressures generated by universal education—that an intelligentsia of great numbers has become possible. This intelligentsia writes the literature, produces the programs, edits the news, and very largely sets the styles and forms, the tastes and habits of the masses. Yet in the non-Communist world the intelligentsia, despite the importance of its role, seems to have a tendency toward rootlessness.[2] This tendency explains in part why segments of the non-Communist world's intelligentsia have been so susceptible to the Communist propaganda about atomic warfare that there exists an observable nuclear neurosis in some quarters. But whatever phantasmagoria Soviet propagandists conjure up about nuclear warfare, or even if Communist word-artists restrict themselves to the truth about this subject, the intelligentsia in the non-Communist world cannot ignore the reality of the lot of the intellectual under Marxism-Leninism. The repression of Boris Pasternak in the Soviet Union and of Milovan Djilas in Yugoslavia are, unhappily, only the leading examples of the servitude that is the fate of the true intellectual in Communist-controlled countries.

2. *The Revolution in Communications*

Equally important and accompanying the changes in education have been the technological transitions affecting the communication of ideas. Thus in the battle for the minds of men, the invention of the typewriter, the teleprinter, duplicating machines, radio, and television have been as significant as the spread of universal education. Today the ability of man to transmit information instantaneously and to reproduce written materials, pictures, and photographs in innumerable copies permits the propagandist to place his message before a mass audience on an unparalleled scale. Every day sees a new advance in the technology of communications, and science seems certain to continue to arm the propagandist with the most Orwellian of weapons for affecting the mind of the individual. While many motives have impelled the Soviets to send vehicles into space, not the least would appear to be the present overwhelming propaganda impact and the future communications advantage for psychological warfare.

But in addition to increasing the facility of spreading information—and misinformation—the revolution in communications has given the totalitarian state the tools with which it can control all, or almost all, communications within its borders. Scientific advances permit jamming of radio transmissions, mass censorship and control of all news media, and the employment of electronic and other devices to close off frontiers. Thus when communications media in the West were widely concerned with disseminating the story of Red Chinese attacks on the Chinese Nationalist offshore islands, the people in the great province of Canton on the mainland of China read or heard only Communist propaganda about advances in industrial production.[3]

3. *The Revolution in Weapons*

The development of nuclear weapons has overturned previous concepts of mass destruction. The H-bomb is not merely a far-reaching addition to the field of weapons but is a device, as Sir Winston Churchill stated in the House of Commons, whereby "the entire foundation of human affairs was revolutionized." The advent of the intercontinental ballistic missile has been almost equally portentous. Yet of still greater moment is the fact that the *threat* of the use of weapons of mass destruction immeasurably extended the political nature of warfare.

4. *The Revolution Effected by the Politicization of Warfare*

The revolutions in education, in communications, and in weaponry have contributed to the merging of political affairs and war. But the prime mover toward this end has been the combination of the Marxist-Leninist theories of struggle with the hard facts of Communist experience in world revolution. Especially from the time of Trotsky's *no war, no peace* pronouncement in 1918 the Communists have directed their efforts toward the development of a new form of warfare which blends violent and non-violent techniques. It is not that they have been alone in recognizing war's changing face. Rather it is that, placing such intense emphasis on the political, they have grasped more quickly and more surely than others the fact that in the past war was a continuation of politics by other means, but today the political struggle *is* the true act of war. Much as Marx boasted that he had stood Hegel on his head, Lenin and his successors have stood Clausewitz on his head and have politicized warfare.

THE COMMUNIST SYNTHESIS OF WAR AND PEACE

From the revolutions in education, communications, and weapons, and the revolution effected by their own politicization of warfare the Communists have produced a synthesis of war and peace. They have carried both war and peace to a higher threshold in a supreme effort to disintegrate all existing societies and cultures. Past conquerors with designs for world hegemony have sought primarily to *explode* their ideas or their forces against the outer shell of the peoples or countries they were attacking. The Communists intend not to *explode* but patiently to *disintegrate* all non-Communist societies. They aim at nothing less than the creation of a new civilization for the entire world, a civilization in which they will be the self-ordained cosmocrats. They have con-

275

joined both war and peace so that all of man's activities—art, science, literature, music, the drama, the technics of warfare— are harnessed to Marxist-Leninist canons that delineate precisely what a totally new world ought to be on every plane. They are engaged in a conflict of *civilizations* that is of such magnitude that it should be called *polyreconism,** the fusion of war and peace.** This is the essence of Communist grand strategy; this is the Communist synthesis of war and peace.

A New Stage in Soviet Policy?

Increased Soviet emphasis on cultural exchanges and on more extensive participation in international organizations[4] —symbolized in many ways by the Khrushchev visit and by the visits of other Soviet officials to the United States—would seem to have opened a new stage in Soviet policy. There is some evidence to suggest that the Communists believe this to be the culminating phase of their grand strategy of *polyreconism.*[5] The development of Soviet grand strategy in terms of stages or periods of specific strategic aims is not new. Long ago Lenin indicated Communism's broad strategic flexibility when he said: "In all countries, the revolution grows by channels which in different countries differ widely. In some the revolution can come one or two years later than in others. All have to pass certain political developments. . . ."[6]

Undoubtedly additional time is required for a regrouping

Polyreconism is a word coined from Greek roots to convey the concept of the merging or the fusion of war and peace.

**Compare Lenin's view that "the dictatorship of the proletariat is a persistent struggle—sanguinary and bloodless, violent and peaceful, military and economic, educational and administrative—against the forces and traditions of the old society."

of Soviet forces for the final phase of the struggle against the non-Communist world. Soviet difficulties can be viewed as extending into the latter 1960's and are threefold:

(1) Deficiencies in agriculture, in consumer goods, and in important segments of heavy industry such as chemicals and electric power production. The 21st Congress of the Communist Party of the Soviet Union was critical of failures in a number of these areas, and Khrushchev has since been even more specific in his criticism. The October, 1959, decree of the Party's Central Committee on increasing consumer goods also indicates the Soviet need for a breathing space to strengthen the regime internally. Reports of labor unrest and even of strikes in the U.S.S.R. because of heavier work loads, pay cuts, and consumer goods shortages further underscore Soviet difficulties.[7]

(2) Unrest in Eastern Europe. The Hungarian Revolution of 1956 seems to have made a more profound impression on the rulers of the Kremlin than it did on Western statesmen. Many indicators in the Soviet press point up the fact that perhaps a decade (1957-1967) will be required fully to reassert Communist authority in Eastern Europe and effectively to curb the continuing nationalistic aspirations of the people. The frankest admission of Soviet difficulties in the captive nations was made by Khrushchev when he stated: "The principle of peaceful coexistence signifies a renunciation of interference in the internal affairs of other countries with the object of altering their system of government or mode of life or for any other motive."[8]

He further indicated Soviet sensitivity about the restlessness in the Communist-controlled Eastern European countries by these words: "Real facts of life in the last ten years have shown convincingly that the policy of 'rolling back' Communism can only poison the international atmosphere, heighten the tension between states and work in favor of the cold war. Neither its inspirers nor those who conduct it can turn back the course of history and restore capitalism in the socialist countries."[9]

(3) The third factor that Soviet strategy must seek to overcome is the roadblock placed in the way of further Communist expansion by American refusal—thus far—to be blackmailed by nuclear threats. Once again it would appear that President Eisenhower's no appeasement address to the nation on September 11, 1958, was studied more carefully in Moscow and Peking than in Washington. Not only did Chinese Communist threats against Formosa subside following this speech, but the softer Soviet approach in world politics can be dated from the latter part of 1958 and early 1959. The new stage in Soviet grand strategy is apparently based on the thought that it will be necessary to effect additional reductions in the military power of the United States and to soften up the will of the United States to resist. Soviet proposals on disarmament are being tailored toward reducing American military capabilities in the knowledge that once a democracy starts to disarm it does so openly and with great rapidity. It is well known that immediately after both World Wars the United States rushed with almost indecent speed to destroy the great military machine it had constructed during wartime. To this end it is possible that the Soviet Union might offer certain real concessions on disarmament, secure in the knowledge that it can reverse its position much more

quickly than can the democracies and that the democracies will permit their research teams, now so vital a part of modern defense, to enter private employment where they cannot be quickly assembled when the need arises.

The Soviet record of violation or evasion of signed treaties and agreements makes it appear more likely that the U.S.S.R. will agree to adhere only to disarmament agreements through which the Soviets can circumvent the Western democracies. This is especially probable in the field of nuclear testing and nuclear disarmament. Scientific advances have made feasible the masking of kiloton explosions of nuclear devices in such ways that inspection would be effective only if control personnel could travel with complete freedom and inspect *all* facilities whether labeled "nuclear" or not.[10]

Furthermore, *any* disarmament concessions will be, on the part of the Soviet bloc, in the nature of a *detente*. But the democracies, by contrast, have in the past tended to consider such arrangements on a permanent or semipermanent basis. Marxist-Leninist thinking in this regard has not changed from the idea of one-time Politburo member Grigori E. Zinoviev who said on February 2, 1919: "We are willing to sign an unfavorable peace with the Allies. . . . It would only mean that we should put no trust whatever in the *bit of paper** we should sign. We should use the breathing space so obtained in order to gather our strength. . . ."[11]

The new phase of Soviet strategy does not imply an abandonment of the ultimate goal of a Communist world. This is clearly spelled out by Khrushchev's statement immediately preceding his American visit: "We Communists believe that

*Emphasis supplied.

279

the idea of Communism will ultimately be victorious throughout the world, just as it has been victorious in our country, in China and many other states."[12]

The idea of a breathing space during which Soviet strategy will call for the struggle against the non-Communist countries to be conducted in a more sophisticated form was also pointed out in a *Pravda* editorial that laid down the line in these words: "Today we are living at a time when the historic transition from socialism to communism is taking place. . . . At the United Nations Comrade Khrushchev put forward the principles of U.S.S.R. foreign policy and on behalf of the Soviet Government submitted proposals for universal and complete disarmament of all states, which *opens up a new era in the struggle for world peace.*"*[13]

A breathing space in the cold war between the Soviet Union and the NATO allies will also permit the Chinese Communist junior partner to step up cold war activity in the Far East while the U.S.S.R. regroups its forces in the other half of the globe.

The apparent new phase in Soviet policy can be expected to last only as long as it offers advantages to the Kremlin leadership. Undoubtedly there will be those in the Soviet high command who will urge a harder policy against the West, for they will see signs that will confirm their belief that the capitalists are sufficiently decadent and weakened to be eliminated sooner rather than later. From time to time the non-Communist world will be threatened, and "incidents" will be manufactured to test its strength. The United States will remain the principal barrier to Soviet bloc aspira-

*Emphasis supplied.

tions. Nineteen hundred and fifty-eight saw the beginnings of a subtler policy by the Soviet Union to dissipate American determination to maintain this barrier. The decade to 1968, and especially the years from 1961, will be the crucial period in the development of Soviet strength and the attempted softening of the American will to resist and of the ingredient that chiefly supports that will, our military strength. Signs of weakness on the part of the United States will no doubt increase the momentum of the Soviet advance and lead the Kremlin to believe that it need not delay the last stage of the Communist offensive.

THE UNITED STATES:
DANGER AND PROMISE OF THE FUTURE

What are the implications of the Communist fusion of war and peace for the United States? What are the more immediate implications of the new tack in Soviet policy?

The years 1961-1968 may well be the most critical years ever faced by the American Republic. It is during this period that the most severe testing of our national character and courage will take place. The apparent new phase in Soviet policy for this period calls for a softening-up process, during which the non-Communist world, but the United States especially, will be propagandized on a scale never before witnessed.

Unless we fully understand the continuous warfare under the guise of peace that the Communists wage against us, the following picture of the next eight years may well come true.

Cultural exchanges will emphasize the peaceful nature of the U.S.S.R. and the Soviet bloc countries. An attempt will be made to sell Americans the idea that *all* war is futile, and hence that *any* kind of peace is preferable even to the *risk* of war. Communist propaganda will place heavy emphasis on the point that the American people do not have a variety of choices to make. Instead, Americans will be told that there are only two ways out of their dilemma: "Either war—and war in the rocket and H-bomb age is fraught with the most dire consequences for all nations—or peaceful coexistence."[14] Massive propaganda based on scientific or pseudo-scientific claims will emphasize the achievements of the Soviet Union and will portray the United States as a second-class power in the space age.

After endless conferences on disarmament, the Soviet conferees will at last make certain concessions that will be widely hailed in the world press, and the non-Communist powers will hasten to disarm. Utilizing its vast land area and with its unparalleled experience in propaganda and in clandestine operations, the Soviet Union will be able to conceal the extent of its own pledged disarmament and will be able further to develop its weapons systems. With the advantage of such a breathing space, the Soviet Union will undoubtedly be able to secure a marked relaxation or a complete abandonment of export controls and will probably be able to get generous grants of economic aid or long-term credits from the Western democracies. These measures would enable the Kremlin to satisfy the desires for consumer goods in the Soviet bloc without slowing well-screened research and development efforts to achieve superiority in new weapons.

The extension of long-term credits, economic aid in some form, and increased trade with Russia will also be urged on the ground that Soviet leaders can "restrain" the Chinese Communists. During this time the Chinese Communists will continue their role of saber rattlers in the Far East, and Soviet diplomacy will be portrayed as exerting a calming influence on the Chinese. The Kremlin will also employ this breathing space to make a final consolidation of its power in the satellite countries of Eastern Europe and to stamp out the last vestiges of opposition there and in the fully incorporated captive areas such as Latvia, Lithuania, and Estonia.

The years 1961-1968 will be years of decision for the United States because present Soviet disadvantages in nuclear military power are likely to be overcome gradually and may even disappear completely by 1964-1965.[15] Moreover, the current Soviet Seven Year Plan will have been completed as of December 31, 1965, and the Party leadership will have had time to assess fully the results and get the new research, arms, and related heavy industry programs under way by 1967. If, then, the Soviet Union has also received the long breathing space that it needs, the time may be considered ripe by 1968 for the final blow against the leader—in Communist eyes—of the camp of imperialism, the United States. While Marxists-Leninists (believing as they do that history is on their side) have never adhered to any rigid time-table of conquest, the November, 1957, Joint Communiqué of the Communist Parties of the Soviet Union, China, and the satellite countries seems to have been cast in terms of the not-too-distant future. The communiqué proclaimed: "The world Socialist system, which is growing and becoming stronger, is exerting ever greater influence upon the international situation in the interests of peace and progress and the freedom of the peoples. While socialism is on the upgrade, imperialism is heading toward decline. . . ."[16]

If, therefore, the softening-up process that seems to be

283

projected by the new stage of Soviet policy continues to 1968, that year would offer the Communists an opportunity (having by then consolidated their forces and weakened ours) for putting into practice all of the techniques that they have developed in their fusion of war and peace. For 1968 is a Presidential election year. Believing, as Marxists-Leninists do, that the Western democracies are essentially decadent, they could well use—after nearly a decade of preparatory preparation—the American Presidential campaign in 1968 as the occasion for a bold stroke in political/psychological warfare. During September and October, 1968, the Soviet leadership could launch a massive propaganda campaign with the object of urging one—or both—of the candidates to "form a more broadly based government" when elected. The term "more broadly based government" is, of course, Communist jargon for a government whose Cabinet would include Communists or Communist sympathizers. It could be expected that such proposals would follow immediately upon the publicity attendant on some new or claimed Soviet scientific achievement. Possibly the Soviets will choose this time to launch some new type of space vehicle. For example, one that would be equipped to broadcast both simultaneous radio messages and television pictures in many languages to countries around the globe. Whatever the special circumstances that attend the propaganda campaign, the world will be told: "The aggressive imperialist circles of the United States by pursuing the so-called 'positions of strength' policy, seek to bring most countries of the world under their sway and to hamper the onward march of mankind in accordance with the laws of social development."[17]

It will then be suggested to the American people that they

certainly do not wish to "hamper the onward march of mankind." Accordingly, they should demand that one or both of the Presidential candidates show his devotion to the "cause of peace" by pledging that, if elected, he will eliminate the influence of the "aggressive imperialist circles" through the formation of a "broadly based government" in which Communists or Communist followers can actively participate as Cabinet members and in other high goverment posts in order that: "Everything that obstructs peaceful coexistence between states with different social systems . . . be swept out of the way. . . . We must eliminate the things that tend to aggravate the international situation and to obstruct peaceful coexistence."[18]

In the background to this orchestration of peace will be a less sophisticated note. Americans will be given to understand that the alternative to forming a "more broadly based government" will be sudden nuclear devastation. Their will sapped by a decade of propaganda on the horrors of nuclear war, the futility of resistance, the idea of peace at any price, people may ask themselves why not? Why not accept the "reasonableness" of the Soviet demand for a "peace-loving" American government? Pressures (beginning with a vocal minority) will soon be reflected in the utterances of one of the candidates. He will instantly be hailed in the press as a man with "vision," one "truly democratic," "progressive," and, above all, "forward looking." It will be capitulation, but only a few will use the word.

The American experience will touch off a great landside in the other non-Communist nations. Then throughout the world Moscow will indeed be able to say: "The events taking place in the capitalist countries serve as historic proof that capitalism is doomed. No matter how much the reformists and revisionists may strive to beautify and adorn capitalism, they cannot forestall its death, just as nothing is strong enough to contain the mighty advance of Communism."[19]

While millions still fearfully scan the skies for the missiles that never come, freedom will expire "not with a bang, but with a whimper."

Is this idle fancy? Perhaps. Yet as recently as 1916 Communism was merely the subject of long-winded discussions in European coffee houses by theoretical revolutionaries who had never met a payroll. And little more than a decade ago the Czechoslovak democracy was taken over by the Communists with never a shot fired in anger.

The Communists say today that "revolutionary theory is not a collection of 'frozen' dogmas and formulas, but a fighting guide for practical activity for the transformation of the world, for the building of Communism." The Moscow-Peking Axis believes that through the application of the Marxist-Leninist synthesis of warfare to concrete situations it can disintegrate all existing non-Communist civilizations. So long as opposing civilizations do not effectively and steadfastly oppose them, so long especially as the United States—the natural leader of a freedom-seeking world—does not revivify the ideas that have made an American civilization, and made it great, who would venture to contend that the Communists mislead themselves?

WHAT IS TO BE DONE?

1. *The Politico-Psychological Front*

"What is the individual? Who cares about him? His little

286

voice is no stronger than the squeak of a mouse." So said Soviet writer Mayakovsky. Disclaim this view though the Communists may, the record of Communism stamps them with it. Not so long ago the Soviet treatment of their own poet and writer Boris Pasternak indicated more loudly than words the true standing of the individual in Communist society. Marxists-Leninists seem at times aware of this weakest of links in their system, and yet the inner compulsion of that very system prevents them from doing anything about it even if they would.

Would we not profit by a reexamination of America's own greatness? Rather than neon lights and pastel-colored automobiles has not our greatness been in higher things? The belief that man has an innate dignity and an eternal destiny was what wise old John Adams meant when he said that "the American Revolution was in the minds and hearts of the people." Is there any better guide in a Western world that today has a surfeit of goodies?

A calm appraisal of our own strength and of that of the Moscow-Peking Axis would seem to be very much in order in this age of nuclear-missile blackmail. We need not take so dim a view of Soviet scientific achievement as that of British Police Constable Trevor Davies who, after catching a glimpse of Sputnik II, is said to have told a reporter, "Personally, I was rather disappointed." This exhibition of the traditional British phlegm might well be one of the answers to panic-thinking about how to surrender gracefully. Surely a fear psychosis about the terrors of a possible nuclear war is utterly alien to our American national character. How strange that the Communists—who have never really insisted on the importance of *will* in human affairs—should be able to conduct a warfare of *will* against that nation whose inheritance has been the Judaeo-Christian tradition of faith that moves mountains.

While we have been reluctant to meet our adversaries in the arena of unconventional warfare, especially on the politico-psychological front, we are better equipped than the Communists to engage in a battle of *wills*. And we are definitely stronger in the political warfare field. Let us recall that national self-determination and the freedom of peoples really to be free politically were first proclaimed by the great innovator of political warfare in its modern sense, our own Woodrow Wilson. Could not Americans once again move boldly ahead in this, Communism's most vulnerable area? As baseball's great Willie Keeler once said, "Hit 'em where they ain't." We have generally shied away from this engagement despite our huge stockpiles of potential ideological weapons that could carry the struggle onto the Communist terrain. The late Secretary of State John Foster Dulles suggested the most potent of these weapons of political warfare in a speech in Cleveland, Ohio, on November 18, 1958, when he pledged the support of the United States to "political independence for all peoples who desire it and are able to undertake its responsibilities." The light of freedom continues to beckon powerfully to the captive nations of Eastern Europe, the former states of Latvia, Lithuania, and Estonia, to Tibet, and to other nations and ethnic groups subjugated by the new colonialism of the Moscow-Peking Axis. Yet the United States has failed to exploit the centrifugal forces that continue to tear at the Communist empire. The United States has both the assets and the ideas to engage successfully in that vast and shifting conflict which is unconventional warfare and nowhere more than on the politico-psychological front.*

2. *The Economic Front*

The economic front is closely related to the politico-psychological front. It was not without reason that the first thing the Kremlin did after the East German uprising in June, 1953, was to ship a trainload of butter to East Germany.

We Americans have often displayed a special genius in the economic field at home and in our external relations. The magnificent work of Herbert Hoover as President Wilson's Director of Relief after the First World War illustrates on the broadest scale the significance of the American economy as an agency for world peace and world order. It will be recalled that the Hoover mission by relief and reconstruction work not only promoted the recovery of stability on the continent but actively rolled back Communism from Eastern and Central Europe.

Today the first task on the economic front appears to be the provision for a sound and growing economy in the United States. With an expanding economy, there is no reason why we cannot support defense needs as well as vigorous foreign policy. In order to grow, the economy should be kept free; and additional incentives should be earnestly sought to this

*American ingenuity at the tactical level of politico-psychological warfare is illustrated by an incident that took place during the measures short of war period before Pearl Harbor. In November, 1941, the U.S. Navy seized the *Odenwald*, a Nazi vessel which was running the British blockade with a highly valuable cargo of strategic goods. The Navy was able to employ this inventive gambit by using an old order that provided that any ship *suspected* of being involved in the slave trade could be searched and detained.

end.[20] To adopt rigid controls for the American economy would be to accept battle on the enemy's terms. The adoption of measures that would strengthen and expand our free enterprise system, however, would be to meet the Communist bloc on economic warfare grounds least advantageous to *them*. The erosion of an economic system that stresses competition and private enterprise would as surely lead to defeat as would our unilateral disarmament.

There are many factors that could be considered, but it might be well to explore the possibilities inherent in three:

(1) There have been few meaningful changes in the income tax deductions that industry has been allowed to make for depreciation during the past quarter century. Would it not be wise to provide much more liberal depreciation credits in our income tax structure? Most if not all of our obsolescent and inefficient industrial plant would be rapidly replaced if the powerful incentive of heavy depreciation allowances were offered. The advances by American business that would surely follow such stimuli might well make our past industrial achievements look small by comparison. It can be argued that while all business should be encouraged by depreciation incentives, the railroads ought to be specially favored. The modernization of their physical plant would go a long way toward curing the sickness that afflicts this major industry and would equally be a definite contribution to our national defense. In view of the role of the railroads in providing highly mobile launching sites for the newest family of guided missiles, their defense value is greater than ever.

(2) Special incentives should also be written into our tax laws to encourage much greater expenditure by industry for basic research. Such basic research by business is not only a

major factor in providing new products and new or more efficient processes for an expanding economy, but also has a direct bearing on a sound defense posture.

It might also be well to consider reforming the income tax structure generally with a view to encouraging money to flow into business expansion, the stimulation of new industries, and the encouragement of private capital to invest outside the United States. After all, it was Marx himself who considered an increasingly steep tax on income to be a device for exerting "despotic inroads on the rights of property, and on conditions of bourgeoisie production."[21]

(3) Labor ought to be encouraged to see that cooperation with management in efforts to increase over-all productivity is an imperative for our times. Labor needs to accept the fact that outmoded work rules and objections to labor-saving devices block increased industrial capacity. For its part, management ought to adopt both the sense of justice and the flexibility of procedures required to find positions for those displaced by more efficient work rules and methods. We need not be frightened by increases in hourly wages. Increased efficiency means the productivity that will absorb proper wage increases and still provide for growth and a sound economy.

Proposals such as these have validity in ordinary times. They possess a special sense of urgency in the war of civilizations in which we are now engaged. Most importantly, there is little possibility that they will ever be adopted unless there is the belief that they are musts for the survival of the American system as we have known it. Labor and management alike are vitally interested in that survival.

Such proposals will not only help varied segments of the

American economy but will also contribute significantly to its over-all growth. And the evidence shows that the United States, often used as the example of a full-grown or "mature" economy, is actually increasing its long-term growth. Thus revised figures issued by the Federal Reserve Board have shown for 1959 an industrial growth index 7 per cent above that of a decade before. Our rate of economic growth, then, appears to be much better than some past pessimistic opinions would have suggested.[22] This fact should, if combined with a program of incentives to aid our free enterprise system, permit the higher defense expenditures that we need and still allow us to maintain a sound economy.

Additionally, there should be no relaxation in the present system of export controls and other economic safeguards as they effect the Moscow-Peking Axis. Instead, some consideration should be given to the imposition of more effective measures. If there be even a remote possibility of a more moderate group getting control in either Moscow or Peking, such a group will certainly have little chance of gaining power so long as we do anything that assists the present leadership to maintain its rule. There are signs of hope in the fact that the more intense the economic difficulties that the Moscow-Peking Axis encounters, the more likely there will be internal dissension within the Communist bloc and perhaps friction between Moscow and Peking. During the year 1959 the Chinese Communist Party disclosed that there were serious shortcomings in the economy and that there had been gross exaggerations made by certain Party officials with respect to increased production. In the Soviet Union both the 20th and 21st Party Congresses brought out economic shortcomings. Some of the statements made at the 21st Party Congress are unconsciously revealing. For example, "the main agricultural task during the seven-year plan will be reaching a production level which *will wholly meet the population's demands in the way of foodstuffs and industry's demands for raw materials. . . .*" And "during the seven-year plan, *cement output will increase about 50 million tons, which almost equals the current U.S. output.*"*[23] Other weaknesses in Russia's industrial complex were brought to light in 1960 when *Pravda* indicated that bungling and mismanagement in the huge Donets Basin coal fields was so bad that it took more men to produce a ton of coal than twenty years previously.[24] Should one of our tasks be to strengthen the imperfect economy of those who would "bury" us?

As previously pointed out, one of the most devastating critiques of increased trade with the Moscow-Peking Axis has been made by Mr. O. V. Tracy, Vice-President of the Esso Standard Oil Company: "Businessmen everywhere," he reminds us, "should remember the blandishments with which Hitler wooed Britain and the United States in the years before the last war. The bait now offered to the West is not unlike the bait that Hitler dangled before our noses twenty or so years ago. . . . The Europeans who do business with the Soviets . . . are subsidizing their competitors with advanced machinery—for there is a deadly iron fist hidden in this velvet glove of so-called 'peaceful trade.' Two world wars have proved that trade alone is not the road to peace. . . ."[25]

On the positive side of what is to be done on the economic front there is this cogent reasoning: "The crucial battle in the economic war will be fought in providing the peoples of the world with improved standards of living. Today America

*Emphasis supplied.

has the lead. We must do all in our power to maintain this lead."[26]

3. *The Defense Front*

The founders of our government were well aware that in world politics we should have to deal not with angels but with men. Wisely they understood that only power can check power. Their grasp of this basic and unchanging fact was stated lucidly in these words: "We are not to expect that they [other nations] should regard our advancement in union, in power and consequence by land and by sea, with an eye of indifference and composure. The people of America are aware that inducements to war may arise out of these circumstances, as well as from others not so obvious at present, and that whenever such inducements may find fit time and opportunity for operation, pretences to color and justify them will not be found wanting."[27]

How to provide for keeping ourselves in *such a situation that, instead of inviting war,* we will be able to repress and discourage war? The Founding Fathers had the answer. The answer was practical; it had been tested and has been tested by time. That situation, they held, "consists in the best possible state of defence."[28]

If today we do not want to invite war but to repress and discourage it, is there any more certain method than by providing the best possible state of defense? Do we not need to re-examine the entire question of the relationship between armaments and aggressive war? In the past has it been so-called armaments races that caused war? Or has it been rather that when a non-aggressor nation fell seriously behind an aggressor nation in the quality and capabilities of its defense, it encouraged the aggressive-minded nation to accept a risk that would not otherwise have been undertaken?* This would seem to be especially true of the totalitarian state. Did an armaments competition bring about the Soviet attack on Finland in 1939 or Hitler's invasion of Poland in that same year? The Soviet Union and Communist China have conducted a long and vigorous propaganda campaign against what they term the American position of "situations of strength." Is this because the Moscow-Peking Axis is truly desirous of world peace, or is it because continued or increased American defense capabilities stand in the way of a Communist world order?

From the post World War II period down to the present time the Soviet Union has constantly talked disarmament and has sometimes claimed that it has made reductions in its armed forces. Conclusive evidence as to real reductions has, however, been difficult if not impossible to obtain. The evidence that is available suggests that the Soviet Union has been increasing its over-all military capabilities. During the Department of Defense Appropriations Hearings for 1960, an exchange between the Chairman of the Appropriations Subcommittee, Mr. George H. Mahon, and the Secretary of Defense, Mr. Neil McElroy, was revealing:

Mr. Mahon: In this arms race which we despise because we are freedom-loving people, the Soviet Union has been closing the gap since World War II, very markedly. Would you agree to that statement?

*A cogent argument can be made that the Second World War was the result of the failure of the democracies to maintain strong armed forces rather than that there was an armaments "race." Aggressors are encouraged by signs of weakness but checked by power.

Secretary McElroy: Yes. . . .

Mr. Mahon: Our position has been deteriorating since World War II relatively speaking, with respect to the U.S.S.R.?

Secretary McElroy: Only relatively speaking.

Mr. Mahon: Of course, we are getting stronger, but they have been getting stronger faster.

Secretary McElroy: That is correct.

Mr. Mahon: How long is this trend going to continue?

Secretary McElroy: *It cannot continue to the point where this country is unable to protect its national security.**29

From the founding of the American Republic to the nuclear age one salient fact has been proved again and again: it is difficult to avoid concluding that "the best possible state of defence" is the surest safeguard of liberty. Did not the myopia of the United States and the other Western democracies toward proper defenses during the Munich period encourage aggression?

Today with the advent of nuclear weapons and of both intermediate range and intercontinental missiles, orthodox armed force appears to have taken on a new role. The existence of army, navy, and air components in being, in numbers, and in a high state of readiness now plays a dual role. In part such forces provide the reserves and also form an umbrella for the conduct of conflict by unconventional methods such as propaganda, political warfare, guerrilla warfare, and similar forms of the new warfare. The other aspect of the role of orthodox armed forces in being is the deterrent aspect. For the quality and the numbers in which such forces exist in the United States largely determine the Soviet bloc's willingness

*Emphasis supplied.

to speak and to act softly rather than to proceed more bel-
ligerently.

While military power today has thus assumed a rather
different role than it had in the past, the *capability* of waging
war in its relation to America's national strategy is little
changed from the earliest days of the Republic. George Washington might well have been addressing the America of today
when he said: "There is a rank due to the United States
among nations, which will be withheld, if not absolutely
lost, by the reputation of weakness—if we desire to avoid in-
sult we must be ready to repel it; if we desire to secure peace,
one of the most powerful institutions of our rising prosperity,
it must be known that we are at all times ready for war."[30]

Today as then, if adequate armed strength is coupled with
wise and bold statesmanship, there need be no reason why
we cannot look forward to the establishment of an era of
peace with justice.

In the post World War II years we have directed our military resources more and more toward being able to fight and
win an all-out atomic war, and it was probably essential that
we do so in order to reach a massive capability that would
deter the Moscow-Peking Axis. For the decade of the 1960's
it would seem that we have sufficient deterrent power in a
total war situation so long as we continue to maintain this
capability. This was indicated during the 1960 Defense Ap-
propriation Hearings when the Subcommittee Chairman put
the following question to the Chairman of the Joint Chiefs
of Staff:

Mr. Mahon: This is the same question which has been asked
in several different ways. In your opinion, which country,

U.S.A. or U.S.S.R., at an agreed given moment, so I am knocking out the element of surprise attack, could deliver upon the other today the most destructive attack utilizing all presently available weapons?

General Twining: There is no question about that.

Mr. Mahon: What is your answer?

General Twining: The United States.[31]

We can accept the assurance of the Chairman of the Joint Chiefs of Staff that we are currently well prepared for a possible total war, or at least one from which the element of surprise by the aggressor is disbarred. But are we prepared for the Communist synthesis of war and peace? This Communist synthesis or politicization of warfare embraces a broad spectrum of struggle and encompasses a multitude of border incidents, guerrilla warfare, local insurrections, and small wars. To these situations the Marxists-Leninists apply their theory of *no war, no peace* so that there are no declarations of war, no clearly defined issues between war and peace. Many responsible authorities have warned that we lack the proper type of military forces in being—especially conventional ground and sea forces—ready and able to move swiftly to stop such trouble before it spreads.[32]

The need for increased ground, sea, and tactical air forces to meet the situation of local, limited struggles of the Communist *no war, no peace* type was suggested by the following interchange between Congressman William E. Minshall and the Chairman of the Joint Chiefs of Staff at a Congressional hearing on defense appropriations:

Mr. Minshall: What is the enemy's capability as far as con-

ducting these limited wars? How many could he conduct
through satellite nations?

General Twining: He probably could conduct quite a few
through satellites.

Mr. Minshall: In other words, they could limited war us to
death as well as have an all-out war, could they not?

The answer was listed as: (Off the record).[33]

We need, therefore, increased ground forces equipped with
the most modern weapons and vehicles and supported by
fully adequate sealift and airlift. This transport capability,
the very essence of mobility, will enable ground forces to be
dispatched expeditiously to areas in which aggression in the
form of war-by-proxy, local insurrection, or other forms of
no war, no peace occur. Increased naval surface support craft,
such as guided-missile-firing destroyers and cruisers, are also
indicated. Increased tactical air forces and bolder experimentation in possible new techniques for their employment
would likewise provide an increased margin of safety for our
national security. It may well be a dangerous delusion to assume that the day of manned aircraft is past in warfare. On
the contrary, new developments may open up new areas
for the employment of tactical aircraft in situations short of
an all-out war or, equally, in the recovery and countering
phases of total war itself. Vertical take-off aircraft, convertiplanes, hovercraft, improved helicopters—all of these suggest the development of new ideas and new tactics that can
be applied to the new modes of conflict that face us. The
United States Army has gone forward with boldness and
ingenuity in experimenting with aircraft especially adapted
to close support of ground forces and to employment in

localized situations. It should be encouraged to continue and to expand the scope of such experimentation.

The Army should also be aided unstintingly so that (through its own research and development facilities and with the help of industry) it can proceed more rapidly in the development and quantitative purchase of the widest possible range of land and amphibious vehicles. These should encompass all types of personnel carriers, self-propelled artillery and missile launchers, tanks, and transport vehicles and should be *military* vehicles. We must beware of the specious arguments that we can adapt civilian transport to military needs. Commercial automobiles, busses, and trucks are, in general, roadbound and are either worthless or very unsatisfactory for operations in the arctic and antarctic regions, in swampland,* in desert country, and across unbridged or unbridgeable waterways. The possession of such a vast range of vehicles will add to the inherently greater flexibility of ground forces that permits them to cope with situations ranging from rioting in city streets to total nuclear war. Additionally, as the most automotive-minded nation in the world, the United States can hardly afford to consider vehicular mobility to be a luxury. It is, instead, as Henry Ford considered machinery, a necessity which frees men from the drudgery—and hence from the waste and inefficiency—of manual operations.

Above all, our military power—land, sea, and air—must be related to the present and future capabilities of the Soviet

*The development of the swamp buggy by the American oil industry is an example of our potential in the entire field of the equation: flexibility/mobility.

bloc and not to their smile of today or their threats of destruction of tomorrow. To rely solely on the capability of fighting a total war could well be fatal in the face of the Communist grand strategy of *no war, no peace.*

This is not to counsel a downgrading of our powerful retaliatory forces. The Strategic Air Command's manned bombers will constitute a powerful means of deterring the Moscow-Peking Axis for some years. We must maintain this capability, and this maintenance is related to the build up, additionally, of other all-out war capabilities. Increasingly important will be the nuclear-powered, ballistic-missile-firing submarines of the Navy. The USS *George Washington,* the first of a new class of submarines equipped to fire the Navy's 1200-mile Polaris missile was put in commission on December 30, 1959. It represents a new capability that will vastly increase American deterrent capacity. However, only 23 of these fleet ballistic missile submarines are under construction or conversion,* and the Navy believes that forty-five will be required to maintain a fully adequate deterrent position.

There are, of course, many other factors in a fully credible deterrent. Active and passive defensive measures, a secure communications network, and civil defenses—all would give survivability and residual power. The maintenance, then, and in some areas the strengthening, or, in other areas the building, of deterrent capacity must be combined with our ability to retaliate with deadly effect against any direct attack by the Moscow-Peking Axis as a necessary defense requirement. Again, however, these are not the *only* requirements. In this age of technology *man* is not obsolete—he has ac-

*Nine were in commission as of July, 1960.

quired, by virtue of the complexity of the age itself, an even higher role in the control and direction of this complex technology. And not least is this true in the area of defense. By preparing a broad spectrum of defense capabilities we will instead of inviting either direct attack or nibbling aggression, avoid a general war. At the same time we will have the capacity to engage the Communist bloc on unconventional ground of our own choosing. In this manner we can safeguard, as well as it is given to men to do, the heritage of freedom so dearly bought by past generations. Since we know of no way to judge the future but by the past, can we afford anything less than the best and most flexible defense?

THE EDGE OF WAR

Edge: "A place or time of critical danger"*

On the politico-psychological front, on the economic front, and on the defense front our national existence is threatened by the same continuing challenge that threatens all of Western civilization. For the Communist fusion of war and peace seeks not so much to atomize that civilization with nuclear weapons as it does to disintegrate it with the weapons of unconventional warfare. The continuing vitality of the Communist ideology is not the least of the threats we face and it explicates for us many of the reasons why the Communist apparatus can operate successfully by unconventional methods. Indicative of that ideological vitality is the revealing statement made by Dr. Klaus Fuchs, the Communist atom spy who spent ten years in British prisons for handing over

Webster's New International Dictionary, Unabridged.

American and British nuclear secrets to the Soviet Union. Interviewed by a Western journalist at his palatial villa in Dresden in the Communist Zone, Fuchs stated that he would repeat his espionage work once again if necessary because *"whatever helps the Soviet Union is right."**34 This is the essence of the world conflict of the 1960's. The Communists call it the "struggle for peace," which is their euphemism for unconventional warfare. A great American called it the "cold war." But by whatever name it be called, it is not merely the challenge to a system of government—nor even to physical survival, as have been many challenges in the crises of the American past—but a time of critical danger, a mortal threat, to the survival of the United States as it exists in our hopes, our beliefs, and our aspirations, and above all to the continuance of a civilization whose core is—still—Judaeo-Christian.

Though less than bright, the picture is not all dark. We have many and varied assets. Our economy produces such an abundance of food and goods and services that we stand unique in world history in having constantly to deal with the problem of *how to limit production* and *how to dispose of surpluses!* The people in our armed forces are resourceful and courageous, though seldom enough do we pay tribute to them for either of these qualities.** A valuable asset lies in

*Emphasis supplied.

**In Richard O'Connor's perceptive novel of military life, *Officers and Ladies* (Garden City, N.Y.: Doubleday, 1958), there is the interesting sentence: "Soldiering isn't a 'serious' profession in many people's view; it's a mere extension of schoolboy play." Perhaps this helps to explain not only certain American attitudes toward the military but also toward methods of conflict which contain mixed violent and non-violent techniques.

the evidence from the American past, which shows that we will accept any sacrifice if we are convinced of the need and if, as a people, we are offered vigorous leadership by men in whose character and wisdom we can reasonably trust. But our most important asset is that we see man as having an innate dignity and an eternal destiny. Our belief that the state was created to serve man is a major weapon in an era of ideological conflict. Rather than the little voice of a mouse's squeak, man's voice for us has been the majestic tones of Lincoln's "malice toward none, charity for all." This is our past.

But is the evidence of the past meaningful for the present and the future? An American newspaperman has stated that a member of the Senate Foreign Relations Committee said to him, "The American people are for appeasement, although they won't call it by that name. They're scared, and they want an accommodation with the Russians."[35] If we are so enamored of the multitude of good things we possess, we may indeed no longer be the kind of people to make sacrifices, willing to accept even a calculated risk in the arena of world politics. Then indeed our god will be our belly and slavery will seem sweet if it preserves even a few material goods.

Some years ago in an article comparing the policies and world positions of the United States and the Soviet Union, the London *Economist* posed a thoughtful question: "The Americans hand is all trumps. But will any of them ever be played?"

Those trumps will never be played by a people torn by inner doubts, a people that cannot decide whether they want to win, lose, or draw, a people intent on being hag-ridden with the fear of their own system, their own society, a people uncertain as regards their ultimate (eternal) destiny. Such a people are ill-equipped to engage in conflict with a system that—however evil—is led by a general staff of world revolution that knows where it is going and is determined to achieve nothing less than victory.

The trumps, however, can and will be played by an America that calls back again its greatness. That greatness was of the spirit. And there is yet an America that in this conflict of will can draw once more on its spiritual heritage with the call to action of the Prophet Isaias:

> Strengthen Ye the Feeble Hands, and
> Confirm the Weak Knees. Say to the
> Faint-Hearted: Take Courage, and Fear Not.

A people that thus recalls its heritage of courage may yet ensure that *"the edge of war,* like an ill-sheathed knife, No more shall cut its master."

NOTES

1. Jose Ortega y Gasset, *The Revolt of the Masses* (New York: W. W. Norton & Co., 1932), p. 18.
2. See the contributions by Hannah Arendt, Raymond Aron, Russell Kirk, Arthur Koestler, Peter Viereck, Simone Weil, and others toward an understanding of the intelligentsia in general and also as regards the tendency toward a lack of belonging to or a feeling of alienation from Western society. Raymond Aron's, *The Opium of the Intellectuals* (Garden City, N.Y.: Doubleday, 1957), is very good in an under-

standing of the urge many Western intellectuals have to *"ser-rer à gauche*—keep left." See also the interesting study by Neal Wood, *Communism and British Intellectuals* (London: Gollancz, 1959).

3. See the account by a British observer, Lord Windlesham in *Time & Tide,* Vol. 40, October 10, 1959, p. 1088.

4. After failing to take an interest in the United Nations Intergovernmental Maritime Consultative Organization, the Soviet Union joined it at the last moment for the initial session in January, 1959.

5. The proceedings of the 21st Congress of the Communist Party of the Soviet Union are suggestive. See also the new (1959) *History of the Communist Party of the Soviet Union* which replaced the official history of the Stalin era.

6. *Severnaia Communa,* No. 139, as cited in *Senate Documents,* Document No. 62, 66th Congress, 1st Session (Washington: Government Printing Office, 1919), Vol. 3, pp. 301-302.

7. For reports of labor unrest see, for example, the *New York Times,* April 24, 1960.

8. Nikita S. Khrushchev, "The Camp of Peaceful Coexistence," *Foreign Affairs* (October, 1959) as printed in the *Wall Street Journal,* September 4, 1959.

9. *Ibid.*

10. Freeman J. Dyson, "The Future Development of Nuclear Weapons," *Foreign Affairs* (April, 1960), p. 461ff. Thomas E. Murray, *Nuclear Policy for War and Peace* (New York: Crown, 1960), points out various ways in which nuclear tests can be concealed. The former member of the Atomic Energy Commission warns, in this searching analysis, that to make concessions to the Soviet Union on nuclear disarmament without foolproof inspection would be to court disaster.

11. Quoted, U.S. Department of State Press Release, August 18, 1920.

12. Khrushchev, "The Camp of Peaceful Coexistence," *loc. cit.*

13. *Pravda* as quoted by *Moscow Radio,* October 16, 1959; the Soviet and satellite press and radio have found it necessary to remind some of the less perceptive comrades that the "struggle for world peace," that is, the continuation of unconventional warfare, must be waged with even greater vigor but with more finesse.

14. Khrushchev, "The Camp of Peaceful Coexistence," *loc. cit.*

15. Hanson W. Baldwin's, *The Great Arms Race* (New York: Praeger, 1958), is an excellent survey of U.S. and Soviet military power; for many aspects of nuclear weapons see Admiral Elis Biorklund, *International Atomic Policy* (London: George Allen & Unwin, 1956), ch. 5; on the nuclear deterrent and Soviet position see Rear-Admiral H. G. Thursfield, ed., *Brassey's Annual 1959* (New York: Macmillan, 1959), pp. 148-154 and p. 215; see also the testimony of Secretary of Defense Gates before the Senate Preparedness Investigating Subcommittee and the Senate Committee on Aeronautical and Space Sciences (joint hearing), March 16, 1960, and the testimony of General Thomas S. Power, SAC chief, *Department of Defense Appropriations for 1960,* Subcommittee of the Committee on Appropriations, House of Representatives, 86th Congress, 1st Session (Washington: Government Printing Office, 1959), pp. 370-382.

16. *Communique on the Conference of Representatives of Communist and Workers Parties of Socialist Countries,* issued after the Moscow meeting, November 14-16, 1957, as cited by *Pravda,* November 22, 1957.

17. *Ibid.*

18. Concluding Speech by N. S. Khrushchev at the 21st Congress of the Soviet Communist Party, February 5, 1959.

19. Speech by I. G. Kebin, First Secretary, Central Committee of the Estonian Communist Party, delivered before the 21st Party Congress of the Soviet Communist Party as printed in *Pravda,* February 4, 1959.

20. Noteworthy are the proposals of the Cabinet Commit-

tee headed by Vice-President Richard Nixon especially as regards improved ways of managing the national debt. The Joint Congressional Economic Committee has also issued valuable studies on the national economy.

21. "Business and Economic Conditions," *First National City Bank Monthly Letter,* New York, April 1960, p. 43.

22. *Ibid.,* February and April, 1960, *passim.*; Department of State, External Research Division, "The US-Soviet Economic Race," November 25, 1959, p. 1ff; Department of State, Unclassified Intelligence Report No. 8175, "Indicators of Economic Strength of Western Europe, Canada, US, and Soviet Bloc, 1958," December 9, 1959, *passim.*

23. For surveys of the Chinese Communist economy and for statements by Chinese Communist officials see the *Wall Street Journal* and the *New York Times* for the period June-October, 1959; for official Soviet criticism see "On the Target Figures for the Development of the National Economy of the USSR for 1959-1965" as reported by *Moscow Radio,* January 28, 1959.

24. *Pravda* as cited by the *New York Times,* March 30, 1960.

25. Address by O. V. Tracy, June 11, 1959, *loc. cit.*

26. *Ibid.*

27. *The Federalist* (Modern Library Edition, 1937), No. 4, p. 19.

28. *Ibid.*

29. *Department of Defense Appropriations for 1960,* Hearings Before the Subcommittee of the Committee on Appropriations, House of Representatives, 86th Congress, 1st Session (Washington: Government Printing Office, 1959), Part I, p. 68.

30. Message to Congress, December 3, 1793.

31. *Department of Defense Appropriations,* Part I, *op. cit.,* p. 68.

32. See, for example, Gavin, *op. cit.,* and Taylor, *op. cit.*

The contributions to an understanding of the problem made in books, articles, and public statements by Generals Mark Clark, James M. Gavin, Matthew B. Ridgway, Maxwell D. Taylor, and Albert C. Wedemeyer are incisive and thought-provoking. Their writing as well as that of a host of other officers, active and retired, strikingly refutes the picture of the unthinking martinet so popular with a generation of writers of fiction.

33. *Department of Defense Appropriations,* Part I, *op. cit.,* p. 113.

34. *New York Times,* February 28, 1960.

35. *Wall Street Journal,* October 30, 1959.

INDEX

Acheson, Dean, 98
Adams, Henry, 7
Adams, John, 287
Adenauer, Chancellor Konrad, 141
Acsopian language, 72, 180, 263
Africa, 58, 140, 166, 175, 178
Aggression, 70, 194, 216, 239
Aircraft, manned, 299, 301
Aircraft carriers, 12
Airlift, 231, 299
Air power, 10
Alanbrooke, Field Marshal Lord, 229
American Legion, 22, 218
Amphibious vehicles, 300
AMTORG, 147-48
Anglo-Iranian Oil Company, 248-49
Anisimov, Viktor, 148
Anti-Semitism, 141-44
Antonov, Viktor N., 149
Appeasement, 191, 220, 304
Arevalo, Juan Jose, 255-56
Armament inspection, 184
Armas, Col. Carlos Castillo, 261
Armed forces, 9
Armed struggle, 78
Armored vehicles, 106
Arms, control and inspection, 138-39
Asia, 136, 166
Assassinations, 64, 154, 157, 161, 248
Atkinson, James D., 39, 199
Atlantic Charter, 227

Australia, 149, 152
Australian Royal Commission, 152
Azores, 226

Baldwin, Hanson W., 307
Baltic Sea, 140
Baruch, Bernard, 230
Battle Act, 234
Battle of wills, 36, 288
Ben-Gurion, Premier David, 143
Beria, 151
Berlin Blockade, 125, 231
Black Sea, 140
Blitzkrieg, 63, 196, 263
Bolshevik doctrine, 1
Bolshevik regime, 208-10
Bolshevik Revolution, 124
Bourbon whiskey, 213
Braddock, Gen., 35
Brazil, 76, 176
Briand, Aristide, 95
Bridges, Sen. Styles, 233
British Army, 16
Brogan, Prof. D. W., 31, 36
Brooke, Rupert, 21
Brouhaha, 238
Brussels World's Fair, 135
Bryant, Sir Arthur, 117
Burke, Adm. Arleigh A., 242
Burke, Edmund, 103
Burnham, James, 199
Bush, Dr. Vannevar, 115
Buzzard, Sir Anthony, 194
Byrnes, James F., 244

311

The Edge of War

Calculated risk, 117, 304
Calhoun, John C., 99
Canada, 227, 246
Canadian Royal Commission, 148
Canosa, Jaime, 177
Capitalism, 44, 49, 71-72, 286; encirclement of, 74
Capone, Al, 154
Captive nations, 283
Carribean, 168, 217
Castro, Fidel, 167, 177
Castro, Raul, 177
CENTO, 254
Central Intelligence Agency, 261
Chicherin, 52, 163
Chile, 176
Chinese Communists, 78ff., 134, 158, 170, 193
Chinese Nationalists, 274
Churchill, Sir Winston, 223, 245, 274
Civil defense, 301
Civil disturbances, 130, 248
Clandestine operations, 81, 282
Clausewitz, Major Gen. Karl von, 10-11, 46, 53ff., 80, 102, 113
Cold war, 51, 61, 82, 123-24, 127, 152, 215, 229-64, 303
Communications, 273-74; revolution in, 273
Communism: aggression, xi; techniques, xi, 47, 64; dictatorship, 34; synthesis of war and peace, 42ff., 275; violent and non-violent techniques, 51, 75, 114, 126, 155, 275; jargon, 51, 84, 284; imperialism, theory, 72-73; concept of law, 92ff.; infiltration, 255; ultimate victory, 280
Conflict, 276
Congress, U.S., 214; Joint Resolution on Formosa, 236; Joint Resolution on the Middle East, 238-39

312

Convertiplanes, 299
Cosmocrats, 275
Craig, George N., 218
Cuba, 167-69, 177-78
Cultural exchange, 152, 235, 264, 268, 276, 281
Czechoslovakia, 76, 169, 179, 286

Dallin, David J., 201
Dean, Gen. William F., 33
Deane, Cong. Charles B., 196
Defeatism, 28
Democratic slogans, 67
Denmark, 76
Deterrent force, 122, 296-97, 301
Dignity of man, 304
Dillon, C. Douglas, 167
Diplomacy, 110, 162, 172; position of strength, 98
Diplomatic immunity, 133, 148
Disarmament, 29, 94, 132, 137-39, 162, 278, 280, 290, 295
Djilas, Milovan, 82, 85, 273
Dodd, Sen. Thomas J., 143
Dominican Republic, 216
Donovan, Gen. William J., 123
Douhet, Gen. Giulio, 10
Dukes, Sir Paul, 209
Dulles, Allen, 250
Dulles, John Foster, 98, 260, 288
Duran, Carlos Manuel Pellecer, 257
Durkin, Rev. Joseph T., S.J., 39
Durocher, Leo, 36

East Germany, 52, 169, 289
Economic front, 289
Economic sanctions, 214
Economic warfare, 106-107, 114, 130, 161-71, 290
Edge of War, 302-305
Education, 272-73
Egypt, 179
Eisenhower, Dwight D., 235-40, 250, 253

5

The Edge of War

Psychological warfare, 73, 107
Public opinion, 107, 111, 218; control of, 274

Quemoy, 236

Radford, Adm. Arthur W., 116
Red Sea, 241
Resistance movements, 113, 158
Ridgway, Gen. Matthew B., 35
Rieber, Torkild, 253
Roadbound vehicles, 300
Rommel, Field Marshal Erwin, 101
Roosevelt, Elliott, 182
Roosevelt, Franklin D., 221-29
Roosevelt, Theodore, 219-21
Royal Air Force, 151
Royal Navy, 34, 101, 104
Ruge, Vice Adm. Friedrich, 140
Russo-Polish War, 53

Sabotage, 154
Salazar, Lt. Col. Jose Luis Cruz, 261
Satellites, Soviet, 144, 283
Satow, Sir Ernest, 110-1
Schwarzkopf, Brig. Gen. H. N., 250
Schweppenburg, Gen. Geyr von, 63, 225
Scott, Gen. Winfield, 18
Sealift, 299
Sea power, 10ff., 104, 245
Sears, Prof. Louis M., 214
Serrano, Felixberto M., 237
Shah of Iran, 251
Shaposhnikov, Marshal Boris, 56
Shatov, Michael, 150
Shepilov, Dmitrii, 76, 78
Sheridan, Gen. Philip, 32
Sherman, Gen. William T., 18, 112
Sherwood, Robert, 25
Sino-Soviet bloc, 86, 93, 242
Soviet Union: strategy, 1, 52; industrial weakness, 41, 277, 293; theory of war, 52, 65ff.; two

Soviet Union (Cont.)
camps theory, 58, 61; ebb and flow theory, 59ff.; Red Army, 65-66; children, treatment, 92; Jews, 93, 143-46; AGITPROP, 131, 147; treaties and agreements, 139, 181, 279; secret police, 147, 188, 265; electric power production, 165, 204; agriculture, 165, 277; Seven Year Plan, 166, 283; breathing space, 181, 188-89, 280; missiles, 190-91; Red Army forces in Iran, 243; economic shortcomings, 292
Space vehicles, 284
Spain, 81
Spengler, Oswald, 108
Sprout, Prof. Margaret Tuttle, 10
Stalin, J. V., 34, 48, 52, 53, 56ff., 145, 174, 182, 228
Stark, Adm. Harold R., 226
Stassen, Harold, 69, 182
Strategic Air Command, 116, 301
Strauss, Dr. Franz Josef, 141
Struggle, violent and non-violent techniques, 51, 75, 114, 126, 155, 275
Struggle for peace, 50, 53, 62, 72, 83
Submarines: nuclear powered, 11; ballistic missile firing, 301
Subversion, 80, 84, 146-53
Surprise, element of, 298
Surprise attack, 117-18
Survivorship, 192
Suslov, M. A., 75, 153
Swamp buggy, 300
Sweden, 76, 134, 148
Switzerland, 150
Swope, Herbert Bayard, 230

Tactical air forces, 299
Taft, Sen. Robert A., 233
Taracouzio, Prof. T. A., 44
TASS, 133, 148-49

The Edge of War